THE ARMCHAIR GENERAL WWI

THE ARMCHAIR GENERAL WWI

CAN YOU WIN THE GREAT WAR?

JOHN BUCKLEY & SPENCER JONES

CENTURY

1 3 5 7 9 10 8 6 4 2

Century
20 Vauxhall Bridge Road
London SW1V 2SA

Century is part of the Penguin Random House group of companies whose addresses can be found at global.penguinrandomhouse.com.

First published by Century in 2023

www.penguin.co.uk

A CIP catalogue record for this book is available from the British Library.

ISBN 9781529901016

All images in the public domain

Maps by Roger Walker

Typeset in 12/15pt Times LT Std by Jouve (UK), Milton Keynes
Printed and bound in Great Britain by Clays Ltd, Elcograf S.p.A.

The authorised representative in the EEA is Penguin Random House Ireland, Morrison Chambers, 32 Nassau Street, Dublin D02 YH68

www.greenpenguin.co.uk

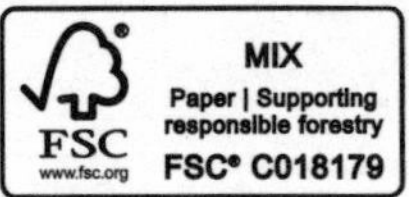

Penguin Random House is committed to a sustainable future for our business, our readers and our planet. This book is made from Forest Stewardship Council® certified paper.

Spencer Jones: *To my great-grandfathers,*
in memory of their service in the First World War.

Edward Astley Carless, Royal Field Artillery.
Rice Davies, 7th South Staffordshire Regiment,
wounded at Gallipoli.

John Buckley: *To my great-grandfather Ewald Lauffer,*
a baker of Manchester, interned by the British
in the Great War, and who, in 1920, returned
disenchanted to Germany.

CONTENTS

INTRODUCTION

It's a Thursday evening on campus and, across a floor of one of our teaching buildings, two groups of History and War Studies students are feverishly studying maps, operational briefing notes, plans and ship schematics. Some are issuing orders, others discussing possible consequences and still more are administering decisions and calculating outcomes. Command structures are under stress and there are many furrowed brows. Between these two groups, we, the staff team (Spencer Jones and John Buckley), administer the event, provide feedback and consult a hidden master map, which captures the full picture of what is taking place. Everyone is engaged in playing out a war-game simulation of a possible encounter between the British Grand Fleet and the German High Seas Fleet in the North Sea in 1917 – one group of students has taken the role of the British, the other group the Germans, while the staff oversee the flow of the battle, which plays out across a number of hours. Teams have developed plans with clear objectives, all based on detailed research on the strategic situation facing the respective powers in 1917. Now they are prosecuting their plans and stratagems on maps, but with only limited information – the German team sees what their naval commanders have knowledge of, while the British team get to see only what they would be aware of. The fog of war is re-created to a degree, and only the staff team gets to see the complete picture. How will the teams fare? Can the Germans score a victory of sorts? Will the Grand Fleet chase down the High Seas Fleet and inflict crippling losses on them? Or will the British jailer simply lock up the German prisoner once more, as had occurred at Jutland in 1916?

In these simulations we aim to draw out the interaction between the wider political strategy, operational methods and tactical capabilities. Why do these North Sea actions in the First World War play out as they do? On what basis were decisions taken? Why were alternative choices not made? What would be the implications of different types of outcome? Was Admiral Jellicoe, the Grand Fleet commander at the Battle of Jutland, the only man who could lose the Great War in an afternoon, as Winston Churchill later stated in the 1920s? If so, how?

Such evenings highlight for us once again the role of the crucial pivotal decision in military and strategic history, the effect of the commander's choices and the enduring fascination with the impact of alternative outcomes, if those choices and decisions had been different. For some historians this remains little more than an absorbing parlour game and cannot be viewed as real or serious history; the discipline of history, after all, concerns itself with interpreting the past through evidence, and there cannot be 'evidence' of things that did not happen. There is enough debate and argument over establishing convincing arguments for why events occurred as they did; dealing with the potential implications of alternatives – or 'counterfactuals' as they have been labelled – is a further step into the unknown that is fraught with uncertainty and a step too far for some.

For some academic historians, 'what if?' or counterfactual history is often politically motivated by those who want to argue that history is driven by major players and key decisions, rather than by broader political, economic and social pressures. Richard Evans in *Altered Pasts: Counterfactuals in History* (2014) argues that most modern counterfactual histories have been written by right-wing historians lamenting the fact that Britain would have been better served by its leaders taking smarter decisions – for example, staying neutral in 1914. In other words, the decision-makers in the British Cabinet made a gross error in judgement by committing Britain to the war. This is certainly a line taken by Niall Ferguson in *The Pity of War* (1998), in which he proposed that European and global (and particularly British) prospects would have been much improved if Asquith's government had stayed out of the war in 1914 and, in effect, let Germany win quickly (a scenario explored in this volume in 'The July Crisis' on p. 13).

Ferguson, a keen advocate of counterfactual history, published *Virtual History* in 1997, an edited collection of counterfactuals in which he staked out a rationale for the genre. Yet many such counterfactual histories do quickly unravel if they are taken too far down a single route; more often than not, wider and deeper strategic, economic and political pressures funnel decision-making back in particular directions. It was interesting that some responses to the first *Armchair General* book, which explored the Second World War, pointed out that certain decisions did not change the outcome of the war, or of campaigns, a great deal. That was a point we wanted to make: that decisions vary in impact, and not that many radically alter the overall flow of the war. Ultimately, the idea of the right-wing 'great men of history' (and it is usually men they refer to) versus the left-wing inevitable-determinism approach is unsatisfying: history is a variable mix of both, and not all counterfactual histories seek better choices that result in happier national stories for established groups.

In addition, although such approaches take us on journeys into alternative possible histories, they are in essence linear – the reader is completely at the mercy of the author. Although these counterfactual histories are interesting and can be useful in understanding why critical decisions may, in certain circumstances, have major repercussions, they do not capture the essence of the intense pressures playing on decision-makers at pivotal moments, particularly in conflicts. One of our key aims in this book is to bring together the pressure of military, political and strategic decision-making with explorations of the outcomes of such decisions.

We have used gaming methods in teaching for many years to explore how, and on what basis, commanders and leaders make crucial decisions, and the implications – both short- and long-term – of those choices. We have had students conduct research, create grand strategies and devise battlefield plans across a whole series of wars in order to get them to better understand the reasons behind the decision-making process, the pressures at work on commanders, the incomplete data that leaders have to work with, and the possibility that the enemy might react in different ways. Opposing teams of students have refought the Agincourt campaign of 1415, battles in the Thirty Years War, Antietam in the American Civil War and Pacific naval battles of 1942, such as Midway and the Eastern Solomons. All have offered fascinating (and sometimes amusing) insights into command and leadership, and into the psychology and pressures at work, even in teaching rooms that are insulated from the life-and-death struggles of war. Games and simulations have, of course, been used by the military for centuries as a means of teaching lessons, but also as a way of getting officers to think about how and why command decisions are made. Students of history similarly get much from the same approach – frustration and bewilderment sit easily alongside incisive thinking and great perspicacity.

In this book, therefore, we have brought the notion of 'what if' history together with the essence of decision-making. Each scenario set in the Great War lays out the context and environment in which crucial and pivotal command and leadership choices were made, both at political and military levels. You will be placed in the position of evaluating evidence, balancing the possible outcomes and making the critical decision that will either lead you along the historical path or into alternative timelines, with the differing ramifications and potential outcomes of both. Some might yield great success, but others might lead to crushing defeat, with dramatic and calamitous outcomes. We have presented the counterfactual alternatives as much as possible as 'real' historical accounts, and have used contemporary pieces of evidence and material to colour the alternative outcome in order to add real flavour. So, in the alternative-history sections, Lloyd George did utter those words, albeit in a slightly different context; and Kerensky did write that memo, though not quite at that time. We have only tinkered with history.

We have also kept as much as possible to the plausible rather than the fantastical. Naturally, events have to be tweaked to offer alternatives, and more often than not there were compelling reasons why the historical path was the most obvious and logical; commanders and leaders generally only made foolish decisions that appeared so in hindsight. But we did not inject completely ahistorical elements into the scenarios – no Flying Fortresses, or indeed atomic bombs (notwithstanding the evidence of H. G. Wells' novel *The World Set Free* of 1914). Everything that will inform your decision-making as you follow a timeline will appear to be a realistically possible outcome; it will just be a path that did not quite make the cut in history, but could have done so without stretching credibility too far. Hopefully the scenarios will illustrate that the historical paths that were taken were adopted for what appeared to be legitimate reasons at the time, even if the alternatives made some sense too.

Yet as we play out our North Sea naval battles with our students, testing their respective plans and tactics, it is all too apparent that escaping the pressures and drivers that shaped historical outcomes is remarkably difficult, certainly without adopting decisions that should have been better consigned to the list of implausible alternatives.

John Buckley and Spencer Jones

PROTAGONISTS

1 THE JULY CRISIS

You are:

Gavrilo Princip, a Bosnian Serb student and a member of the radical revolutionary movement called Young Bosnia (p. 15)

Sergei Sazonov, the Russian Empire's Foreign Minister (p. 23)

Sophie, Duchess of Hohenberg, wife of Archduke Franz Ferdinand (p. 31)

Serbia's Prime Minister, ***Nikola Pašić*** (p. 37)

David Lloyd George, the dynamic and charismatic Chancellor of the Exchequer in the Liberal government (p. 45)

Harold Nicolson, a civil servant and diplomat at the Foreign Office (p. 52)

Queen Mary, King George V's wife and confidante (p. 61)

2 THE GUNS OF AUGUST

You are:

Field Marshal Lord Roberts, VC, one of Britain's most famous soldiers and an unofficial advisor to the British government (p. 72)

General Sir Horace Smith-Dorrien, commanding II Corps of the BEF (p. 78)

Field Marshal Sir John French, Commander-in-Chief of the British Expeditionary Force (p. 86)

Lieutenant-Colonel George de Symons Barrow, the GSO1 (Intelligence) officer for the BEF's Cavalry Division (p. 94)

Brigadier-General John 'Johnnie' Gough, VC, serving as the Chief of Staff for Douglas Haig's I Corps (p. 100)

Major Tom Bridges, commanding C Squadron of the 4th Royal Irish Dragoon Guards (p. 106)

Charles à Court Repington, the military correspondent of *The Times* newspaper (p. 110)

3 GALLIPOLI

You are:

Secretary of State for War ***Lord Kitchener*** (p. 118)

Vice Admiral John de Robeck, commander of the Eastern Mediterranean Squadron (p. 126)

Lieutenant-General Frederick Stopford, commanding IX Corps (p. 135)

First Lord of the Admiralty ***Winston Churchill*** (p. 142)

Captain Rudolf Miles Burmester, captain of HMS *Euryalus* (p. 148)

Lieutenant-Colonel Henry Glanville Allen Moore, commanding officer of the 6th East Yorkshire Battalion (p. 154)

Lieutenant-General William Birdwood, commander of the Dardanelles Army (p. 161)

4 JUTLAND

You are:

Rear Admiral Hugh Evan-Thomas, commander of the 5th Battle Squadron (p. 171)

Admiral John Jellicoe, commander of the Grand Fleet (p. 176)

Captain Algernon Boyle, commanding HMS *Malaya* (p. 182)

Rear Admiral David Beatty, commander of the Battlecruiser Fleet (p. 188)

Vice Admiral Cecil Burney, commander of the 1st Battle Squadron (p. 192)

Vice Admiral Doveton Sturdee, commander of the 4th Battle Squadron (p. 198)

Captain John Green, commanding HMS *New Zealand* (p. 204)

5 BATTLE OF THE SOMME

You are:

General Sir Henry Rawlinson, the commander of the Fourth Army (p. 214)

Major-General Archibald Montgomery, currently serving as the Chief of Staff to Henry Rawlinson at Fourth Army (p. 222)

Lieutenant-General Aylmer Hunter-Weston, the commander of VIII Corps (p. 226)

General Sir Douglas Haig, the Commander-in-Chief of the British Expeditionary Force (p. 233)

Lieutenant-General Walter Congreve, VC, the commander of XIII Corps (p. 238)

Colonel Hugh Elles, commander of British tank forces on the Western Front (p. 244)

Lieutenant-General Sir Hubert Gough, the commander of the Fifth Army (p. 252)

6 LAWRENCE OF ARABIA

You are:

Gertrude Bell, famed author, explorer, linguist and archaeologist (p. 263)

Faisal ibn Hussein, the third son of the Sharif of Mecca, Hussein bin Ali, and the de-facto military leader of the Arab Revolt (p. 268)

***Captain T. E. Lawrence*,** later to be known as Lawrence of Arabia (p. 276)

The legendary desert bandit ***Auda abu Tayi*** (p. 282)

Ronald Storrs, an experienced politician from the British government of Egypt (p. 286)

Abdullah bin Hussein, the thirty-three-year-old son of the Sharif of Mecca, Hussein bin Ali (p. 291)

***Captain T. E. Lawrence*,** later to be known as Lawrence of Arabia (p. 294)

7 THE ZIMMERMANN TELEGRAM

You are:

Captain Reginald Hall, the charismatic Director of the Intelligence Division (DID) at the Admiralty (p. 305)

Charles Hardinge, (Lord Hardinge of Penshurst) Permanent Undersecretary at the Foreign Office (p. 312)

Arthur Balfour, the British Foreign Secretary (p. 318)

Josephus Daniels, United States Secretary of the Navy (p. 326)

Cándido Aguilar, the Foreign Minister for Mexico (p. 332)

Robert Lansing, US Secretary of State (p. 339)

Robert 'Fighting Bob' La Follette, Republican Senator from Wisconsin (p. 344)

8 REVOLUTION

You are:

General Mikhail Vassilievich Alekseyev, Russian Army Chief of Staff (p. 354)

Lord Jellicoe, First Sea Lord (p. 362)

General Aleksandr Ivanovich Verkhovsky, Minister for War (p. 369)

Leon Trotsky, Foreign Minister (p. 374)

Alexander Kerensky, President of the Russian Republic (p. 382)

General Lavr Kornilov, Commander-in-Chief of the Imperial White Russian forces (p. 390)

Grigory Sokolnikov, member of the new Soviet regime and the first Politburo (p. 398)

1

THE JULY CRISIS:

THE ROAD TO WAR, SUMMER 1914

SECTION 1
GAVRILO PRINCIP: THE ASSASSIN

Sunday 28 June 1914, Sarajevo, Bosnia, Austro-Hungarian Empire

It is a warm, sunny day in central Sarajevo, the capital of Bosnia, a territory that, since 1908, has been formally part of the long-standing Austro-Hungarian Empire, though in reality Vienna has ruled here since the 1870s. Today dense crowds are lining the streets of the city, hoping for a fleeting glimpse of the Archduke Franz Ferdinand, heir to the throne of the Austro-Hungarian Empire. He is visiting Sarajevo, accompanied by his wife Sophie, as part of a formal visit to Bosnia to observe military manoeuvres, and thus far all has gone well. He and his wife are travelling in a cavalcade of six cars carrying the elite of Sarajevo alongside some of Franz's own staff. Yet security appears lax and there is little evidence of bodyguards and, curiously, unlike on many other formal state occasions such as this, the streets are not lined with soldiers.

In many ways, though, it is an idyllic scene, with the convoy of cars trundling slowly along Appel Quay, the wide boulevard running alongside the bank of the River Miljacka. Along the route, rising above the well-wishers lining the pavements, are numerous mosques, evidence of Bosnia's heritage as part of the Ottoman Empire. The royal couple seems relaxed and the visit appears to be proceeding well, despite previous warnings that its timing was ill-advised. Indeed, the visit coincides with the Feast of St Vitus, an important commemorative date in the history of Serb national identity, known in Serbia as *Vidovdan*. Disturbingly, it in part marks the date in 1389 when the Ottoman sultan was assassinated by a Serb. It is also the first St Vitus' Day since the liberation of Kosovo from Ottoman rule by Serbia's forces in the recent Balkan Wars. Some advisors had indicated that demonstrations in favour of flourishing Serb nationalism (Bosnia's population is a mix of different ethnic and religious groups, including many Serbs) might erupt, but so far nothing appears to have developed.

1. Gavrilo Princip

Yet all is not well, for dotted throughout the crowd are a small number of revolutionaries intent on marking the visit of the Archduke with extreme violence. You are one of them, nineteen-year-old ***Gavrilo Princip***, a Bosnian Serb student and a member of the radical revolutionary movement called Young Bosnia. Armed with hand-bombs and revolvers, you and your fellow would-be assassins are intent on killing the Archduke, to make a profound statement against Austrian colonial rule and in support of Slavic independence. You are from a poor, rural family in Bosnia and, despite being in less-than-robust health, you travelled to Sarajevo at the age of thirteen and, through schooling and interaction with others, had become involved with anti-imperialist and radical groups. You joined Young Bosnia, a group made up of Serbs (such as yourself), Muslims and Croats, which seeks to establish a new pan-Slavic state, independent of Austrian rule. Having been expelled from your school in Sarajevo in 1912 because of your open, determined and aggressive activism, you travelled on foot the 170 miles to Belgrade, the capital of independent Serbia, to try and continue with your studies. When conflict broke out across the Balkans, and Serbia went to war against Ottoman Turkey, you volunteered for military service. Much to your bitter disappointment, you were rejected because of your small stature and weak physical condition, but Serbia was successful in the war, causing alarm in Vienna, which was fearful of the spread of Slavic nationalism.

In fact you had been back in Sarajevo when, in May 1913, the Austrian governor, General Oskar Potiorek, had declared a state of emergency to clamp down on any Slavic nationalist fervour. Martial law was imposed and Serb societies and groups were banned, generating yet more resentment against Austrian rule. Back in Belgrade, you and your fellow radicals were enraged by Austria's heavy-handed attitude and when, in the spring of 1914, you became aware of the impending visit to Sarajevo of Franz Ferdinand, you decided to act. For you the Archduke is a prime target, as it seems he wants to reform

Map 1: Map of the Balkans, 1914

the structure of the Austro-Hungarian Empire in an effort to buy off the moderate Slav community: if he succeeds, it could end the chances of creating a truly independent 'Yugoslavia'.

You formed a team with Nedeljko Čabrinović and Trifko Grabež and planned to head to Sarajevo to assassinate the Archduke and Governor Potiorek. An old and more senior confidant, Danilo Ilić, who had links with the Black Hand organisation – a secretive and unofficial Serbian-army military society – became involved and he organised your team. All of you were Bosnian citizens. After receiving equipment (bombs, guns and cyanide) and training (you were the best shot), you and your comrades made your way carefully into Bosnia in preparation for the attack. Ilić also recruited three more radicals to the operation, although you had little to do with them, not even knowing their identities until the day before the attack.

By the morning of 28 June you and the other five assassins were in position along the route to be taken by Franz Ferdinand's entourage; Ilić moved through the crowds to offer words of encouragement to you all. At around 10.10 a.m. you hear an explosion on the Appel Quay before the motorcade reaches your position. Has one of your comrades been successful? You run towards the position of Čabrinović, only to see him being dragged away in agony; it looks as though he has tried to use his cyanide to kill himself, but has been unsuccessful. You think for a moment about shooting him to put him out of his pain, but then see the Archduke's cars speeding past. You move to intercept, but there is a quite a commotion in the crowd and although you spot Franz Ferdinand in his ostentatiously plumed hat, you are unable to get a shot at him.

You watch in frustration and despair as the motorcade speeds away, carrying the Archduke and his party, apparently unscathed, towards Sarajevo Town Hall. The attack has clearly failed. You have little idea what has become of your fellow conspirators, but you think it is likely the Archduke will return along the Appel Quay, so you move to a position outside Schiller's Delicatessen, opposite the Latin Bridge, to bide your time.

At a little before 11 a.m. your luck appears to change dramatically when the Archduke's motorcade returns and turns off Appel Quay

2. Franz Ferdinand and Sophie as they leave Sarajevo Town Hall at 10.45 a.m.

3. Schiller's Delicatessen

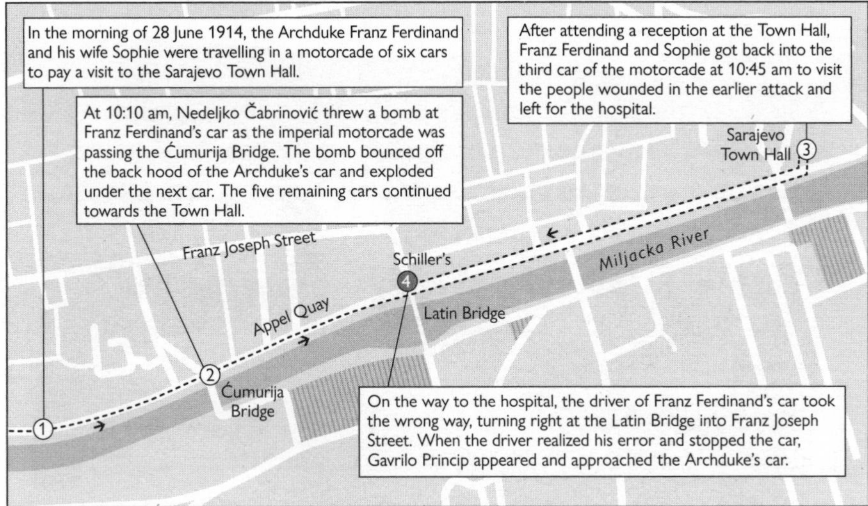

In the morning of 28 June 1914, the Archduke Franz Ferdinand and his wife Sophie were travelling in a motorcade of six cars to pay a visit to the Sarajevo Town Hall.
At 10:10 am, Nedeljko Čabrinović threw a bomb at Franz Ferdinand's car as the imperial motorcade was passing the Ćumurija Bridge. The bomb bounced off the back hood of the Archduke's car and exploded under the next car. The five remaining cars continued towards the Town Hall.
After attending a reception at the Town Hall, Franz Ferdinand and Sophie got back into the third car of the motorcade at 10:45 am to visit the people wounded in the earlier attack and left for the hospital.
Sarajevo Town Hall
Franz Joseph Street
Schiller's
Miljacka River
Appel Quay
Latin Bridge
Ćumurija Bridge
On the way to the hospital, the driver of Franz Ferdinand's car took the wrong way, turning right at the Latin Bridge into Franz Joseph Street. When the driver realized his error and stopped the car, Gavrilo Princip appeared and approached the Archduke's car.

Map 2: Route taken by Franz Ferdinand's motorcade

around the street corner where you are standing. There in the third car, which is open-topped, and clearly visible is Franz Ferdinand himself. You see Governor Potiorek in the car, who shouts at the driver, 'What is this? This is the wrong way!' The driver halts and begins to reverse, passing slowly, very close to where you are standing. A security guard is positioned on the running board on the other side of the car, but he is too far away to intervene.

This is your moment of truth: just a few metres away sits the Archduke Franz Ferdinand, static and in the open, and you are armed with a revolver. This could be the moment to strike down a man who represents all that you detest – a moment that could decide the future of the Slavic people. You reach for your gun but, as you begin to advance, you notice that the Archduke's wife, Sophie, is sitting next to her husband; she will surely be caught in the gunfire. Is this the way to make your mark, killing a defenceless woman just to be sure of hitting your target? What should you do?

AIDE-MEMOIRE

* The Archduke Franz Ferdinand, your primary target, is there in front of you. You will never get a better opportunity to strike down a hated oppressor.
* Sophie is not the target - shooting her or, worse, killing her could have serious repercussions.
* If Franz Ferdinand lives, you might never see a unified, independent southern Slavic state.
* Your cause could be severely compromised and weakened by a cold-blooded killing of a woman and mother.
* Sometimes the ends justify the means, and many innocent Bosnians have died at the hands of the Austrian imperialists.
* Surely you can find a way to avoid the calamity that might befall Europe, should you assassinate Sophie?

THE DECISION

Should you go through with the attack without hesitation and gun down the Archduke and whoever is around him? Or should you take sufficient care to ensure that you shoot only the Archduke? You have a split second to decide.

- If you want to shoot immediately, go to **Section 2** (p. 22).

OR

- If you want to be cautious and target only the Archduke, go to **Section 3** (p. 30).

SECTION 2
MOBILISATION IN ST PETERSBURG

Friday 24 July 1914, Council of Ministers meeting, Mariinsky Palace, St Petersburg, Russia

Nearly a month has passed since the assassination of the Archduke Franz Ferdinand in Sarajevo and the Great Powers of Europe have waited for Austria–Hungary's response. In St Petersburg, the capital of Russia, alarm has ebbed and flowed in anticipation of Vienna's next steps. Despite assurances from the Austrians, Russian ministers have remained concerned that Vienna will squarely blame Serbia for the assassination and insist on harsh recriminations. Yet, as far as the Russian government knows, although the assassins were acting in support of a wider pro-Slav ideal, there is no evidence of a direct conspiracy involving Belgrade and the Serbian government. As far as Russia is concerned, Austria might well use the assassinations as a ruse or pretext to bring Serbia to heel, quite possibly through the use of force. It is widely believed in St Petersburg that Vienna is intent on pushing back against the growth of Serbian power in the Balkans, and the murder of the Archduke might well have given it an opportunity to achieve its aims. Russia, with close cultural ties to Serbia, will resist Austrian expansion in the Balkans. Knowing that Austria would call upon Germany, its close ally, for support, and that Russia would in turn call upon its close ally, France, for aid, Europe stands on the brink. How far is Austria willing to push Serbia and risk an outbreak of war?

4. Sergei Sazonov

By the morning of 24 July it has started to become apparent that Austria is unwilling to compromise and is going to push Serbia all the way. Around 10 a.m. the text of Vienna's ultimatum to Serbia arrives in St Petersburg: it is unrelenting in tone and insists on the near-capitulation of Serbia, in the face of Austrian demands. Moreover, Belgrade has been given just forty-eight hours to respond.

It is crunch time. You are ***Sergei Sazonov***, the Russian Empire's fifty-three-year-old Foreign Minister; it is your job to oversee Russia's response to this inflammatory Austrian initiative. You have been in post for almost four years, before which you had served in a series of high-ranking positions around Europe. During your time as Foreign Minister you worked to improve Russo-German relations and to reach a better understanding with Japan – a task made all the more difficult after Russia's humiliating defeat against the Japanese in the war of 1904–5. In Balkan affairs you have generally taken a more moderate approach than some, much to the irritation of those who have promoted an even stronger pan-Slav line, but you have always strongly supported Serbian independence and have hoped for the expansion of Slav power in the region.

Following the assassinations a few weeks earlier, and in light of the diplomatic hints emanating from Vienna, you have increasingly come to the view that military action by Austria against Serbia is imminent, and that Russia might well have to intervene. As you read Austria's uncompromising ultimatum, you start to wonder if war is

Document 1: The Austrian ultimatum to Serbia

Deutsche Übersetzung

der Note, die der k.u.k. Gesandte in Belgrad der kgl. serbischen Regierung am 23. Juli 14 nachmittags überreicht hat.

Zur Veröffentlichung in den Morgenblättern am Freitag den 24. Juli 1914

Euer Hochwohlgeboren wollen die nachfolgende Note am Donnerstag, den 23. Juli nachmittags jedenfalls zwischen 4 und 5 Uhr der königlichen Regierung überreichen:

„„Am 31. März 1909 hat der königlich serbische Gesandte am Wiener Hofe im Auftrage seiner Regierung der k.u.k. Regierung folgende Erklärung abgegeben:

„Serbien anerkennt, daß es durch die in Bosnien geschaffene Tatsache in seinen Rechten nicht berührt wurde und daß es sich demgemäß den Entschließungen anpassen wird, welche die Mächte in Bezug auf den Artikel 25 des Berliner Vertrages treffen werden. Indem Serbien den Ratschlägen der Großmächte Folge leistet, verpflichtet es sich, die Haltung des Protestes und des Widerstandes, die es hinsichtlich der Annexion seit dem vergangenen Oktober eingenommen hat, aufzugeben, und es verpflichtet

./.

I 1811 76

unavoidable. After absorbing the contents of the ultimatum, you telephone Tsar Nicholas II to inform him of the developments. It is, in fact, the first time you have used the device to report to the Tsar. Nicholas orders Russia's Council of Ministers to discuss the situation that very afternoon.

You then call in the Austrian Ambassador, Frigyes Szapáry, and give him a severe ticking off about the ultimatum: 'You want to make war on Serbia!' you declare. Szapáry tries to fend off the criticism, but you brush him off and send him away with a flea in his ear. It is essential now to assess the attitudes of the French and British to the unfolding crisis.

Over lunch at the French embassy, you discuss the matter with the French and British Ambassadors, Maurice Paléologue and George Buchanan. As you expected, Paléologue urges a tough line against Vienna and Berlin. 'But suppose that policy is bound to lead to war?'

5. Council meeting, Mariinsky Palace

you enquire. Only if the Germanic powers have already decided it will lead to war, Paléologue retorts. Buchanan, as is usual for the British, is more equivocal. The combative French tone is perhaps a result of the very recent visit by the French President, Raymond Poincaré, to St Petersburg, where he was bullish in his support for Tsar Nicholas and Russia.

At 3 p.m. the Council of Ministers meeting starts, and you look around the room to assess the situation; you must evaluate what Russia's response to the Austrian ultimatum to Serbia should be. You start by pointing out that the risks are great, because it is clear to you that Germany is squarely behind Austria's belligerent attitude towards Serbia, and that war with Austria will inevitably mean war with Germany also. While Russia can count on the support of France, Britain's position as usual remains vague, you suggest. It is also the case, you point out, that on previous occasions, when confronting Austro-German diplomatic aggression (in 1908, for example), Russia has backed down. 'Germany had looked upon our concessions as so many proofs of our weakness and, far from our having prevented our neighbours from using aggressive methods, we had encouraged them,' you claim. 'Russian prestige in the Balkans' might 'collapse utterly' if you do not respond robustly to Berlin and Vienna.

The most powerful and influential man in the Council of Ministers, Alexander Krivoshein, the Agriculture Minister and a close confidant of the Tsar himself, speaks next. Russia is financially and economically much better off than just a few years ago, he declares, though militarily our rearmament programmes will not be completed until 1917. War would be very risky, 'so our policy should aim at reducing the possibility of a European war'. However, 'if we remained passive, we would not attain our object'. He pushes for a robust response, with the aim of causing Vienna and Berlin to hesitate and step back from war. The Army and Navy Ministers confess that Russia's military strength is still limited and that military superiority over the Central Powers (Germany and Austria–Hungary) could not be guaranteed. War has possibly come too early.

One problem confronting you all is the time it will take Russia to mobilise its armed forces for war. Because of the need to move so

Map 3: Europe in 1914

many hundreds of thousands of troops around a vast empire during mobilisation, it will take some weeks to get everything ready. In contrast, Germany can mobilise faster, having superior railway systems and shorter distances to travel. So if Russia does not start mobilising soon, the Germans might mobilise quickly and strike first, before you are ready. If you intend to offer a strong response in support of Serbia, you will therefore need to mobilise almost immediately. But if you mobilise first, it could be viewed across Europe as a very escalatory and hostile act, possibly making the likelihood of war even greater.

As you reflect on the possibilities, you consider a conversation you had that morning with the Chief of the Russian General Staff, General Nikolai Yanushkevich. You had discussed the idea of partial mobilisation – that is, preparing the troops necessary for war with

Austria–Hungary, but not those that would move to the borders with Germany. This might look much less inflammatory, but the army has no facility for this; everything is based on the plan for general mobilisation, Mobilisation Schedule 19. The man who would know if partial mobilisation was really viable is General Yuri Danilov, the army's Quartermaster-General and a strong and impressive personality – but he is far away in the Caucasus. In contrast, General Yanushkevich is a man of dubious quality, more of a courtier who owes his position to being a favourite of the Tsar rather than to actual ability. He claims that a partial mobilisation is possible, but can you trust him? However, you both agree that such a measure might be viewed as less aggressive than a full mobilisation.

As the Council of Ministers meeting rumbles on, the idea of partial mobilisation is raised. Might it offer a solution? Or is it still too aggressive in tone and likely to provoke Germany into a robust response? Any outcome of this meeting will have to be taken to the Tsar, probably tomorrow. What will you advise? Partial mobilisation or conciliation?

AIDE-MEMOIRE

* Russia cannot afford to back down again in the face of Austro-German aggression – it would destroy Russia's reputation as a Great Power and result in an end to Serbian independence.
* Russia is not militarily prepared for a war – you need another two or three years.
* Not standing up to Berlin and Vienna might make war more likely. Your previous compromises appear to have emboldened the enemy, not satisfied them.
* Is a major European war worth the risk?

* There is no direct evidence linking Serbia to the assassinations. The perpetrators were Bosnians, not Serbian citizens. You have to back your friends in the Balkans.
* Partial mobilisation has never been attempted. It could still provide Berlin with reason to act, and leave your defences unprepared against Germany.

THE DECISION

Should you seek alternative diplomatic measures in order to avoid war, even if this means risking support in the Balkans? Or should you order partial mobilisation to force Germany and Austria to back down, even if it risks a wider war?

▶ If you want to negotiate and force Serbia to concede everything to the Austrians to avoid war, go to **Section 4** (p. 36).

OR

▶ If you want begin partial mobilisation to demonstrate your resolve, go to **Section 5** (p. 44).

SECTION 3
FRANZ FERDINAND'S NEW AUSTRIA

Thursday 8 February 1917, Festsaal (Festival Hall), Hofburg (Imperial Palace), Vienna, Austro-Hungarian Empire

A grand ceremony is taking place in the vast Festival Hall of the Austro-Hungarian Emperor's Hofburg Palace in central Vienna. Many of the great leaders and elite of the Empire are present to watch the ceremonial signing of a grand treaty, which will establish a new constitutional settlement for Austria.

6. Sophie, Duchess of Hohenberg

The recent weather has been bitterly cold, with heavy snowfall causing widespread disruption, but the occasion in the hall, it is hoped, will bring about a thaw in relations throughout the Empire.

The most important figure attending the ceremony is the new Emperor, Franz Ferdinand himself, resplendent in his finest uniform. Around him are the most senior figures of the various nationalities and groups drawn from across the Empire, all there to see the beginning of a new semi-federal Austria–Hungary, one that it is hoped will put an end to the waves of violence and agitation that have riven the Empire for the last few years. Among the vast crowd is you, ***Sophie, Duchess of Hohenberg***, wife of the Emperor. You look on with admiration and contentment; after years of near-exclusion and humiliation, you (alongside your husband) are having a significant and, hopefully, long-lasting impact on your empire and society. Franz acceded to the throne last November after the death of his uncle, the ailing, stubborn eighty-six-year-old Emperor Franz Josef. They had rarely seen eye-to-eye on many issues, and you always suspected that the old man harboured deep reservations about the suitability of either of you for the highest office. He had certainly done his best to dissuade your husband from marrying you, back in 1900, as you were not of the noblest rank, even though you came from one of the most high-ranking Czech families. However, you were not wealthy and had taken a post as a lady-in-waiting before you and Franz Ferdinand had met. Franz insisted on marrying you, however, though he had to sacrifice the future prospects of your children: yours was to be a morganatic marriage, and your children would never be allowed to accede to the throne. Throughout your marriage you had been forced to stand in the shadows and had been shunned by the elite of Austria's nobility, never allowed to travel in public alongside your husband or to sit or stand alongside him at official or state events. Despite these difficulties, you have been described (by a man) as a 'woman of high intelligence, extraordinarily ambitious, resolute yet vain'.

But now, after years of standing in the background, never allowed to play a major role in the life of the Austro-Hungarian court and the monarchy, you are at last able to be fully part of state occasions, albeit at your husband's side.

For your husband and other reformers, it is not a moment too soon for new, modern policies to be implemented. Unrest throughout the Empire has grown in recent years, with various nationalities and ethnicities jostling for greater recognition and rights. Some radicals and revolutionaries had even resorted to extreme violence, leading to the awful events in Sarajevo back in 1914. An assassin had attempted to murder your husband, but had hesitated on seeing you alongside him.

Map 4: The Austro-Hungarian Empire under Franz Ferdinand

Nonetheless, Franz was wounded and Governor Potiorek had been killed before the assassin was cut down.

Your husband's vision for reform and change was fuelled by the attack, however. As well as cracking down on revolutionary violence and forcing Serbia into severe concessions, Franz had pushed even harder for a new constitutional structure, one that offered greater recognition and equality for the discontented factions across Austria's sprawling empire, particularly the Czechs – all of which you viewed very positively, being of Czech heritage yourself. The summer crisis of 1914 had nonetheless brought Europe to the brink of war: Vienna had implicated Serbia in the assassination attempt, something Belgrade strenuously denied. Russia had supported Serbia, prompting Germany to back Austria. Yet no one was willing to go to war over the death of a governor and an *attempted* assassination: Berlin reined in Vienna's demands, and calm voices in St Petersburg persuaded Serbia to acquiesce. The sting was drawn.

You have heard from your husband that, in Berlin, the Kaiser is now more fearful than ever of war with an ever-strengthening Russia, particularly as the Russians are still allied to France. Berlin's relations with London might have thawed a little between 1914 and 1917, but the Kaiser remains keen for Vienna to modernise the Austro-Hungarian Empire sufficiently to avoid further Balkan conflicts. The ailing Ottoman Empire might yet destabilise the Eastern Mediterranean, but for the moment Vienna's agenda – in part prompted by your husband's initiatives – might bring about a calmer international order.

AFTERMATH

Although hopes were high for the Vienna Settlement, hostile forces were arrayed against it. Hungary, which had been afforded a higher status alongside Austria back in 1848 as part of the newly created Empire, now found itself comparatively reduced in rank, and nationalists in Budapest were decidedly unhappy with Franz Ferdinand's new constitution. Hungarian Prime Minister István Tisza was furious about the rights afforded to Transylvania, which he considered to be clearly part of Hungary. To the south, although moderate opinion had momentarily been satisfied, those seeking a pan-Slavic union, perhaps linked with Serbia, were dismayed at the limited extent of federal powers distributed to the various parts of the empire.

7. Alexandru Averescu

By 1918 agitation was growing in Bosnia and Transylvania in particular. Under the direction of Prime Minister Tisza,

Hungarian forces deployed directly into Transylvania to suppress Romanian separatists and radicals; the crackdown was brutal. In independent Romania the response, headed by the newly appointed populist Prime Minister Alexandru Averescu, was to send supplies and equipment to the rebels, a stance supported by the Russians and the French. This infuriated Budapest, and Tisza demanded support from Vienna. In Bosnia in the autumn of 1917, a revitalised Young Serbia movement had begun a campaign of violence and disruption against Austro-Hungarian domination, with the long-term aim of bringing about full independence for the Slavic peoples. Vienna was convinced Belgrade was behind the insurgency, and in 1918 martial law was reimposed. Support for the new Austro-Hungarian constitution began to haemorrhage and the spectre of civil war loomed large.

In July 1918 Hungarian forces entered Romania in pursuit of Transylvanian rebels, causing an international crisis. Vienna's hand

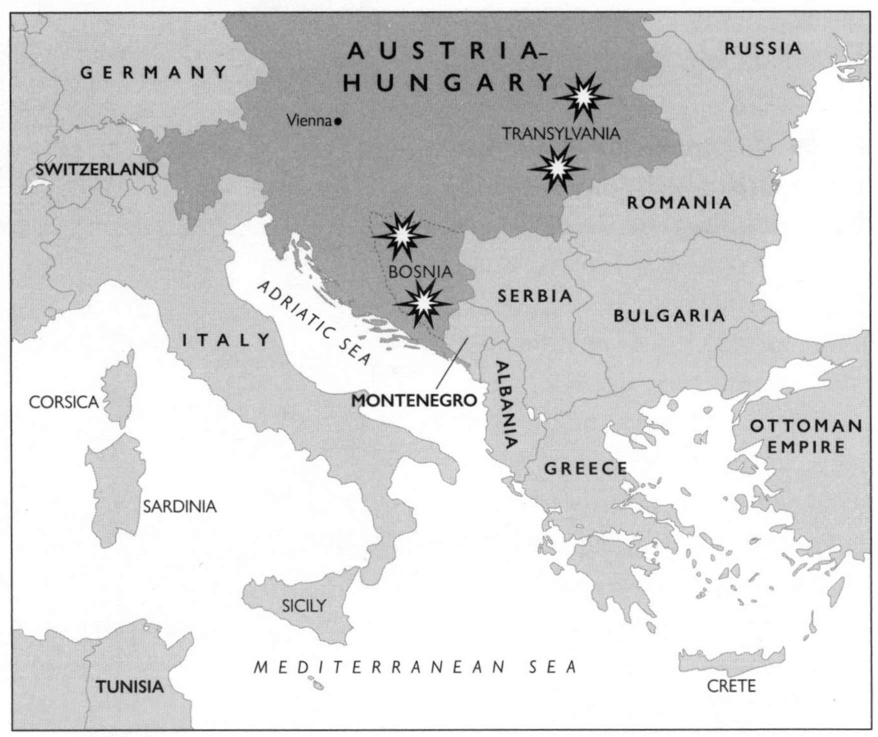

Map 5: Balkans Conflict, 1918

was forced into backing the incursion, while Russia offered strong support to Bucharest. Within weeks, Germany and France had been drawn into the affair and soon the Balkans was ablaze. When Russian forces began to mobilise in support of Romania against Austria, Germany mobilised also, then France. Confronted by a much stronger Russia than a few years earlier, Berlin's hopes of quick success appeared limited indeed. Yet Britain, still riven by civil war in Ireland over the Liberal government's attempts to impose Home Rule, remained neutral. As war erupts across the continent, Europe's future hangs in the balance.

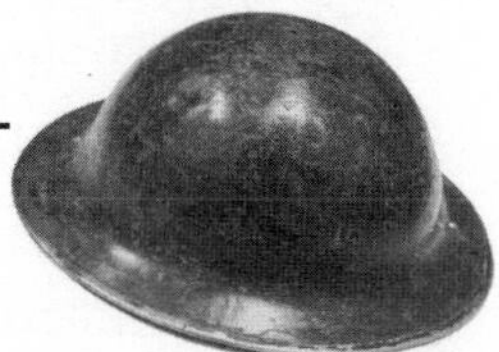

THE DECISION

- ▶ To explore the alternative route go to **Section 2** (p. 22).

  OR

- ▶ To explore the history of the July Crisis go to the **Historical Note** on p. 65.

SECTION 4
CONGRESS OF BUDAPEST

Monday 10 August 1914, Royal Castle, Budapest, Austro-Hungarian Empire

More than a month has passed since the appalling assassinations of the Archduke Franz Ferdinand and his wife in Sarajevo, and until just over a week ago the prospect of a pan-European war loomed large. Austria's ultimatum to Serbia had almost pushed the Great Powers into open conflict, with Russia supporting Serbia, and Germany supporting Austria. France had also been more than likely to be dragged into any war to honour its alliance with Russia. Britain too might well have been drawn in, if Germany attacked France, especially if Belgian neutrality had been violated. Near-panic had swept across the capitals of Europe; Berlin and Paris, in particular, looked askance at St Petersburg for the Russian government's reaction to Austria's arguably heavy-handed attitude to Serbia. The Tsar and his staff, however, held back and,

8. Nikola Pašić (left), confers with a military advisor

thankfully, disaster had been temporarily averted. Now the major players in the drama have assembled in Budapest at the grand Royal Castle to thrash out a way forward, to search for a formula that might defuse tension in Eastern Europe and allow the Great Powers to step back from war without losing face. It will not be easy – something you are only too aware of, for you are Serbia's Prime Minister, sixty-eight-year-old ***Nikola Pašić***.

You had been the recipient of Vienna's highly confrontational and escalatory ultimatum, which had been delivered to your government in Belgrade a little after 6 p.m. on 23 July. You had been campaigning in the south, ahead of elections planned for 14 August, and it was not until the following day that you had become fully involved in formulating Serbia's response. By then Austrian troops and ships had begun assembling along the northern banks of the River Sava directly opposite Belgrade, preparatory to bombardment and attack, it seemed to you and your fellow Serbian leaders.

Now, more than two weeks later, as you look around at some of the conference attendees assembling in the Royal Castle – Bethmann Hollweg (the German Chancellor), Leopold Berchtold (Austria's Foreign Minister) and Sergey Sazonov (the Russian Foreign Minister) – you

9. The Royal Castle, Budapest

reflect upon how close you had all come to calamity. You are used to combative politics and to fighting for high stakes, ever since you moved into politics in the late nineteenth century, despite being a qualified engineer. You had led the People's Radical Party in Serbia, working to establish Serbia as a major player in the Balkans and to resist the encroachment of Austrian expansion against the backdrop of the crumbling Ottoman Empire. You had also fought against elite opponents in Serbia, bringing down a death sentence imposed by King Milan. Exile, imprisonment and rehabilitation followed in later years, but you have since become the dominant, if still controversial, figure in Serbian politics. Not a great speaker – indeed, your stumbling speeches laced with discursive anecdotes, delivered with a thick rural accent, are a source of amusement – you are nevertheless forceful, respected by the wider population and grudgingly admired by the elite. For years you had sought closer ties with Russia to counterbalance the threat of your much larger Habsburg neighbours.

You had been made informally aware of a potential plot to attack Archduke Franz Ferdinand and had even indirectly and vaguely alerted Vienna to the threat. Of course you could not openly give a warning, as this would both implicate you in the plot and infuriate the more radical elements in Serbia and Bosnia, whose broader case you largely supported. In the aftermath of the assassination, you of course denied all knowledge, but you were deeply concerned that a forensic investigation might expose how much Serbia was involved in the atrocity. You recognised how destabilising the whole situation could be for Serbia – and this at the moment when Belgrade was basking in the success of the Balkan Wars that had raged on and off since 1912. You believed

10. Theobald von Bethmann Hollweg

that you could count on Russia's support, as you were its major ally in the Balkans, especially after St Petersburg had broken with Bulgaria in the Balkan Wars.

Rumours had spread in July, with news from Austria that the 'hawks' in Vienna seemed hell-bent on war with you, and that Berlin appeared to support Austria. The big question therefore was how much would Russia back you if it came to open conflict, and how much would Berlin stick its neck out for Vienna? Would the Germans risk war with France and Russia at the same time? And how much control was being wielded by 'sensible' leaders?

You had had very little time to respond to Vienna's ultimatum, but thought it best to concede, to avert a war with Austria. After all, the Russians had persuaded you to stand down in previous confrontations with Austria, so they would probably do so again. Grudgingly you and your staff composed a response to Vienna in which you accepted their terms, though with many clever nuances to deflect attention and evade direct responsibility. You had hesitated over the demand for Austrian involvement in the internal Serbian investigation into the assassinations – what might they uncover? – but when news arrived from St Petersburg that Russia was holding back from open support for you, you had little choice but to comply. You had delivered your government's response to the ultimatum in person (as no one else would do it) to the Austrian Ambassador in Belgrade, but you did not hold out much hope – the Ambassador's staff were already packing bags, in expectation of a hasty departure. By then you had given the order for the Serbian army to mobilise and ready itself for war. Prospects for peace were bleak.

Yet the mood changed when news from St Petersburg emerged that the Tsar was holding back from mobilising the vast Russian army and was seeking a diplomatic solution. Despair descended in Belgrade – Russia had let the peoples of the Balkans down before, so would this be a repeat? Would they merely let the Austrians march in? Russian Foreign Minister Sazonov then cabled you to say that he had received information that in Berlin Chancellor Bethmann Hollweg and the Kaiser were also hesitating. As Russia held back from mobilisation, the Kaiser lost his nerve – the incident in Sarajevo and

Austria's demands on Serbia were not causes enough for Germany to go to war with Russia and France, he appears to have told his officials. The Tsar had written to his cousin Wilhelm, urging him to rein in Vienna; Russia would likewise prevail upon Belgrade to concede.

Bethmann Hollweg and Sazonov then proposed that an 'independent' inquiry be set up in Serbia to seek out the truth behind Serbia's links with the assassination – this would hopefully fulfil Vienna's demands – and while Belgrade would have to submit to the investigation, it would not be driven by Vienna. Although this was still a violation of your independence, in the circumstances there was little alternative. The ball was now back in Vienna's court – would they still go ahead with war, knowing that Berlin was less than squarely behind them?

Edward Grey, the British Foreign Secretary, had already proposed holding a conference to resolve the crisis, but Berlin and St Petersburg now seized the initiative and called for a congress of the interested and involved powers to establish a longer-lasting settlement. So now you have all assembled in Budapest to seek a way forward. You know that there are military hotheads working behind the scenes to destabilise the Congress, as they want war. The Austrian and German militaries in particular are fuming at the 'missed opportunity', you have heard. Yet moderates in Vienna, Berlin and St Petersburg appear to be momentarily in the ascendant, and you must work to defuse the crisis – concessions around your hopes for a pan-Slavic state might have to be temporarily accepted. At the same time, radical elements in Serbia and Bosnia must not be allowed to think that their ultimate hopes and dreams have been permanently shattered, or your own position may be under threat. You are also hopeful that the moderate voices from Britain and France – however much on the fringes of this Congress they may be – will help to moderate the discussions. As the main speeches begin, you are optimistic that the moment for war has passed and that Serbia will soon be able to return to a path of indirectly, yet forcefully, supporting pan-Slavic independence.

AFTERMATH

The Congress of Budapest proved successful in diffusing European tensions, at least in the short to medium term. Russia was greatly relieved at having avoided direct military confrontation with Germany and Austria at a time when the army chiefs in St Petersburg were aware of their own limitations. Any prospect of war was best avoided until at least 1917, they had argued. In Berlin, although the military were dismayed, the Kaiser and the Chancellor were pleased that better relations with Russia had been temporarily secured. Moreover, better links with London developed over the next few years, and so Germany's fear of encirclement eased. In Vienna the hardliners were dismayed at their inability to use forceful means to snuff out notions of Slavic independence in the Balkans; Serbia remained, albeit in a temporarily chastened form, a source of resistance to the long-term security of the Austro-Hungarian Empire.

In the following years there were further eruptions in the Balkans, which served to weaken Vienna's power. Russia and Serbia continued to support these movements surreptitiously, but Russia itself was convulsed by social and political upheaval in 1920, which almost swept the Tsar from power. Forced to accept a more constitutional position, Nicholas II's role in international affairs diminished. As the new regime in Russia endeavoured to bring stability, so further wars broke out in the Balkans, and the Austro-Hungarian Empire teetered on the brink of collapse. London, dealing with the fallout of civil war in Ireland, stood aside, while in Germany internal confrontation between political parties such as the Social Democrats and conservative nationalists simmered, rendering forceful action unlikely. As Europe moved into the 1920s there were still many social, political and strategic differences to be resolved.

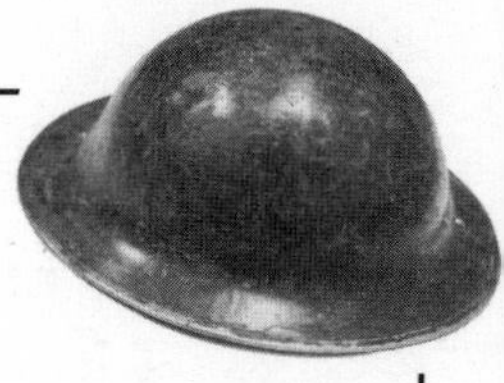

THE DECISION

- To explore the alternative route, go to **Section 5** (p. 44).

OR

- To explore the history of the July Crisis go to the **Historical Note** on p. 65.

SECTION 5
POOR LITTLE BELGIUM

Sunday 2 August 1914, Cabinet Room, 10 Downing Street, London

Tumultuous events have swept Europe since Austria issued its ultimatum to Serbia on 23 July. As Belgrade reeled under the diplomatic assault and attempted to concede as much as it could, in St Petersburg, Berlin and Paris frantic toing and froing ensued. To onlooking nations, it has become increasingly unclear who is trying to exploit the situation for their own ends and who is actually trying to hold Europe back from the brink of war. To the Liberal government in London, headed by the Prime Minister, Herbert Asquith, the Balkans furore has appeared distant and of limited immediate importance; the British Cabinet is far more concerned about the deteriorating political position in Ireland. There Home Rule is soon to be enacted, something bitterly resisted by the Conservative opposition in Britain, and which some believe is likely to cause civil war. The British Cabinet had not even discussed foreign affairs following the Sarajevo assassinations until a short briefing on 24 July by the fifty-two-year-old, rather understated Foreign Secretary, Edward Grey. Grey is of aristocratic stock (his country estate in Northumberland has been held by the family since the time of Edward III), but he is rather stilted in his delivery and is a less than engaging speaker. Yet Grey is a powerful figure in foreign affairs; he has led the British Foreign Office since 1908 and is thus, by some distance, the longest-serving Foreign Minister in Europe. After such a long tenure, his and the Foreign Office's view of global affairs have become one and the same.

Listening in, you start to become more aware of the growing crisis in the Balkans; you are ***David Lloyd George***, the dynamic and charismatic Chancellor of the Exchequer in the Liberal government. You have been MP for Carnarvon Boroughs since 1890 and have served in various ministerial roles since the formation of the great reforming Liberal government in 1905. A noted orator with great wit and charm fused with a firebrand personality, you are also known as a radical, unwilling to bend to convention or to staid institutions.

11. Edward Grey

As Grey hints at the work he has been doing with the great capitals of Europe, it starts to become clear that the Foreign Secretary views the unfolding situation with pessimism. His attempts at mediation have fallen on deaf ears, particularly in Berlin, which seems set on backing Austria's overbearing stance towards Serbia. Even the Russians, supposedly now in a loose association (or Entente, as some call it) with Britain and France, appear dubious about Grey's overtures. Now, with the Austrian Ultimatum, the crisis has deepened. Grey describes the Ultimatum as 'the most formidable document I have ever seen addressed by one State to another that was independent', while Churchill claims it to be 'the most insolent document of its kind ever devised'.

12. David Lloyd George

Grey warns that if Serbia does not acquiesce to Austrian demands, war between them is likely and will probably draw in Russia, Germany and France. Yet most of the Cabinet (including you) are opposed to Britain becoming entangled in this affair – your agreements with Paris, and certainly with St Petersburg, do not amount to formal alliances and do not compel you to become involved. Grey appears less than happy with this view; you suspect that he would prefer a stronger commitment to intervention, should it become necessary. He and the other interventionists obviously see Germany as a major strategic problem to be confronted, and it is true that when the Germans started to expand their navy at the turn of the century, for no obvious reason, it represented an aggressive move against Britain. But Russia also offers a major threat to British interests, mainly in the Middle East and India, and we have reached an understanding with them. Oddly, Asquith, the Prime Minister, seems distracted by his personal correspondence.

Matters deteriorate over the next few days, despite Grey's efforts to push for a diplomatic solution, and on 28 July Austria declares war on Serbia. In talks between the Germans and Edward Goschen, the British Ambassador in Berlin, the Germans claim they would not be seeking territorial gains against France, should war come; this might prevent the Channel ports falling into German hands. However, if Germany goes to war against France, it seems likely to want to attack through Belgium; if Belgium did not resist, Berlin would guarantee its future territorial integrity also. And if the Germans passed through the southern region only, that might be palatable. Obviously this is an effort merely to secure British neutrality. Can the Germans be trusted? And nothing was made clear about the French overseas empire, should the Germans prove triumphant.

By Thursday 30 July the Russians had begun to mobilise against Austria, prompting the Germans to demand that they back down; the Tsar (under some pressure from his government) rejects the German request and begins general mobilisation. The Germans follow suit, and war is now imminent. Grey's efforts to minimise the spread of war by offering to guarantee French security if Germany only attacked in the east comes to nothing; the Germans seem intent on forcing

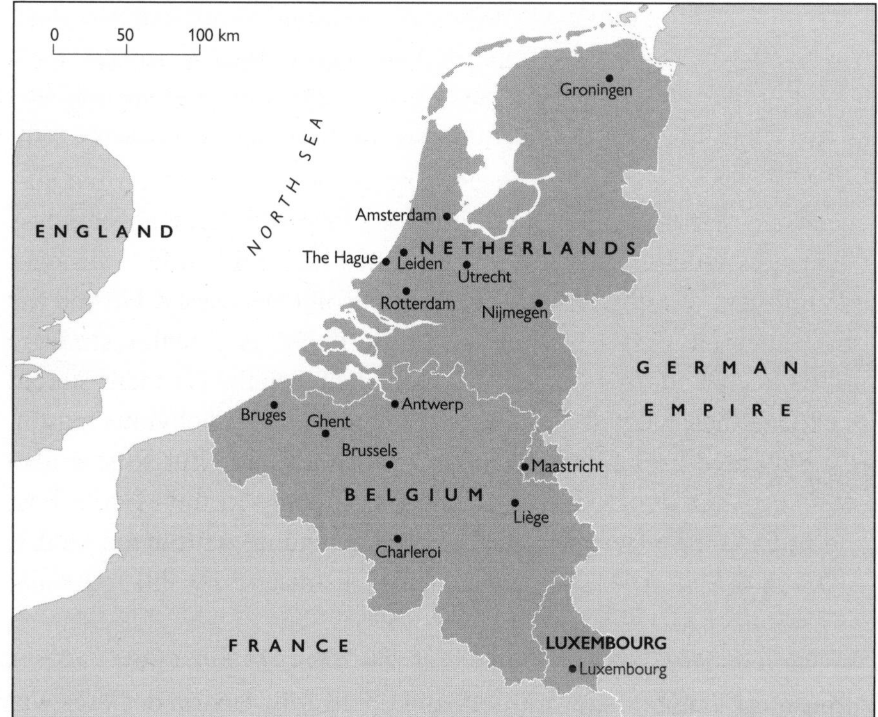

Map 6: If Germany attacks France, it could well be through Belgium, but how much territory will it violate?

WAR EXTRA! The Evening World. WAR EXTRA!

"Circulation Books Open to All." "Circulation Books Open to All."

PRICE ONE CENT. NEW YORK, SATURDAY, AUGUST 1, 1914. 10 PAGES PRICE ONE CENT.

GERMANY DECLARES WAR; ALL EUROPE IS IN ARMS

ST. PETERSBURG, Aug. 1—The German Ambassador, in the name of his Government, sent to the Russian Minister of Foreign Affairs at 7.30 o'clock a declaration of war.

The announcement is made by the St. Petersburg telegraph agency, which is considered the official news agency of Russia.

RATE DECISION PROVES PARTIAL VICTORY FOR 52 EASTERN RAILROADS

Flat Horizonal Increase Is Refused, But 5 Per Cent Granted in Some Cases.

WILL ADD TO INCOMES.

Raise Granted Between Buf-

BANKERS CONFER TO KEEP AMERICAN GOLD AT HOME

ATLANTIC LINERS PARALYZED IN RUSH FOR PASSAGE

English Liners Refuse to Take Any Passengers for Continental Europe.

BASEBALL

NATIONAL LEAGUE.

AT PHILADELPHIA.

CHICAGO—

1 0 0 0 0 2 0 0 1—4

PHILADELPHIA—

6 0 0 0 2 0 2 0 —10

AT BOSTON.

ST. LOUIS—

BOSTON—

AMERICAN LEAGUE.

AT DETROIT.

WASHINGTON—

ITALY BREAKS THE TRIPLE ALLIANCE; FRANCE CALLS OUT HER WAR ARMY

7,474,000 ANSWER FIRST CALL; 7 WARRING NATIONS CAN PUT 32,541,000 MEN IN THE FIELD

FRANCE has called to the colors every available reserve.

AUSTRIA already has her complete strength in the field.

SERVIA has called out every able-bodied man into the army.

England Gives Formal Notice That She Will Side With France and Russia and Back Up Her Agreements to the Full Extent of Her Power and Resources.

PARIS, Aug. 1.—A crucial stage in the war situation was reached to-night when the British Ambassador called at the Elysee Palace and pledged

Paris into backing down. On Saturday 1 August the Germans declare war on Russia, and rumours are rife that they are beginning to prepare troops in the west to strike against France, presumably through Belgium. There are even reports that German troops have moved into Luxembourg.

At the British Cabinet meeting on the morning of Saturday 1 August the mood is very much for Asquith's government to stay neutral, though Grey blocks the formal announcement of such a policy by threatening to resign. The First Lord of the Admiralty, Winston Churchill, one of the few 'hawks' in the Cabinet, asks for permission to mobilise the Royal Navy, but is rebuffed. Such is the strength of the anti-interventionist group that John Morley, Lord President of the Council, declared to Churchill, 'We have beaten you after all.'

Yet at the first Cabinet meeting the next day, between 11 a.m. and 2 p.m., you note a change in the mood. A measure drafted by Herbert Samuel, the President of the Local Government Board, is proposed, stating that if war were to break out in the west, the Royal Navy would intervene to prevent the German fleet attacking French ports in the English Channel or through the North Sea. Grey strongly urges you all to support this policy. He argues: 'We have led France to rely on us, and unless we support her in her agony, I cannot continue at the Foreign Office. We cannot take half-measures – either we must declare ourselves neutral, or in it. If we are to be neutral [I] will go.'

Tension mounts. Asquith also appears to be siding with the pro-interventionists: 'I shall stand by Grey in any event,' he states to one Cabinet colleague. The Tories have naturally thrown in their lot behind intervention, setting out their support for such a measure to Asquith. And yet most of the Liberal Party, the wider membership and the liberal-leaning press are generally opposed to entering any war.

The leading 'doves' in the Cabinet – Burns, Simon, Morley and Beauchamp – become alarmed. Earlier this morning you and several of your colleagues had met at your offices at Number 11 Downing Street (you are the Chancellor) to discuss the situation – there you had concluded that you 'were not prepared to go to war now, but that in certain events we night reconsider [the] position'. The outright violation of a neutral power (possibly Belgium) could be a game-changer for you. Yet it had been established as policy a few days earlier that Britain is not compelled by the Treaty of London of 1839 to intervene to secure Belgium's independence, only that there may be a moral obligation.

During the fraught Cabinet meeting you are handed notes by Churchill and Charles Masterman, Chancellor of the Duchy of Lancaster urging you to stay loyal to the Cabinet and to stand by Asquith and Grey: 'For Heaven's sake let us all stand together.' As the meeting breaks up, with another planned for 6.30 p.m., you convene at Number 11 with colleagues to thrash out a collective middle-ground view. Samuel attends and it is apparent that a proposal to intervene in the war if Belgian neutrality is substantially violated is going to be proposed. Such a policy would almost certainly mean war, for Germany is likely to force a passage through Belgium, although there is some lingering hope that it will not be too great an incursion. But Grey and the other hawks are certain to use it as a cause for intervention on the side of France: war with Germany will inevitably follow. As the leading figure of the middle group of ministers, it could well be down to you. If you rebel against Grey and the hawks, you might bring down the government and that could let in a coalition, with the Tories back in power – they would certainly press for war. It might mean elections and paralysis, just as the war spreads across Europe. What should you do?

AIDE-MEMOIRE

* There is no great desire in the country, or in the Liberal Party, for war against Germany over this Balkan affair. Few people in Britain have even heard of Serbia.
* Britain has the entente cordiale with France – to step aside now would be disastrous for British standing and would risk leaving Britain isolated.

* Is it worth going to war to protect Belgium? The Germans might simply pass though some southern regions and not cause too much damage (see Map 6).
* If you stand aside, Germany might well defeat France and then dominate the continent. That would be hugely damaging for British security (see Map 7).
* The leading bankers and financiers of London have urged the government not to intervene.

Map 7: A worst-case scenario?

* The Germans have been aggressive towards Britain for years. They have built up a big navy, with little obvious strategic need, to try and rival the Royal Navy. Who is to say they won't try again? They must be stopped.
* There has been a recent thaw in relations between London and Berlin. Perhaps there is a way forward?
* Mass resignations from the Cabinet, by anti-war ministers, could bring the government down.
* If you stay and support Grey and Asquith in their war, will you be betraying liberal ideals?

THE DECISION

Should you stay loyal to Asquith and Grey and guarantee Belgian independence? Or should you lead a peace faction, with the aim of keeping Britain out of the war, even if it risks collapsing the government?

▶ If you want to prepare to go to war if Germany substantially violates Belgian neutrality, go to **Section 6** (p. 52).

OR

▶ If you want to stay neutral, go to **Section 7** (p. 60).

SECTION 6
THE LAMPS ARE GOING OUT: BRITAIN JOINS THE WAR

11.10 p.m., Tuesday 4 August 1914, German embassy, London

Since the British Cabinet decided to lay down a clear statement to Germany just two days ago, that if German troops entered Belgium by force of arms Britain would intervene, the slide to war has progressed at a dizzying speed.

13. Harold Nicolson

You are ***Harold Nicolson***, a twenty-seven-year-old civil servant and diplomat at the Foreign Office. Born into a diplomat's family (your father is, indeed, currently the Permanent Secretary at the Foreign Office), you have travelled the world with your father and attended Balliol College, Oxford, where, although you hardly excelled, you at least graduated, albeit with a third-class honours – a 'gentleman's degree'. Yet you surprised everyone, including your father, by passing the competitive entrance exam for the diplomatic service with ease. You spent your early diplomatic career in Madrid and Constantinople, but are now back in London. Recently married to the writer Vita Sackville-West (this is best described as an unconventional union), you are being confronted with the looming conflict in Europe. Now, however, very late on 4 August, you have been handed a very delicate task, despite being a young and junior member of staff at the Foreign Office in London. Bizarrely, you have been despatched to the German embassy in London to meet the Ambassador, Prince Max von Lichnowsky, both to deliver a declaration of war and to retrieve one.

14. Edward Goschen

Yesterday Edward Grey, the Foreign Secretary, had delivered what many regarded as the greatest speech of his career. In the House of Commons he had set out British policy regarding German military activity in the West. In short, he had laid down a red line that if German troops forced their way through Belgium to attack France, Britain would intervene. It seemed that this position carried the weight of support of both Parliament and, increasingly, the wider population of the nation. This morning Grey had instructed the British Ambassador in Berlin, Edward Goschen, to inform the German government that unless they guaranteed Belgian neutrality, Britain would feel the need to 'take all steps in their power to uphold the neutrality of Belgium'. Failure to comply by midnight in Berlin on 4 August (actually 11 p.m. in London) would result in a British declaration of war on Germany. Ominously, few in the Foreign Office believed that Germany would respond to such an ultimatum, let alone comply.

In expectation of this eventuality, officials in the Foreign Office began assembling the paperwork necessary for a declaration of war. This involved preparing telegrams to be issued to governments across the world stating that Britain was declaring war on Germany, alongside writing a letter to be delivered to the German Ambassador in London, Prince Lichnowsky, instructing him of the situation and returning his passport, so that he might depart London forthwith. Curiously, the Foreign Office always had pre-prepared telegrams available for this situation, which merely needed to be stamped with the name of the country that Britain was to be at war with. Additionally there were two cupboards of telegrams: Cupboard A contained telegrams stating that Britain was declaring war, while Cupboard B contained telegrams outlining that London had received notice that war had been declared upon Britain. As it was assumed in the Foreign Office that Britain would be declaring war upon Germany later that day, staff – including you – began stamping up the telegrams from Cupboard A, and by 9.30 p.m. all was prepared and ready to be issued when the moment came.

Yet at 9.40 p.m. all hell broke loose when an official scurried across from Number 10 Downing Street with news that the Admiralty had intercepted a German message to its fleet stating that a war with Britain was already under way: it seemed as though Berlin had already declared war on Britain. You and your colleagues in the Foreign Office

15. The German embassy, London

realised, with some dismay, that this now required you to switch the telegrams from Cupboard A with those from Cupboard B, and all would need stamping up in double-quick time, ready to be issued in the next couple of hours. It did, however, mean that Britain would not be the first to declare war and diplomatically this was good news, as London did not want to appear to be the aggressor.

As you and your colleagues began stamping the new telegrams, the letter to the German Ambassador Prince Lichnowsky, stating that as Germany had declared war on Britain he would have to leave London, was despatched to the German embassy, carried by a senior official, Sir Lancelot Oliphant, who returned at 10.15 p.m.: the deed had been done.

But a further twist followed, for ten minutes later an urgent message arrived from Edward Goschen, the British Ambassador in Berlin, stating that the German government was not going to respond to the British ultimatum and that war would follow, if London so desired it. For you and your colleagues, therefore, it was clear that Berlin had not yet declared war on Britain after all, and so all the paperwork you had been frantically preparing over the last hour was redundant. In fact you now needed to revert to the original telegrams from Cupboard A that you had stamped up earlier that day – the ones setting out that Britain was declaring war on Germany. You all groaned and sighed, in recognition of the wasted effort, and officials were despatched to the telegraph room down the corridor to withdraw the Cupboard B telegrams that were about to be sent out. More importantly, the letter that had been carried by Lancelot Oliphant to Prince Lichnowsky was now the wrong one, for it stated that Britain was responding to a German declaration of war on Britain: in reality, the opposite was true and London was declaring war on Berlin.

An awkward meeting takes place, led by the Permanent Secretary at the Foreign Office, and as you listen it becomes clear that you are being volunteered to go back to the German embassy, hopefully to recover the first letter and to issue the correct letter to Prince Lichnowsky. It is all hugely embarrassing, but as none of the senior officials wants to carry out this potentially humiliating task, it falls to you. Leaving behind your colleagues, who are assembling the correct telegrams to be issued to the governments of the world, you slip out into

16. Prince Max von Lichnowsky

the night onto Horse Guards Parade, clutching the replacement letter. You ring the bell on the side-door of the German embassy at the bottom of the Duke of York steps and eventually rouse some of the suspicious and disbelieving German staff. 'I have a message of the gravest importance from Sir Edward Grey,' you announce. At first they try to refuse you entry but, putting on your best air of importance, you implore the doorman, 'Young man, you don't know what you are doing . . . this matter is of the highest importance.' Eventually they allow you in to see the Ambassador.

Prince Lichnowsky has retired to his bedroom and, when you eventually manage to see him, he is sitting in bed, looking rather puzzled and bemused. As you explain yourself, he points to a large Chippendale writing table, on which sits the letter brought over by

17. Prince Lichnowsky and his wife (and their pet dog) depart from London just after the start of the Great War

Oliphant earlier that evening; to your relief, you see that it has only been partially opened. You surmise that the Ambassador had begun to open the first letter and, on seeing the passports inside, had concluded that it was a declaration of war and had put it to one side in despair. You quickly swap the documents and then ask the Ambassador to sign a receipt form, while in the background you both hear cheering crowds in the Mall and the singing of 'God Save the King'. As you leave, Prince Lichnowsky murmurs, 'Please remember to give my regards to your father [the Permanent Secretary at the Foreign Office]; I shall not see him again.' Britain is now at war with Germany.

AFTERMATH

As Edward Grey had gloomily confided to a friend on the evening of 3 August 1914 as they gazed across St James's Park and watched the gas-lights being lit: 'The lamps are going out all over Europe, we shall not see them lit again in our lifetime.' Europe was being plunged into

Daily

Daily Net SALE Six Times as Large as That of Any Penny Lon

WEDNESDAY, AUGUST 5, 1914 — LONDON — MANCHESTER

GREAT BRITAIN DECLARES WAR ON GERMANY

The following announcement was issued at the Foreign Office at 12.15 a.m.

'OWING to the summary rejection by the German Government of the request made by His Majesty's Government for assurances that the neutrality of

SUMMARY REJECTION OF BRITISH ULTIMATUM

Britain had sent an ultimatum to Germany which expired at midnight.

This was due to Germany's refusal to leave Belgium neutral and her invasion of that country.

The German Ambassador went to 10 Downing Street at 12.10am to receive his travel papers. He looked a broken man.

Sir Edward Goschen, the British Ambassador in Berlin, demanded his

Historic d

18. Headlines in Britain, 5 August 1914

a calamitous war, and by the end of the following day Britain had been drawn in.

The British Expeditionary Force (BEF) was quickly despatched to the continent to aid the French in their battles against the German attack, spearheaded by a dramatic thrust through Belgium, without Brussels' consent. Although the BEF was small, its intervention, alongside some misjudgements by senior German commanders, resulted in the Allies surviving the Battle of the Marne, enabling Paris to be rescued from the clutches of the Germans. With no likelihood of securing a knockout blow against the French, the German armies fell back onto defensive positions and within weeks the spectre of trench warfare had descended upon the Western Front. British intervention was by no means the only factor in preventing a decisive blow being delivered to France in 1914, but it was certainly a major contributor in bolstering the Allies and sustaining their efforts over the next few years. For the Germans, the failure of the western offensive in 1914 to compel French surrender consigned Berlin to a two-front war, in which they would have to tackle the British and the French in the west and the Russians in the east for the foreseeable future. It forced them into an attritional and protracted war in which it became increasingly difficult to see a route to victory.

THE DECISION

- To explore the alternative route go to **Section 7** (p. 60).

OR

- To explore the history of the July Crisis go to the **Historical Note** on p. 65.

SECTION 7
A NEW EUROPE?

Saturday 1 July 1916, Kaisersaal, Hamburg City Hall, Germany

A grand ceremony is under way in the Emperor's Hall in Hamburg, an occasion that appears to be setting out a new rapprochement for European diplomatic affairs and the balance of power. A crucial new treaty of understanding and friendship is about to be signed.

In the room are assembled many of the great leaders of Germany and Britain, the two most powerful nations in Europe – one a great and growing economic continental powerhouse, the other the head of a vast global maritime trading and finance empire. The two heads of state, Kaiser Wilhelm II and King George V, exchange pleasantries, although in truth they do not get on that well; the Kaiser remains a difficult character, bumptious and unpredictable, while his cousin, the British King Emperor, is shy and reserved, at least in public. It does not seem to have helped that they are first cousins. Alongside them are the political chiefs of the two Great Powers, Chancellor Theobald von Bethmann Hollweg and Prime Minister Herbert Asquith, both relieved to have reached this point after years of Anglo-German bickering and suspicion. Officials bustle around, and everywhere one turns there are powerful and dynamic figures: here Winston Churchill, First Lord of the Admiralty, there Grand Admiral Alfred von Tirpitz, Chief of the German Naval Staff. Everyone is assembled to witness the signing of a new agreement between the two Great Powers, the Treaty of Hamburg. It is hoped that this treaty will herald a period of better relations and the easing of tensions.

19. Kaiser Wilhelm II and King George V

Watching on, as the ceremony reaches the point at which the documents will be signed, are many associated political, social and family members of the two nations, including you, ***Queen Mary***, George's wife and confidante. For you, and indeed for George, this is a difficult moment. Although George's grandmother, Queen Victoria, would have been greatly pleased by the rapprochement with Germany, the rest of the family are less than amused. George's father, Edward VII, loathed Kaiser Wilhelm, while Edward's wife, Queen Alexandra, was Danish and therefore had little time for the Germans who had attacked her home nation in the 1860s. In truth, you and the rest of the British royals favoured links with the Russians, headed by Tsar Nicholas – also a first cousin of George and Wilhelm. Ties were further strengthened by the Tsar's mother also being a Dane, and the sister of Queen Alexandra. Such had been the closeness that George and

20. George V and Queen Mary

Nicholas and their families had holidayed together in Denmark; Wilhelm had not been invited.

Yet service and duty had prevailed, and you and George had accepted that the political leaders of Britain saw greater strategic benefit in closer links with Berlin than with St Petersburg. George had grumbled at the thought of having to be friendly to Wilhelm while links with Nicholas were loosened. But you had persuaded him that your personal views could not prevail; unlike Nicholas, and even Wilhelm, you were constitutional monarchs and real political power sat with Asquith, the Prime Minister, and his Cabinet. And the status and power of both Nicholas and Wilhelm had been weakened in the last few years, ever since the war of 1914. You certainly did not want the British monarchy similarly to undermine its position by attempting to influence government business too openly: London had gone through enough turbulence in the last two years as it was.

Back in 1914, as war erupted across Europe, Asquith's government had almost collapsed. David Lloyd George had led a rebellion against Edward Grey's efforts to push Britain into intervening on the side of France against Germany. Riven by dissent, Asquith's administration was paralysed. Grey resigned, and Asquith and Churchill almost went with him. German forces poured across Belgium into northern France, headed for Paris. When German troops moved perilously close to the Channel ports, London protested. Churchill mobilised the fleet and British troops landed on the coast of northern France, securing ports from the clutches of the Germans. Paris tried to draw the British into the conflict, but Berlin, despite protesting, focused on the matter in hand: defeating France quickly.

As General Alexander von Kluck's First German Army swept around Paris, panic broke out in the French government: was it to be a repeat of 1870? For a time Russian efforts on the Eastern Front forced the Germans to turn their attention away from France, but a spectacular German victory at Tannenberg, commanded by Paul von Hindenburg, changed everything. Berlin appeared to be in the ascendant. The French government fled to Bordeaux, and in St Petersburg the Russian government appeared to be on the point of collapse. To the Tsar and his ministers, it seemed as though the French had collapsed, exposing Russia alone to war against Germany and Austria.

Yet Austria had made little headway against Serbia, financial markets were in uproar and the British were calling for an end to hostilities. Since German forces had brutally violated Belgium, and with reports of atrocities perpetrated against civilians, Asquith's government had coalesced around a much stronger policy towards Berlin. The French had been badly beaten, but they had not surrendered, and the speed with which Russia had mobilised had worried Berlin, despite Hindenburg's victory. Negotiations opened and the French conceded some imperial possessions, while the Russians stepped back to bide their time, trading some border provinces to Berlin. Belgium was forced to hand over its empire to Germany and to demilitarise its forts.

But Berlin was convulsed by political change in the years after the war of 1914. Far from securing the position of the right-wing establishment and elites, the wider political body was traumatised by how close the militarists had pushed Germany into a potentially calamitous war with France, Russia and Britain. The major party in the Reichstag, the Social Democrats, instituted a process of significant reform. The Kaiser, alarmed at the prospect of further conflict and war, and believing that Germany's position had been boosted by imperial and territorial acquisitions, acquiesced to a degree to the Reichstag. Vienna meanwhile battled on against Serbia, but Austrian military incompetence was dramatically exposed and soon the Balkans was in uproar, with growing calls for Slavic independence; Vienna's regime teetered and Berlin seemed less willing to intercede.

The Russians, deflated by the stinging defeat at Tannenberg and chastened by the near-collapse of the French in 1914, turned once more to confrontation with the Ottoman Turks and the British in Asia. Relations with London deteriorated, and those in Britain who had always stated that Russia represented a greater threat seemed to have won the argument. In St Petersburg the Tsar's status had been undermined by the near-calamity of 1914; you have heard that Cousin Nicky continues to resist significant reform, but that pressure continues to grow. Surely he must realise that he will have to adapt, just as the British monarchy has and as even the Kaiser appears to accept?

For now, British interests lie in working with Berlin, containing Russia, defusing the Balkans and re-establishing stability in France, which has been convulsed by political change in the wake of the war of 1914. There are even whispers of sweeping revolutionary change once again in France. You and your family may well despair at this realignment in international affairs, but it has a cold, unchallengeable realpolitik logic all of its own. You and George must smile, carry out your duty and accept the situation. You hold your tongue and watch as the leaders shake hands, smile thinly and sign the new Treaty of Hamburg.

AFTERMATH

The age of Anglo-German cooperation captured in the Treaty of Hamburg lasted for many years. For London and Berlin, Russia presented a greater threat, and although their interests clashed over the Balkans as well as over economic and industrial rivalry, for London, controlling Russian expansion in the Middle East and the borders of India was much more pressing. Germany had broken the encirclement it had long feared since the days of Bismarck, but there was still grumbling resentment at British status; the Kaiser and other ultra-nationalists complained about the scope of the British Empire compared to German overseas territories, despite the acquisitions made at the expense of Belgium and France in 1914. For the moment the newly emerging dominance of the political parties in Germany might contain lingering nationalist and militarist sentiment, for that has not yet abated entirely. The ageing Admiral Tirpitz has even been talking about another wave of naval expansion, something that will surely bring a hostile reaction from London.

For France, the consequences of the defeat in 1914 were tumultuous. Although total collapse had been averted, belief in and support for the ailing Third Republic drained away. Resentment at German dominance in Europe and at Britain's duplicity in 1914 grew, and conflicting paths lay ahead – social change and reform versus nationalist rebirth. By the 1920s it was France that looked the most unstable Great Power in Europe. There has even been talk of another revolution.

In the years after the war of 1914 the Austro-Hungarian Empire grew weaker and fragmented in the 1920s, leading to further confrontation with Russia, which continued to support Slavic independence. Britain supported Greece and Turkey in order to keep the Russians out of the Eastern Mediterranean, and war loomed once more. Great Power politics and rivalry remain as potent as ever.

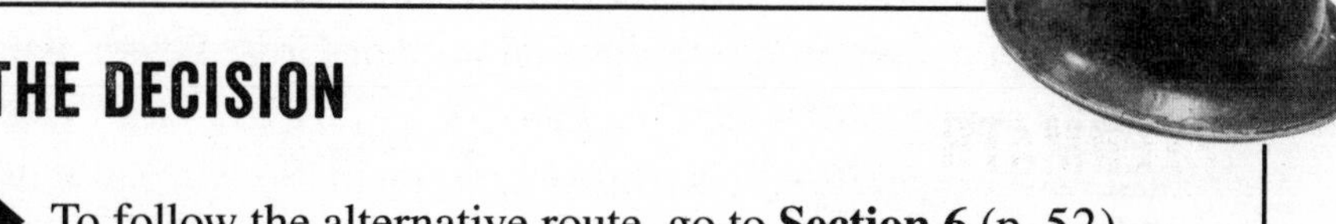

THE DECISION

▶ To follow the alternative route, go to **Section 6** (p. 52).

OR

▶ To explore the decision of the July Crisis, see the **Historical Note** below.

HISTORICAL NOTE

It is obviously the case that war broke out in the summer of 1914, a war that engulfed the Great Powers of Europe and drew in Turkey and Italy by 1915. But was it inevitable? Some historians have long argued that a major war in Europe was a near-certainty and that the political and international situation was a tinderbox almost certain to ignite.

The obvious starting flashpoint was the assassination of Archduke Franz Ferdinand in June, though of course there were many other underlying reasons why the Great Powers went to war in 1914. Princip later recorded that at the moment of the shooting he momentarily hesitated, as he had not expected the Duchess Sophie to be in the firing line; his intended targets were, of course, Franz Ferdinand and Governor Potiorek. For a variety of reasons, it is worth considering the outcome if Princip had failed to assassinate Franz and Sophie – the route explored by going from Section 1 to Section 3. Vienna would of course have been outraged at the attempt, and at the brazenness of what it would have described as Serbian-inspired terrorism. Yet if Franz and Sophie had survived, it is unlikely that Austria would have been able to garner enough support from Berlin to risk war with Russia, merely to subjugate Serbia.

The historical route takes you to Section 2 and the likely fallout of the assassinations and of Austria's ultimatum to Serbia. For many, the key turning point in the July Crisis was Russia's decision to begin mobilisation – a decision taken by the Council of Ministers in St Petersburg and conveyed to the Tsar for his agreement. In recent confrontations with Vienna and Berlin, the Russians had backed down but, fearful of a continuing diminution in their Great Power status by continually conceding to their neighbours, in July 1914 they provided a robust response to Austria's confrontation with Serbia. But it is quite possible that the Russian ministers, knowing their own weakness and lack of preparedness for war in 1914, might have held back. Their resolve had probably been fortified by the recent visit of the French President, who had offered his fulsome support to the Tsar in any dealings with Berlin or Vienna. Yet wise heads in St Petersburg knew full well that military reforms in Russia were not due to be completed until 1917 – it would of course be damaging to Russia's Great Power status not to defend Serbia in 1914, but if the Tsar and his ministers had not mobilised, it is possible that Berlin might have hesitated also, or that the situation might not have escalated so far, something explored by going from Section 2 to Section 4.

A wider European Congress, perhaps held in Budapest, is a possible outcome, and one suggested in 1914. In this context the likely crises confronting some of the European Great Powers lead in a different direction from the historical route of open warfare. Afforded more time to continue its military and economic development, Russia might have looked a more challenging opponent by the end of the decade than it did in 1914, and this might have forced a reassessment in Berlin. Nonetheless, the contradictions in Russia's development and political structures may well have seen internal division, and further social upheaval during this period. Britain would have been distracted for a period of time by a likely outbreak of conflict in Ireland, as the Liberal government of Asquith attempted to enforce its Home Rule Bill. The long-term prospects for the Austro-Hungarian Empire remain uncertain, and further confrontations with Serbia and other Slavic groups were distinctly possible.

In Section 5 we are confronted with the much-debated issue of whether or not Britain should have intervened in the war of 1914. Historically, of course, Asquith and Grey nudged the Cabinet into a position from which war was almost inevitable (go to Section 6), but many historians have long argued that this was the wrong choice. They claim that British interests were best served by standing aside in 1914, and that a German-dominated Europe was tolerable. In such a scenario, Anglo-German relations, which were already thawing a little by 1914, might well have improved – a scenario explored in Section 7. It is argued that Britain had many more links with Germany than it did with Russia, with which Britain had formed a loose association in the years leading up to the Great War. This scenario assumes that Germany would decisively defeat France in 1914 if Britain did not intervene (and this is by no means certain) and that an enhanced imperial Germany was an entity that London could deal with. With the Kaiser still directly involved in foreign policy, this is by no means an obvious outcome. It is certain that George V would have been less than pleased to have broken his relationship with the Tsar in favour of the Kaiser, with whom he had a difficult relationship.

In Section 6 we explore the outcome of Britain's decision to deliver what amounted to an ultimatum to the German government in August 1914 – one that would lead to war. The almost comic confusion in how a state actually declares war on another in the early twentieth century conceals the enormity of the act. The reasons behind Britain's decision centre on the necessity of containing German aggression and expansionism, which might well have led to Berlin dominating the continent and thus threatening Britain's position. The long-held policy in London of maintaining the balance of power in Europe was a primary factor in this decision; in reality Germany's decision to attack France through Belgium, and the consequent violation of Belgian neutrality, was merely the reason to allow Britain to intervene. Nonetheless, the subsequent atrocities perpetrated by German forces in Belgium perhaps underscore the wider reasons and justification for British intervention.

Gavrilo Princip was only nineteen at the time of the assassinations and therefore, although he was convicted by the Austrian authorities, he could not be executed. Nonetheless, his less-than-robust health was sorely tested by the difficult conditions in which he was incarcerated. He deteriorated badly over the next few years and eventually died of tuberculosis while in custody in April 1918.

Sergey Sazonov continued to serve as Russian Foreign Minister until he was forced from power in 1916. He later worked with Admiral Kolchak's regime against the Bolsheviks, before living out his years in exile, dying in France in 1927.

Sophie, Duchess of Hohenberg was of course assassinated on 28 June 1914 by Gavrilo Princip. She had been treated badly by senior elements of the Austrian elite, who looked down upon her supposedly lowly status. Had she survived, it is unlikely she would have played a significant role in Austrian society, even if her husband had eventually become Emperor.

Nikola Pašić remained a dominant figure in Serbian politics in the early decades of the twentieth century. He may well have been aware in advance of the assassination of King Alexander in 1903, which eventually brought him to power, and there is convincing evidence that he was informed of the impending assassination attempt of Franz Ferdinand. He remained in a position of power during the war and eventually was a key figure in the creation of Yugoslavia. He stayed at the heart of politics in Belgrade and was still vying for power when he suffered a heart attack and died, just before his eighty-first birthday in 1926.

David Lloyd George headed the British coalition government from December 1916 and remained as Prime Minister until he was forced from office in 1922. A major figure in British political life for much of the early part of the twentieth century, he was highly regarded for his oratory and his dynamism.

Harold Nicolson continued at the Foreign Office until the late 1920s when, after a short period as a journalist, he turned to politics, joining Oswald Mosley's recently formed New Party in 1931. However, when Mosley formed the British Union of Fascists, Nicolson, who was already warning of the perils of Fascism, switched to become a National Labour MP. After losing his seat in 1945 he turned to literary works and maintaining Sissinghurst Castle in Kent until his death in 1968.

Queen Mary supported George V throughout the First World War and into the 1920s and 1930s. She despaired of her son, Edward VIII, and his willingness to abdicate the throne in order to marry Wallis Simpson. She took a particular interest in the upbringing of her granddaughters, the Princesses Elizabeth and Margaret, and died at the age of eighty-five, a few weeks before Elizabeth's coronation in 1953.

2

THE GUNS OF AUGUST:

THE BRITISH ARMY GOES TO WAR, 1914

SECTION 1
THE EXPEDITIONARY FORCE

5 August 1914, 10 Downing Street, London

It is August 1914 and Europe is at war. London is buzzing with nervous energy. Mobilisation notices recalling soldiers and sailors dot the walls. Excited Londoners share gossip on every street corner and crowds gather around the newspaper sellers, desperate for any scraps of information. Even the weather seems uncertain. Weeks of scorching July sunshine have given way to a cool, cloudy day.

1. Lord Roberts, VC

You observe all this from the staff car that is carrying you to Number 10 Downing Street. Prime Minister Herbert Asquith has summoned a 'Council of the greatest soldiers in the country' to discuss Britain's military options. You are ***Field Marshal Lord Roberts, VC***. Although eighty-two years old, you have a razor-sharp mind and matchless military experience. You began your British army career in 1851, won the Victoria Cross during the Indian Mutiny in 1858 and have led armies to victory in Afghanistan and South Africa. You retired in 1904, but remain an influential voice in military affairs. In retirement you repeatedly warned that Germany's belligerent foreign policy would lead to war in Europe. You take no satisfaction from the fact that your prophecies have come to pass.

You arrive to find Downing Street's council room crowded with soldiers and politicians. Every man at the meeting knows that the decisions made here will be crucial. The key question is how to deploy the 120,000 soldiers of the British Expeditionary Force (BEF), an elite force of professional soldiers that stands in contrast to the vast conscript armies of Europe. Its superb training means that it can punch well above its weight, but it lacks numbers, and risks being overwhelmed in a war of attrition. Furthermore, the BEF is Britain's only deployable army. Although reinforcements can be drawn from the Territorial Force and the Indian Army, not to mention volunteers from Britain and the Dominions of Canada, Australia, New Zealand and South Africa, these men will not be ready for action for several months. The BEF will have to shoulder the weight of Britain's war until then. It is imperative that its forces are deployed in a position where they can do the most damage to the Germans without being crushed by sheer weight of numbers.

The Prime Minister opens the meeting with a statement on the current situation. Asquith admits that although the government has 'constantly considered' British options, it does not have an official war plan. There is a pre-existing idea to send the BEF to France and deploy it on the left flank of the French army. But events have thrown this idea into doubt. The German invasion has been delayed by the stout resistance of the Belgian army at Liège, although it is unclear how much longer this defiance can last. Belgium has called for immediate assistance.

Field Marshal Sir John French is the first soldier to speak. He is a diminutive, fiery cavalryman who will command the BEF in the field. He offers an alternative by suggesting that the BEF should deploy directly to the fortified port city of Antwerp in Belgium. This would allow the BEF to combine with the Belgian army, creating a powerful joint force of some 300,000 men. This Anglo-Belgian army could threaten the exposed flank of the German invasion as it scythes through Belgium. The appearance of such a powerful force in the Low Countries might even impress the Netherlands sufficiently to end its neutrality and join the Allies.

French's proposal appeals to the politicians. The Prime Minister and Foreign Secretary Sir Edward Grey see Belgium as the fulcrum of the war and believe that a powerful British army here could prove decisive. But First Lord of the Admiralty Winston Churchill sounds a note of caution: transporting the BEF to Antwerp would be dependent on the attitude of the Netherlands, due to the necessity of navigating the River Scheldt, part of which lies in Dutch territory. French suggests landing the BEF to the south-west of Antwerp and marching to the city, if a direct deployment proves impossible.

French's idea is challenged by Brigadier-General Henry Wilson. He is an intelligent, eccentric officer nicknamed 'Ugly Wilson', due to a vivid facial scar received in hand-to-hand combat in Burma in the 1880s. He has been the driving force behind British and French peacetime cooperation and reminds the council that Britain's mobilisation plans are based on travelling to France, not Belgium. He adds that France's well-developed rail and road network would give the BEF the mobility to respond to any situation. Finally he hints that the French will expect the British to follow this deployment, and that their own plans may hinge upon it.

A fierce debate follows. French's Antwerp proposal intrigues the politicians, but has limited support among the soldiers. Wilson's deployment to France is preferred by the military, but they are not unanimous in their support.

2. Henry Wilson

The ultimate decision rests with Field Marshal Lord Kitchener, an authoritative, experienced but somewhat enigmatic figure, best known for his crushing victory at the Battle of Omdurman in 1898. The Prime Minister made the sensational decision to appoint Kitchener as Secretary of State for War at the outbreak of the conflict, despite the Field Marshal having no previous experience in Westminster politics. Kitchener has spent the last twelve years in India and Egypt and knows little of British war planning. However, his suspicion of the

Map 1: Belgium and France, 1914

French army is notorious. He served as a volunteer in a field ambulance during the Franco-Prussian War (1870–71) and was appalled by the incompetence of French forces. He listens impassively to the debate on 5 August and prepares to make the final decision the next day.

You know Kitchener well. He was your Chief of Staff in the Anglo-Boer War (1899–1902) and he will value your opinion. But what do you recommend? John French's proposal to deploy to Antwerp is innovative and daring. The city's fortifications should provide a secure base of operations, and a combined British-Belgian army will threaten the German advance through Belgium. Yet there is also a risk that Antwerp may become a trap. The Germans might lay siege to the city, and resupplying the BEF will be difficult if the Netherlands maintains strict neutrality. Furthermore, it is not clear exactly how British and Belgian forces will cooperate.

Wilson's plan to send the BEF to France is safer. It is the product of several years of planning and will give the BEF more freedom of action. French rail and road networks are better than those in Belgium and will enable the army to deploy to wherever it is needed most. Yet Wilson's casual assumption that the BEF will operate on the left flank of the French army troubles several council members. What will the army do in this position? How will it influence the war? It may be too late to make an intervention in Belgium, and it risks being made subordinate to French plans rather than making its own meaningful contribution. Wilson's plan offers flexibility, but may become a hostage to events.

What do you recommend?

AIDE-MEMOIRE

* The Belgian army is fighting for its life at Liège and needs immediate support. Deploying to Antwerp is the fastest and most direct way of assisting Belgium.
* Wilson's pre-existing plan is safer. It has been discussed and developed over a period of several years. It has resolved several technical problems and promises to transport the BEF to the continent with minimum risks.
* Antwerp is a fortified port city. It will provide a secure base of operations and a combined British-Belgian army positioned there will be a serious threat to the flank of the German invasion.
* Wilson's plan will allow the BEF to react to a variety of situations. If the Belgians are still holding out, then the British can march to their aid; alternatively, the BEF can form up on the

left of the French army and help them to repel the German invasion of France.

* It is not clear exactly how the BEF will fight alongside the French army. There is a risk that the French will see it as a reinforcement to be used however they wish. After his bitter experience as a volunteer ambulance man in 1870–71, Kitchener has grave doubts about the competence of the French army.
* Although it has not ruled it out, the Royal Navy is concerned about the Antwerp deployment. If the Dutch maintain their neutrality, then the port will prove difficult to supply.
* If it deploys to France, the BEF may arrive too late to help the Belgians and will be forced to react to whatever the Germans choose to do next.

THE DECISION

Do you advise Kitchener to send the BEF to Antwerp where it might play a decisive role? Or do you urge him to deploy it to France where it can react to a range of threats?

▶ To advise that Kitchener approves French's proposal to deploy the BEF to Antwerp, go to **Section 5** (p. 100).

OR

▶ To suggest adopting Wilson's pre-existing plan to send the BEF to France and respond to events from there, go to **Section 2** (p. 78).

SECTION 2
CRISIS AT LE CATEAU

12.30 a.m., 26 August 1914, II Corps Headquarters, Bavai, France

Your horse whinnies in fear as a deafening peal of thunder cracks above you. The rain falls in sheets and makes rivers run between the cobblestones. A flash of lightning illuminates a narrow street jammed with horses, wagons and weary soldiers. Your exhausted men have been marching and fighting relentlessly for the past three days – and the Germans are closing in.

3. Horace Smith-Dorrien

You are ***General Sir Horace Smith-Dorrien***, commanding II Corps of the BEF. Your career began at the Battle of Isandlwana in 1879, a crushing British defeat at the hands of the Zulus, from which you were lucky to escape with your life. Since then you have forged a reputation as a tough, skilled infantry officer with a truly volcanic temper. You have commanded troops in Africa, Egypt and India, but you have never faced a crisis like this.

A groom calms your frightened horse and you head into your ad-hoc headquarters in the small French village of Bavai. As you shed your waterproofs you reflect on what has happened in the last week. Lord Kitchener approved Henry Wilson's plan to deploy the BEF to France, although he added his own twist by holding back two infantry divisions to protect Britain in the event of a sudden German seaborne invasion. Nevertheless, mobilisation proceeded like clockwork, and the BEF took its place alongside the French Fifth Army on the left flank of the Allied line.

Then things began to go wrong. The August heatwave and the stress of war proved too much for the notoriously obese General Sir James Grierson, commanding II Corps, who died of a heart attack. Lord Kitchener assigned you to take his place, and you joined II Corps in France on 19 August. Taking over the formation at such short notice posed many problems. The greatest of these was your stormy relationship with Field Marshal Sir John French. Although you were once close friends, a series of disputes over tactics and training means that French now openly despises you.

The BEF had advanced to the Belgian town of Mons by 22 August. Urgent reports from the Royal Flying Corps warned that an immense German force was converging on the British position, but Sir John dismissed them as alarmist and intended to advance on Brussels. His plans changed only late that night when a message arrived from the French Fifth Army on his right flank. The French had suffered a heavy defeat at the Battle of Guise and were retiring in disorder. They asked the BEF to cover their flank to prevent the Germans encircling them, and to this end Sir John agreed to hold the line at Mons for twenty-four hours. This was a risky decision. The BEF was facing an oncoming German steamroller, and a 30-mile-wide gap had opened between its flank and the retreating French Fifth Army, leaving the British army in grave danger of encirclement. Although this was not yet known at British headquarters, the BEF was standing in the path of the main thrust of the German 'Schlieffen Plan' – an all-out assault through Belgium and into France, designed to crush the Western Allies in just six weeks.

Sir John assigned II Corps to defend Mons. The position was a poor one and you requested permission to fall back from the town to high ground some two miles to the south. But French brusquely denied your request. Your men had to fight where they stood.

The Germans struck your line at the Battle of Mons on 23 August. Your soldiers fought hard, making use of their superb tactics and training, but sheer weight of German numbers eventually told and you were forced to give ground. You achieved your objective of delaying the enemy advance for twenty-four hours, but the BEF was now isolated and locked in close contact with the German First Army – a mighty force that outnumbers the British by almost four to one.

Sir John French ordered a general retreat to proceed under cover of darkness on 24 August. This was no easy matter, for your corps was entangled with German forces who scented blood and harried you

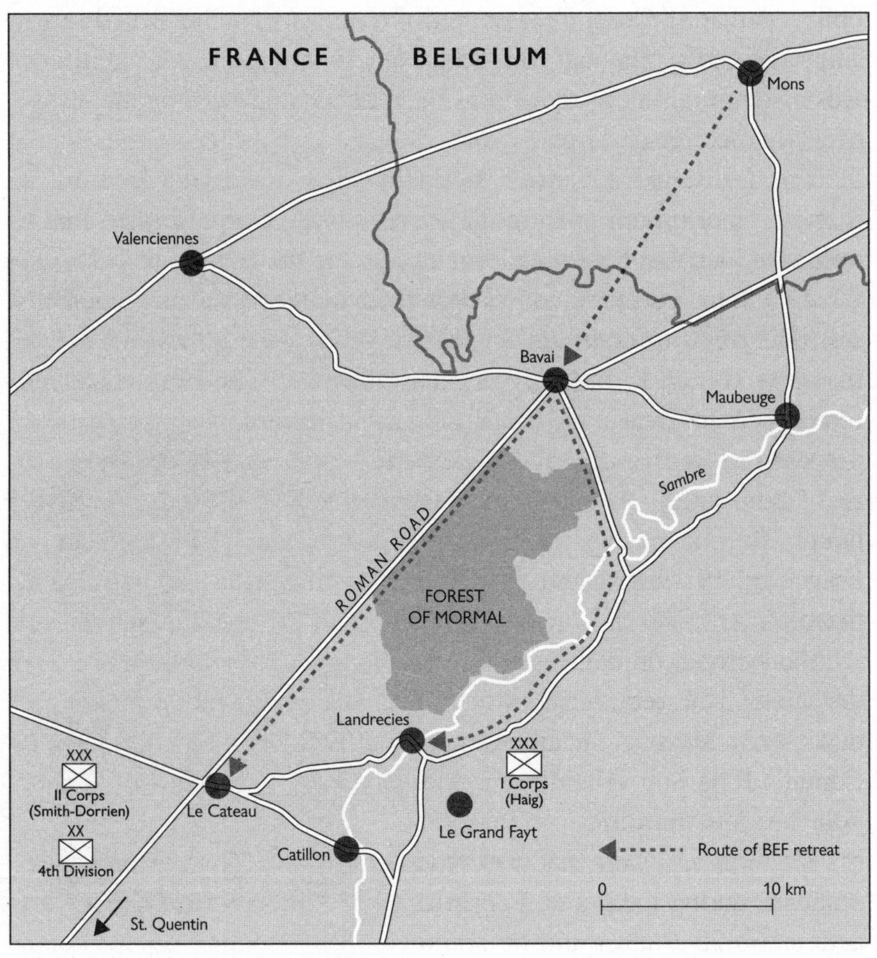

Map 2: The BEF's retreat from Mons

relentlessly. A dangerous German hook that threatened to turn your flank was fended off at heavy cost at Audregnies on 24 August, but the enemy remained in close pursuit.

The situation became critical that night. The BEF was forced to split into two parts to circumvent the impassable Forest of Mormal, which lay astride the retreat route. Your II Corps marched down a Roman road that ran alongside the western half of the forest, while Douglas Haig's I Corps took a more circuitous route along roads to the east of the woodland. You were due to re-form into a single army on the southern side of the forest.

But German forces were unaware of the division of the BEF and believed that II Corps represented the entirety of the British army. They doggedly pursued your force on 25 August. Your withdrawal was made gruelling by the August heat and was slowed by the masses of frightened refugees who blocked the road. Cavalry rearguards did their best to stem the German tide while you urged your soldiers on. Some of your infantry battalions covered a blistering thirty-five miles on 25 August – and yet the Germans are still on your heels.

At 7 p.m. you received orders from Field Marshal French that instructed you to continue the retreat the next day. You passed the information on to your subordinates and prepared to get some much-needed rest. You have averaged just four hours' sleep a night since arriving in France on 19 August and are feeling the strain.

But before you could settle in for the night you received unwelcome news. At 11 p.m. Major-General Edmund 'The Bull' Allenby arrived at your headquarters. He told you that his Cavalry Division had become scattered during the fierce rearguard actions on 25 August and he could not guarantee that his cavalrymen can

4. Edmund 'The Bull' Allenby

protect II Corps on 26 August. He urged you to resume the retreat under cover of darkness.

This unwelcome news prompted you to call an emergency conference with your commanders in Bavai. An endless thunderstorm rages overhead as you lay out the situation. Rain beats against the windows and your discussions are periodically halted by cracks of thunder. In this grim atmosphere you ask your infantry commanders whether it is possible for them to retreat under cover of darkness. Major-General Charles Fergusson shakes his head. The infantry divisions are bone-tired and need to rest, while the appalling weather will make navigation difficult. He believes that the earliest the infantry can march is 9 a.m. Allenby scowls at this news – such a late start will give the Germans several hours of daylight to continue their pursuit, and he does not believe his overstretched cavalry can hold them back. Retreating in daylight will be risky.

You ponder your options for retreat. As II Corps marched past Le Cateau you were heartened to meet the soldiers of 4th Division. Lord Kitchener had held this division back at the outset of war, but rushed them to the battlefront once it was clear that the Germans were not planning naval landings. These reinforcements have significantly increased your strength. Perhaps it would be possible to assemble an improvised rearguard to reinforce the cavalry. These men might be able to buy sufficient time for the rest of II Corps to escape. However, the cost to the rearguard would be great. They would have to fight against overwhelming German numbers and they could be encircled and lost. Worse still, if the rearguard was swiftly overwhelmed, then the Germans would catch the rest of II Corps on the march and destroy it.

There is one other option. Like a cornered animal suddenly turning on its tormentor, you can halt and make a stand against your pursuers, to deal them a 'stopping blow'. The idea has some advantages. After three days of pursuit, the Germans may be overconfident and will not expect you to suddenly turn and fight. They will advance onto the battlefield piecemeal and will be unable to coordinate a full-scale assault for several hours. This will buy you precious time for the Cavalry Division to reorganise, and for you to prepare retreat routes.

But this decision is risky. The battle is certain to be chaotic and bloody. Your corps is exhausted, outnumbered and outgunned. They will be forced to find defensive positions in the darkness and there will be no time to construct anything except the most rudimentary trenches. There is also a risk that the Germans will turn your flanks. There are French cavalry operating on your left, but your right flank is completely open. You hope that Douglas Haig's I Corps will march to cover this gap, but you are unable to establish communication with him and must trust that he will march to the sound of the guns.

You must also consider John French's orders. If you choose to stand and fight, you will be disobeying a direct order from your Commander-in-Chief. This is no small matter. Sir John hates you and will seize upon any opportunity to sack you. Although British *Field Service Regulations* give authority to the 'man on the spot' to implement orders, you do not believe this will save you from French's wrath if you disobey him. Following his orders, even if it ends in disaster, may be the safer career move.

The thunder rumbles once more and shakes you from your thoughts. You look around the table at your subordinates, their faces ghostly and pale in the lamplight. You must make a critical decision.

AIDE-MEMOIRE

* Sir John French has given you a direct order to continue the retreat. Surely you should follow the instructions given by your Commander-in-Chief?
* The Cavalry Division is disorganised and cannot provide a rearguard. Retreating without cavalry protection will be immensely dangerous. The Germans may be able to catch you on the march and destroy you.
* Your infantry is exhausted and will be unable to move until approximately 0900. The Germans will be close on your heels by that time, and you may be unable to escape.

* The reinforcements of 4th Division give you options. You might be able to use them to hold off the German advance for long enough for II Corps to escape.
* Making a stand will surprise the Germans and force them to attack across open ground, where you can inflict heavy losses upon them.
* If you can inflict a heavy enough blow against the Germans, then you may be able to stop their pursuit in its tracks. This would allow you to withdraw unmolested and relieve pressure on the BEF.
* If you make a stand, then your flanks will be dangerously exposed. There is no sign of Haig's I Corps, but you assume they are somewhere on your right flank. Surely they will march to the sound of the guns?

THE DECISION

Do you obey Sir John French's orders and continue the retreat or hold your ground and prepare for battle?

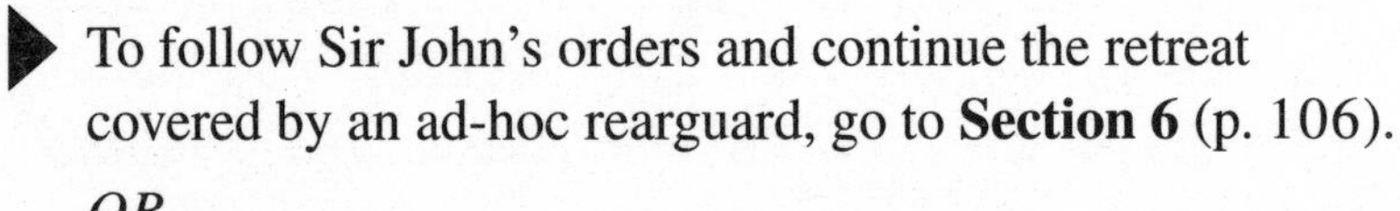

▶ To follow Sir John's orders and continue the retreat covered by an ad-hoc rearguard, go to **Section 6** (p. 106).

OR

▶ To hold your ground and fight your pursuers, go to **Section 3** (p. 86).

SECTION 3
SHOWDOWN IN PARIS

1 September 1914, British embassy, Paris

It is nearly a month since Britain declared war – and the war is being lost. Exhausted, dusty soldiers in British khaki and French blue trudge south along roads crowded with frightened refugees. The rumble of German guns in the distance spurs the retreat onwards. The enemy invasion seems unstoppable.

You survey the survivors of the BEF with a mixture of anger and despair as you pass them on your way to an important meeting in Paris. You are ***Field Marshal Sir John French***, Commander-in-Chief of the British Expeditionary Force. You are an experienced cavalryman who forged a reputation for skill and daring in the Anglo-Boer War (1899–1902). You were the natural choice to lead the BEF into action in 1914, despite concerns about your mercurial temperament and your chaotic personal life, which is marred by infidelity, gambling and unpaid debts. Nevertheless, one of your greatest strengths is your affinity with your soldiers. You have a gift of being able to talk

5. John French

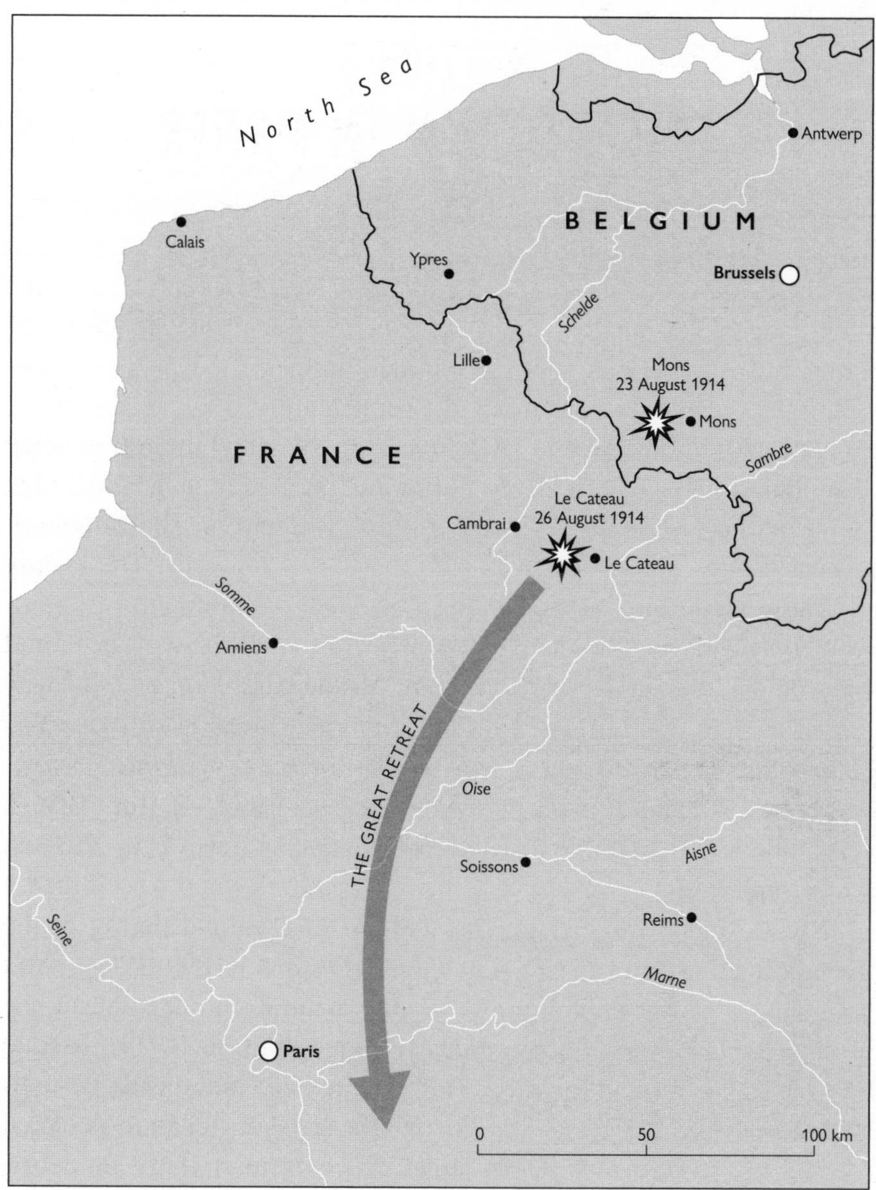

Map 3: The Great Retreat, August–September 1914

to the common man and are immensely popular within the ranks of the army. It is that close connection with your soldiers that makes the current situation so disturbing. You are worried that the BEF has reached its breaking point.

You reflect on the causes of the disaster as your staff car approaches the suburbs of Paris. On your deployment to France, Lord Kitchener gave you confidential instructions that told you to ensure the French did not take command of the BEF, and to avoid risky engagements that might destroy the army. In the event, cooperation with the French has been almost non-existent and your army has been exposed to constant danger. You made a stand at Mons to protect the French Fifth Army, but you feel that your commitment to the Allied cause has not been reciprocated. In your mind, the French army's 'tactics are practically to fall back right and left of me, usually without notice, and to abandon all ideas of offensive operations'. Failed by your allies and facing an overwhelming German assault, you had no choice but to retreat.

The retreat from Mons has been an endless nightmare of fierce combat, relentless heat and sleep deprivation. Amid it all, your hated subordinate, General Smith-Dorrien, disobeyed your orders and turned to fight the Battle of Le Cateau on 26 August. Smith-Dorrien claims that the battle was a victory, points out that the German pursuit was halted and adds that his men are weary, yet unbowed. But you are certain he is exaggerating and you believe that II Corps is in a 'shattered condition'.

By 30 August you had decided that the BEF must withdraw from the fighting line for rest and a refit. General Joseph Joffre, the supreme commander of the French army, urged you to hold your place and promised that he was about to unleash a counter-offensive that would hurl back the German invasion. But you had lost faith in the French high command and were mindful of Kitchener's instructions. You refused his request to join the attack and informed Joffre that you were withdrawing your army to the south for ten days' rest. You sent a telegraph to the British War Cabinet on the same day, stating, 'I have been pressed very hard to remain, even in my shattered condition, in the fighting line but I have absolutely refused to do so and I hope you will approve of the course I have taken. Not only is it in accordance with the spirit and letter of your instructions, but it is dictated by common sense.'

But then events took an unexpected turn. Lord Kitchener telegraphed you to announce that he was coming to France in person to discuss the situation. He has summoned you to this meeting at the British embassy in Paris on 1 September.

A cloud of fear hangs over Paris. The agonies endured during the siege of 1870–71 are still vivid in the city's memory. The French government is preparing to evacuate, and civilians with the means to leave are fleeing in droves. Yet you also notice a steady stream of French soldiers heading towards the front. There are even rumours circulating that Paris will mobilise its large fleet of taxi cabs to rush its soldiers into action. It is clear that France is not yet broken.

On arrival at the embassy, you are enraged to find that Lord Kitchener is dressed in his full Field Marshal's uniform, despite his new role as civilian Secretary of State for War. You feel this is an attempt to undermine your authority, and this is compounded when Kitchener attempts to lecture you about the strategic situation. The mood in the room is tense. There are several embassy staff at the meeting, not to mention French Prime Minister René Viviani and Minister of War Alexandre Millerand, all of whom can sense a thunderous argument looming.

6. Lord Kitchener

Kitchener suggests that you discuss the matter in private, and you leave the uncomfortable politicians behind. The moment the doors are closed you turn your full fury on the Secretary of State for War. You condemn Kitchener's condescending tone, accuse him of ignorance, lambast his failure to understand the reality of the campaign and reiterate your determination to withdraw from the fighting. The BEF is in dire need of rest and you have lost all faith in your French allies. You close your argument by pointing out that your plans are in line with Kitchener's own instructions to preserve the BEF.

Kitchener is unmoved by your statement. He argues that the strategic situation is critical. The Germans are at the gates of Paris – unless they can be repulsed the capital will fall, and France with it. Removing the BEF for a refit is impossible. It will leave a dangerous gap in the Allied line and will fatally weaken Joffre's planned counter-offensive.

The arguments go back and forth. You emphasise your losses and the failures of the French military. Kitchener acknowledges the heavy casualties to the BEF, but stresses the need for Allied unity in the hour of crisis. He shares Joffre's view that the Germans are bloodied, overextended and vulnerable to a determined Allied counter-attack. Such an attack could turn the tide of the entire war, and the BEF must play its part.

As the debate ends, you remind Kitchener that although you value 'his advice and assistance', you will not tolerate 'any interference with my executive command and authority so long as His Majesty's Government chose to retain me in my present position'. You are the commander of the BEF and your decision will be final.

But what should you do? You can see the logic of Kitchener's arguments, but feel he misunderstands the intensity of the war and underestimates the hardships suffered by your army. Questions race through your mind. Can Joffre launch his counter-offensive without your participation? Will the French finally prove reliable allies? Can you ask your weary soldiers for an all-out effort after the gruelling retreat from Mons?

A decision must be made.

AIDE-MEMOIRE

* The BEF is bloodied and exhausted. The retreat from Mons has carried your army almost 200 miles and it is in dire need of rest and refit.
* The German invasion is at the gates of Paris. If it is not halted now, then it will seize the capital and win the war.
* Your French allies seem to have failed you at every turn. Why should Joffre's counter-attack be any different?
* The Germans are becoming over-extended and their soldiers must be weary. They have pursued the Allies for almost ten days and will not expect to face a sudden, determined counter-attack.
* Kitchener's instructions at the outset of war told you to avoid throwing the BEF into risky battles that might lead to heavy casualties. Yet this is exactly what he is telling you to do now. Does he really understand the situation?
* Despite its hardships, the BEF's excellent training means that it remains a powerful force. It could tip the scales if used in the Allied counter-attack.
* Kitchener's decision to wear his Field Marshal's uniform has insulted you. You are not certain you should listen to a word that this jumped-up politician has to say.

THE DECISION

Are you swayed by Kitchener's arguments in favour of joining the French counter-attack or would you rather stick to your original decision to pull the BEF out of the fighting line?

- To stick to your original plan and order the BEF to leave the front line and rest, go to **Section 7** (p. 110).

OR

- If you are convinced by Kitchener's logic and wish to join the counter-attack, go to **Section 4** (p. 94).

SECTION 4
THE MIRACLE ON THE MARNE

11 September 1914, north of the River Marne, France

You and your staff are watering your horses at an abandoned farmhouse when there is a sudden commotion at a nearby barn. Your men have discovered a small group of leaderless German infantrymen who have somehow been left behind as their army retreated. They are disoriented, exhausted and glad to surrender. A quick examination of their shoulder straps identifies their regiment, and you jot the information down in your pocketbook. This book is crammed with information, for you have captured more German prisoners this week than in the previous fortnight.

You are ***Lieutenant-Colonel George de Symons Barrow***, the GSO1 (Intelligence) officer for the BEF's Cavalry Division. You have a reputation as an excellent staff officer, but your role with the BEF came about by chance. Soon after the outbreak of war you encountered Major-General Edmund 'The Bull' Allenby in a War Office corridor and he recruited you on the spot to serve as the intelligence officer for the Cavalry Division. You have performed this role with skill and cunning. On the march towards Mons in mid-August you acquired a Belgian telephone listing and called every train station in the vicinity. If the call went unanswered or if it was answered in German, then you knew that the area was in enemy hands. Unfortunately your warnings that the BEF was facing the juggernaut of the German First Army went unheeded by Sir John French until it was far too late.

But all has changed. A week ago the irresistible German advance had reached the gates of Paris. Your soldiers muttered that the war was lost and that the BEF would soon be withdrawn to the coast, for evacuation back to the United Kingdom. You know that Sir John French seriously considered this option, and wonder what words were exchanged between him and Lord Kitchener in Paris. Whatever was said, it ensured that the BEF remained in the line alongside its beleaguered allies.

7. Joseph Joffre

Staying in the line was one thing, but joining General Joffre's grand counter-attack was quite another. Sir John's confidence in the French army was at a low ebb and he was reluctant to participate in an offensive that might end in disaster. It took a remarkable personal meeting with Joffre at a chateau in Vaux-le-Pénil on 5 September to change his mind.

Joffre arrived in the early afternoon, thanked French for his time and then began addressing him in his 'low, toneless, albino voice'. Despite his name, Sir John was not fluent in French, and several officers offered to translate. Sir John waved all of them away, for he was transfixed by Joffre's expert presentation. The French commander spoke with quiet determination, emphasising that the fate of Europe hung in the balance and stressing the importance of the BEF to his plans. His speech steadily grew in passion. He told Sir John that he was ready to throw his last soldiers into the battle to save France and urged the British to do the same. He ended his appeal with a moment of pure military theatre. He clasped Sir John's hands, looked him squarely in the eyes and said, '*Monsieur le Maréchal, c'est la France qui vous supplie*' ('Field Marshal, it is France that begs you'). Sir John was overwhelmed by the power of the appeal and several witnesses saw tears in his eyes. He attempted to reply in French, but his grasp of the language failed him. Instead he proclaimed, 'Damn it, I can't explain. Tell him that all that men can do, our fellows will do.'

On 6 September, after almost a fortnight of retreat, the BEF turned and began to advance. The Battle of the Marne was under way. French and German forces were locked in combat all along the front. The British army was a small addition to this clash of giants, but it filled a vital part of the line. The BEF operated between the French Sixth Army and the French Fifth Army and ensured that these two forces could advance with their flanks secure. The role was not merely defensive. The BEF was advancing against a weak point of the German line and Joffre urged them to press forward.

The scale and determination of the Allied counter-attack took the German commanders by surprise. The Battle of the Marne would swirl across an enormous battlefront, with advantages won and lost by both sides, but the Allied advance proved irresistible. Sir John French quickly grasped the nature of the battle. On the very first day of the attack he 'got the first inkling that the Germans . . . have walked into

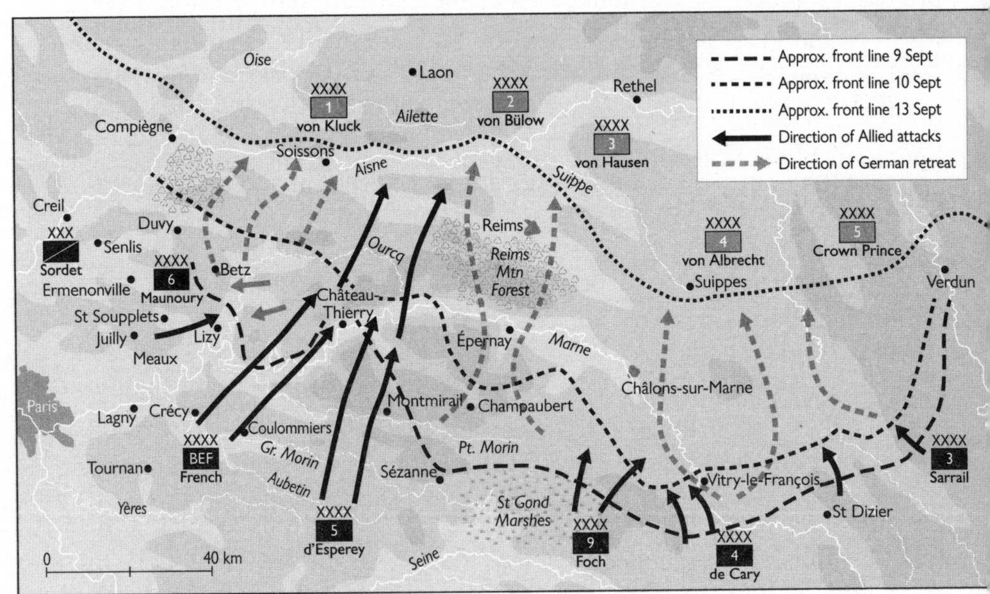

Map 4: The Battle of the Marne

a trap which they are now trying to get out of. All their columns are marching North rapidly and have already begun to recross the Marne.'

Since then the British have advanced steadily, gaining momentum with each passing day and fighting sharp actions against enemy rearguards. The sight of abandoned German equipment and dispirited prisoners inspires your soldiers to press on.

You close your pocketbook and assign an escort to take away the latest German captives. Your cavalry are already in the saddle and eager to advance. In the distance you can hear the steady rumble of artillery as the French advance on either flank. You allow yourself a smile. The Allies are on the cusp of a great victory.

AFTERMATH

The fulcrum of the Battle of the Marne lay with the French Fifth and Sixth Armies and the German First and Second Armies. The Germans initially held their ground, but with Allied troops advancing all along the line, it soon became apparent that their exhausted and over-extended forces were in danger of being encircled. The pressure proved too much for German Chief of the General Staff, Helmuth von Moltke, and on 9 September he ordered his armies to retreat. It was a fateful decision. It signalled the failure of the Schlieffen Plan and brought an end to Germany's attempt to crush France with a single knockout blow. Von Moltke recognised the significance of the defeat and is said to have told Kaiser Wilhelm II, 'Your majesty, we have lost the war.' The defeat at the Marne ensured that Germany would be locked into a long, two-front war – a strategic nightmare that the Schlieffen Plan had been designed to avoid.

The Battle of the Marne saved France, but it did not crush the German invaders. German forces retreated sixty miles to the north and entrenched in strong defensive positions on high ground overlooking the River Aisne. The BEF attempted to break through at the Battle of the Aisne between 12 and 15 September. Although the British skilfully established bridgeheads across the river, they were unable to storm the heights that overlooked the valley and suffered heavy casualties in a battle that was a grim portent of the years of trench warfare to come. The BEF dug in opposite the German positions. A stalemate settled on this part of the front as both sides licked their wounds and considered their next move.

The BEF did not stay here long. Sir John French's army moved to Belgium in early October and was soon locked in deadly combat at the First Battle of Ypres. The line held, albeit at great cost, and Ypres remained in Allied hands. By November 1914 both sides were completely exhausted. Allied and German armies were entrenched opposite one another, from the English Channel to the Swiss border. The Western Front had been formed. Few could imagine that breaking it would take almost four years and cost millions of lives.

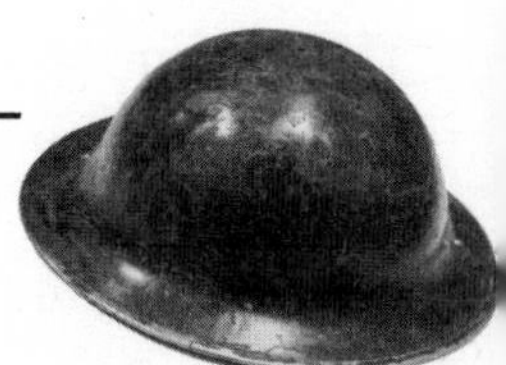

THE DECISION

▶ To follow the alternative route, go back to **Section 3** (p. 86).

OR

▶ To explore the decisions of the campaign, go to the **Historical Note** on p. 113.

SECTION 5

THE ANTWERP EXPEDITION

7 a.m., 1 September 1914, I Corps Headquarters, Antwerp

The guns are thundering to the south of Antwerp. Amid the constant fire you can pick out the sharp crack of rifles and the ominous chatter of machine guns. The BEF's long-awaited offensive against the flank of the German invasion is under way.

You are ***Brigadier-General John 'Johnnie' Gough, VC***, serving as the Chief of Staff for Douglas Haig's I Corps. You are a member of one of the most famous military families in the British Empire. Your father, General Sir Charles Gough, and your uncle, General Sir Hugh Gough, were both awarded the Victoria Cross. You received your own for courage under fire in Somaliland in 1903. Your heroism is matched by intelligence and professionalism, and you are considered one of the finest staff officers in the British army.

8. John Gough, VC

You were dubious about Sir John French's plan to bring the BEF to Antwerp, which saw years of pre-war planning cast aside. The new concept required hasty improvisation. The BEF lacked good maps of the Antwerp area, had no liaison officers with the Belgian army and had to endure frustrating negotiations with the Royal Navy to arrange transport. There was also a tense political dimension. The Dutch were determined to maintain their neutrality, which made passage of the Scheldt estuary impossible for military vessels.

The deployment was chaotic. Dutch neutrality prevented a direct deployment to Antwerp, and the BEF had to land at the much smaller port of Ostend and march to the city. Overworked Belgian stevedores struggled to unload the ships, and the docks were soon packed with soldiers, supplies and equipment. The process took far longer than expected and the Royal Navy's escorts looked on nervously, fearful of a sortie from the German High Seas Fleet. Anxious destroyer captains reported frequent U-boat sightings but, mercifully, there were no attacks on British shipping.

The BEF arrived in Antwerp in dribs and drabs. The rapturous reception from Belgian civilians and soldiers gave you confidence, but your hopes were dampened as you inspected the vaunted fortresses that ringed the port. Although superficially impressive mountains of steel and concrete, the forts dated from the 1880s and had been poorly maintained. Their artillery batteries were now outranged by the latest German heavy guns and you could not rely on them to resist a siege.

The state of the Belgian army also caused concern. Although undoubtedly courageous, its soldiers were poorly trained and ill-equipped. Liaison with Belgian command also proved difficult. There had been no meaningful pre-war discussions between the British and the Belgian military, and arrangements had to be made in the field. The fact that the Belgian army was commanded by the thirty-nine-year-old

9. King Albert I

King Albert I added to the complexities. Sir John French found that he had to defer to the authority of the Belgian monarch without surrendering the BEF's independence. This was a difficult tightrope for any commander to walk and made cooperation difficult.

In a reversal of the famous phrase attributed to Napoleon that 'Antwerp was a pistol pointed at the heart of England', Sir John French had hoped that Antwerp might prove to be a 'dagger to the throat of the Kaiser's armies'. He planned to launch an attack into the flank of the German invasion, but attempts to coordinate this with the Belgians proved taxing. The Belgian army was disorganised after its retreat from Liège and needed time to recuperate. The delay allowed the Germans to detach several corps from their main invasion force and entrench them in screening positions to the south of Antwerp. You raged at the lost opportunity. If you had struck fast, you could have ripped into an exposed flank. Instead you would have to battle through a line of defences first.

On 30 August, King Albert finally informed you that he was ready to join the attack. The next forty-eight hours were a blur of planning as you and Haig prepared for action. Your I Corps would serve as a spearhead that would surge out from the fortress belt, pierce the German forces that were screening the city and advance into the open country beyond.

The attack would begin at 6 a.m. on 1 September. The BEF formed up around the fortresses under cover of dense sea fog, before advancing. The roar of guns soon followed and you knew that the attack had well and truly begun. You and Haig anxiously waited for news at your command post.

Fragmented reports began to arrive by mid-morning. Your forces had crashed into strongly entrenched German positions and were suffering heavy losses. Nevertheless, some lodgements had been made in the German line, and you tried to feed in reinforcements to exploit these successes. By mid-afternoon the battle hung in the balance. Your forces had broken into several points of the German line, but were facing ferocious counter-attacks and a hail of fire from their left flank. The latter point disturbed you, for the Belgians were meant to be attacking on your left. Where were they? Urgent telephone calls eventually confirmed your worst fears: the Belgian assault had been repulsed and they had fallen back to the redoubts.

It was clear that the attack was faltering. Your men clung on in their lodgements until nightfall, repulsing several determined German counter-attacks, but their position was untenable. In the early hours you were forced to withdraw back to your starting point. The Battle of Antwerp had ended in defeat.

AFTERMATH

The Battle of Antwerp was a rude shock to the BEF. The strength of the entrenched German defenders had been unexpected, casualties had been heavy and no ground had been gained. In the aftermath of the battle, BEF intelligence estimated that the Germans were screening Antwerp with sixteen infantry divisions, giving them a numerical advantage over the combined Anglo-Belgian army. Furthermore, they were well entrenched and backed by heavy artillery support. Breaking through this line would be no easy matter.

Attitudes towards the Belgian army soured after the battle. Sir John French was furious that they had retreated without warning the BEF. The Belgians were equally angry with French, blaming him for delays and disorganisation. Relations between Sir John and King Albert were frosty for the rest of the campaign.

Nevertheless, the battle alarmed the German Chief of the General Staff, Helmuth von Moltke, who had always feared a British landing on the Belgian coast, as it would threaten the flank of the German invasion. In pre-war planning he had believed he could screen Antwerp with twelve divisions, but the arrival of the British in August prompted him to increase this number to sixteen. The failure of the Anglo-Belgian attack did nothing to reduce his fears. He convinced himself that it was a feint, and was taken in by faulty intelligence reports that stated the British had landed an additional 40,000 soldiers at Ostend. Fearing for his flank, he detached more divisions from his invading armies to reinforce the screen at Antwerp.

The weakening of his invasion force was a disastrous decision.

The divisions departed for Belgium just as the French were launching their counter-attack at the River Marne. The Battle of the Marne was a confusing, bloody and in some ways indecisive engagement, but it halted the invasion. The Germans remained within striking distance of Paris, but could go no further.

The BEF campaign was also faltering. It had suffered heavy casualties trying to storm the German trenches and its position at Antwerp became dangerous by late September. The Germans brought up their siege guns and began to pulverise the fortress belt. The BEF and the Belgian army held a shrinking perimeter, clinging to a perilously thin overland supply line from Ostend, and suffering under German artillery fire and Zeppelin raids. By early October the position was untenable and the decision was made to evacuate the city under cover of darkness, abandoning a large quantity of stores and equipment. The BEF and the Belgians were able to retreat along the coast towards Ypres.

The decision to deploy the BEF to Belgium instead of France was deeply controversial. The BEF suffered heavy losses and its failure to support France directly damaged relations between the two nations. Its influence on the campaign was due to Moltke's paranoia about British coastal landings rather than any great military brilliance. Nevertheless, Sir John French claimed to his dying day that 'The Battle of Antwerp saved Paris.'

THE DECISION

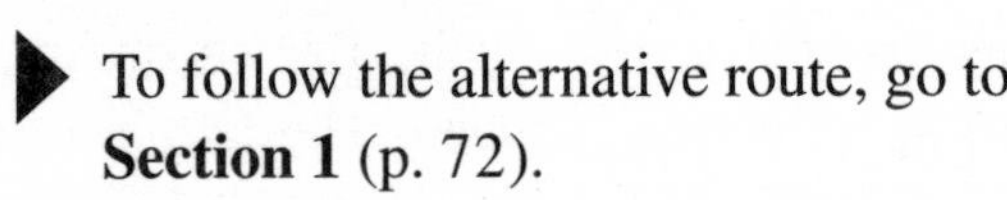

▶ To follow the alternative route, go to **Section 1** (p. 72).

OR

▶ To explore the decisions of the campaign, go to the **Historical Note** on p. 113.

SECTION 6

THE BEF IS BROKEN

5 p.m., 26 August 1914, Bohain-en-Vermandois, France

Your heart sinks as you survey the town square in the small village of Bohain-en-Vermandois. It is packed with bloodied and broken British soldiers. Many are wounded, most have lost their equipment and all are completely exhausted. In the distance you can hear the rumble of guns as the Germans press forward.

You are ***Major Tom Bridges***, commanding C Squadron of the 4th Royal Irish Dragoon Guards. You have had an eventful war. On 22 August, C Squadron had the honour of being the first soldiers of the BEF to engage the enemy when you chased down a German cavalry patrol. You were in action again two days later at Audregnies, where you led C Squadron in a daring but doomed cavalry charge. Your horse was shot from under you and the fall left you concussed. Seconds later you were run over by the regiment's machine-gun section, fracturing your cheekbone and leaving you with a vivid black eye. Your war might have ended there, had it not been for an intrepid staff officer who rushed forward in a

10. Tom Bridges

sports-model Rolls-Royce, rescuing wounded soldiers by bundling them onto the back seats, before racing away to safety at top speed. You resumed command of C Squadron later that evening, despite your injuries.

You arrived at Le Cateau in the early hours of 26 August. Your men were drenched from the thunderstorm and your horses were exhausted. You expected to be directed towards billets and stables, but instead received an urgent message that you were to join a hastily formed rearguard, under the command of Brigadier-General Aylmer Hunter-Weston, which would cover II Corps the next day.

In the storm-racked night you struggled to locate the rest of the rearguard. After several fruitless hours of wandering the farm tracks around Le Cateau, you eventually stumbled upon Hunter-Weston's headquarters. He was struggling to coordinate his new command and had a limited idea of the ground that he was to defend.

The dawn light was soon upon you, and with it came the first German scouts. The enemy probed forward in small groups, trying to determine the strength of your defences. There had been no time to entrench and you felt terribly exposed – a feeling that grew much worse when a German aircraft circled overhead and dropped silver streamers to mark your location. Your cavalry instincts urged you to fall back and take a better position. But you had to hold your ground, for behind you lay a mass of British infantry, artillery and transport that was struggling to retreat.

The Germans were soon pouring fire onto the rearguard. Machine-gun bullets swept over the open ground and artillery rounds burst over your foxholes. Enemy infantry began closing in on your position, while hostile cavalry lapped around your flanks. Hunter-Weston sent increasingly desperate messages to II Corps urging them to speed up their withdrawal before the rearguard collapsed. But the roads were jammed, and units that tried to cut across country were bogged down by the rain-slicked ground. Smith-Dorrien urged you to hold on for as long as you could.

The end was inevitable. Relentless German fire smashed your supporting artillery and tore great gaps in the ranks of the infantry. Hunter-Weston gave the order to fall back at 9.30 a.m., but it was too late, for the enemy had practically surrounded your position. As the rearguard started to withdraw, the Germans seized their opportunity and charged. The British infantry, bloodied and outnumbered, was soon overwhelmed.

You saw the disaster unfolding and had no choice but to mount up and order C Squadron to retreat. You and your men galloped away in the direction of Bohain-en-Vermandois. Your route took you across sodden fields and meandering lanes, dodging German cavalry patrols that were roaming the area looking for stragglers. The sounds of intense combat in the distance made your heart sink as you realised that the Germans must have caught II Corps on the march.

You push your weary horse to carry you a little further and arrive at Bohain-en-Vermandois at around 5 p.m. The town is packed with wounded and leaderless men. They confirm your worst fears. The Germans have swept past the small rearguard and have caught II Corps in marching formation. Smith-Dorrien tried to deploy his soldiers into some form of battle line, but it was too late. After a valiant stand, II Corps was encircled and crushed. The exhausted survivors tell you they are all that remains of the once-proud force.

AFTERMATH

Smith-Dorrien's decision to retreat was disastrous. Hunter-Weston's ad-hoc rearguard was too small to do anything except delay the inevitable. The German pursuit surged down the roads and was soon tearing at the tail of II Corps. Smith-Dorrien attempted to turn his force to face them, but deploying from the congested roads was impossible and his men had to fight where they stood. The BEF fought hard, but the German assault was relentless. By nightfall the bulk of II Corps had been encircled and only a handful of battalions had managed to cut their way out. The remainder of the force had no choice but to surrender.

Haig's I Corps might have made a difference to the outcome. II Corps' last stand was audible at Haig's HQ, and some of his officers urged him to march to the sound of the guns. Had he done so, he might have been able to break the encirclement and allow Smith-Dorrien's men to escape, but Haig, ill and dispirited, refused to act.

The destruction of II Corps broke the BEF. Sir John French was horrified by the outcome and fell into a deep depression. He was convinced that the war was lost and planned to march his survivors to the Channel ports. But the Germans had other ideas. Inspired by their crushing victory over II Corps, they pressed forward and were soon harrying Haig's I Corps. Vastly outnumbered and with little hope of escape, I Corps was forced to make a desperate stand near Guise on 28 August. The battle was a bloodbath. Outnumbered British forces were hit hard from the front and flanks, suffered heavy losses and were routed from the field.

The BEF had been destroyed and the shattered survivors were withdrawn to Britain. France and Belgium fought on, but the destruction of the British army was a devastating blow. Crucially, the fate of the BEF gave Moltke renewed confidence in victory. He kept his nerve when struck by Joffre's last-ditch counter-attack in September and turned the tide of battle. The Germans would lay siege to Paris in the coming weeks. The British looked on helplessly. It would take months to assemble a second BEF and re-join the fight, and by then it would be too late.

THE DECISION

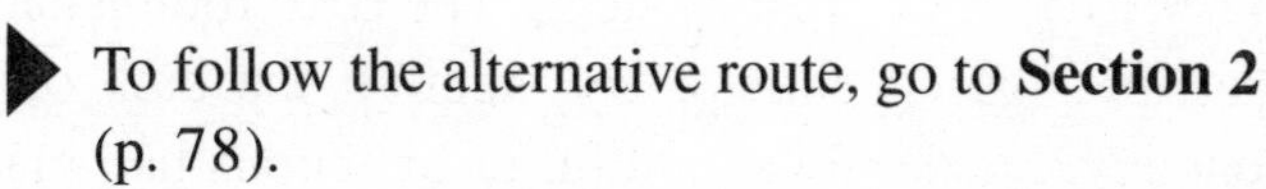

▶ To follow the alternative route, go to **Section 2** (p. 78).

OR

▶ To explore the decisions of the campaign, go to the **Historical Note** on p. 113.

SECTION 7
A CHANGE OF GOVERNMENT

9 March 1915, Oriental Club, London

The tasteful decoration and comfortable chairs in the Oriental Club lounge are as far away from the horrors of the Western Front as you can imagine. It is almost possible to forget that there is a war raging across Europe. The thought sparks a sudden idea in your head and you hastily scribble a line in your notepad: 'The government seems to have forgotten that Britain is locked in a deadly war.' It will be a good byline for the article that you are now itching to write. The information you have at your disposal is scandalous and will rock the establishment.

You know all about scandal, for you are ***Charles à Court Repington***, the military correspondent of *The Times* newspaper. A promising military career was cut short in 1902 when you were caught having a passionate affair with the wife of a senior British official, but rather than hiding in disgrace, you used your notoriety to become a journalist. You are stylish, quick-witted and often involved in mischief. Even your enemies refer to you as 'the gorgeous Wreckington'.

11. Charles à Court Repington

Yet even by your standards, the story that you have now is explosive stuff. As your eyes scan the pages of handwritten notes, you reflect that if even half of this is true, it is enough to put you on the front page of *The Times* for the next week.

Your thoughts are interrupted as the man seated across the table from you speaks to a waiter, 'We need another bottle of claret here.' You wince slightly – it is you who will be paying the bill, and your guest has expensive tastes. But the cost will be worth it, for the man sitting across from you is Field Marshal Sir John French, giving his first public interview since he was sensationally dismissed by Lord Kitchener in September 1914.

The Field Marshal has told you all about the outrageous meeting. His hatred for Kitchener runs deep and is matched only by his rage at Smith-Dorrien's disobedience at the Battle of Le Cateau. Sir John positively seethes with anger at the injustice of it all, but takes a certain crumb of comfort from the fact that his successor and Kitchener's 'pet', General Sir Ian Hamilton, has led the army to several defeats on the Western Front. French has given you dozens of anecdotes that condemn his enemies, with the ultimate blame lying squarely at Lord Kitchener's feet.

The claret arrives and Sir John takes a glass in his hand. His pale-grey eyes are deadly serious. 'Well, Repington, you now have all that I have to tell you. The question is whether you have the courage to print it.'

You smile, for although many say that you lack judgement, you have never been accused of lacking courage. You take your own glass and offer a toast to Sir John. 'To the truth!'

AFTERMATH

The Times ran the story on its front page. Sir John French's revelations about Kitchener's heavy-handed approach, his criticism of Ian Hamilton's command and his insinuation that the war was being badly run by incompetents proved an irresistible cocktail for your readership. You were a wise enough journalist not to give away all the juiciest anecdotes with your first copy and were able to spread out the story over the coming days.

12. Herbert Henry Asquith

The scandal that followed was beyond even your mischievous expectations. Parliament exploded at the revelations of incompetence, ill behaviour and idiocy that French had shared. The opposition demanded answers from the government, and Prime Minister Herbert Asquith could not provide them. Chaos reigned at the despatch box as the Conservatives insisted on the formation of a coalition national government that could steer the nation through the crisis. Even King George V expressed his 'deepest concerns' at the turn of events.

Asquith was forced to bow to the pressure a week after the story was published. The new coalition government made sweeping changes to the running of the war, including removing Lord Kitchener as Secretary of State for War. A new strategic mastermind was required to take his place, and who better than the now seemingly redeemed Sir John French? He had served as Chief of the Imperial General Staff before the war, had commanded an army in the field and had been ill-treated by the government. A clamour grew for his appointment and it was duly confirmed in April 1915.

In the febrile atmosphere of spring 1915 it was easy to forget that, even at his best, French was difficult, erratic and short-tempered. His strategic vision for the war was frequently inconsistent. He flirted with a naval landing in Antwerp, considered opening a Balkan front through Greece and even pondered withdrawing the British army from France, as he had wished to do in 1914. But most of his intellectual energy went into pursuing old feuds. One of his first actions was to unceremoniously sack his old enemy Smith-Dorrien, and he campaigned tirelessly to heap further insult on Kitchener by packing him off to take a minor administrative role in India.

You soon realised that promoting French had been a serious error. But now it was too late to do anything about it, and Britain was bound to follow French's mercurial strategy for the remaining year, with bloody and often disastrous results. By mid-1916 many in the government were wondering how to get rid of the troublesome Field Marshal.

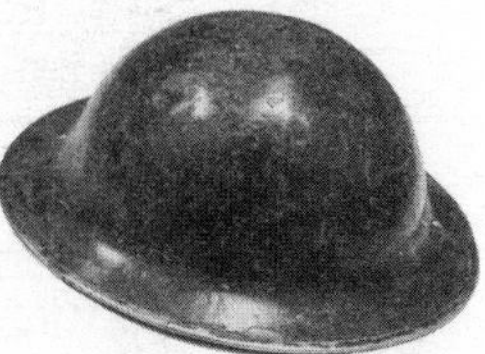

THE DECISION

▶ To follow the alternative route, go to **Section 3** (p. 86).

OR

▶ To explore the decisions of the campaign, see the **Historical Note** below.

HISTORICAL NOTE

The 1914 campaign was Germany's best chance to win a decisive, war-ending victory. Had the Schlieffen Plan fulfilled its lofty ambitions, then Germany might have crushed France within six weeks. Yet the Schlieffen Plan failed, and the Battle of the Marne ended German hopes of a short, victorious war.

Several factors explain the defeat. First and foremost, the French army showed incredible resilience, recovering from crushing defeats in August and launching an unexpected counter-attack at the Marne in September. Second, the Schlieffen Plan itself was wildly ambitious and was wedded to a strict timetable that neglected the friction of war – the accumulation of unfortunate events and unexpected decisions, which serve to foul even the most efficient military plans. One of the main causes of friction was the presence of the BEF. By sheer chance, the BEF found itself standing in the path of the German First Army – the outermost wing of the invasion force – and although it could not stop the invasion, it certainly impeded it. Vastly outnumbered and outgunned, the BEF's survival owed much to its high standards of training and leadership. After surviving the hardships of August, the BEF was then able to join the decisive Allied counterattack at the Battle of the Marne in September. The Battle of the Marne would become known as the 'Miracle of the Marne' in Britain and France. The reversal of fortunes, after the defeats and retreat of August, was stunning.

The historical route is that the BEF adopted its pre-war plan and deployed to France (Section 1 to Section 2). Perhaps the most crucial decision of the campaign then had to be made at Le Cateau. Historically, Smith-Dorrien chose to fight, and the Battle of Le Cateau, although bloody, saved II Corps from complete destruction (Section 2 to Section 3). After breaking contact with the German pursuit at Le Cateau, the BEF retreated south towards Paris. It was there that Sir John had a famous showdown with Lord Kitchener, which ended with an agreement that the army would stay in the fighting line and would fight at the Marne (Section 3 to Section 4).

Yet there were several crucial decisions that could have changed the war completely. The first was Sir John French's suggestion to deploy to Antwerp instead of France (Section 1 to Section 5). The idea had been considered prior to the war, but was discounted as relations between Britain and Belgium were poor. (Major Tom Bridges, who appears in Section 6, led a pre-war liaison mission to Belgium, which ended with him being unceremoniously thrown out of the country.) French's suggestion was daring, but ignored many practical problems, some of which are explored in Section 5. Yet had the BEF deployed to Antwerp, it would have caused an enormous headache for Moltke, who was teetering on the edge of a nervous breakdown throughout August and September, and it might have made a decisive psychological impact. However, the military effectiveness of the BEF and the Belgians would have been limited.

The biggest decision of the campaign lay with Smith-Dorrien in the early hours of 26 August. Facing a dire situation, his decision to turn and fight has been widely lauded (with the notable exception of Sir John French, who hated him already and never forgave him for disobeying his orders). The Battle of Le Cateau cost II Corps dearly, but Smith-Dorrien's men inflicted a stinging blow on the Germans and were able to break contact with their pursuers.

The only alternative to the Battle of Le Cateau was to retreat behind a hastily formed rearguard (Section 2 to Section 6). This decision would have ended in disaster. German forces were too close and too strong for any rearguard to hold them off for long. Furthermore, the exhausted British infantry would not have been able to get far along congested roads and would have been caught by the German pursuit. Unable to deploy properly, Smith-Dorrien would have been forced to fight a broken-backed battle and would have been surrounded and destroyed. The longer-term consequences of this defeat would have been disastrous for the BEF and the Allied war effort.

The final decision of the campaign revolves around Kitchener's astonishing intervention in Paris on 1 September. Sir John French's despairing telegrams had alarmed the War Cabinet and prompted Asquith to send Kitchener to France to 'put the fear of God into them all' and ensure that the BEF did not abandon its allies. Kitchener left no account of the conversation, and Sir John's account is considered unreliable, so we can only speculate about what was said. Historically, Sir John agreed with Kitchener, and the BEF stayed in action. But what if he had refused? In that scenario (Section 7) Kitchener sacks French on the spot. The exact limits of Kitchener's powers were unclear, but he had the full backing of the War Cabinet and this was a moment of crisis when he would not tolerate opposition. Ian Hamilton was the obvious replacement. Historically, in autumn 1914 Kitchener privately suggested to Joffre that Hamilton could replace Sir John, and so it is likely this would have happened, had French been sacked in September. The BEF's actual role in the Battle of the Marne is largely unchanged in this scenario, but I have speculated that French would have proved a huge political problem and would have been able to bring down the government.

Lord Roberts continued to offer unofficial advice to the government and made public appearances to support recruitment. He contracted pneumonia while visiting soldiers of the Indian Expeditionary Force near Ypres and died in France on 14 November 1914.

Horace Smith-Dorrien was promoted to command the Second Army in December 1914, but was sacked by Sir John French at the end of the Second Battle of Ypres in May 1915. Smith-Dorrien was sent to command British forces in East Africa in November 1915, but contracted severe pneumonia on the voyage, which barred him from further active service. He died in 1930.

John French commanded the BEF until he was replaced by his subordinate Douglas Haig in December 1915. He served as the Commander-in-Chief, Home Forces between 1916 and 1918 and then became Lord Lieutenant of Ireland between 1918 and 1921. In 1919 he published his outrageous memoir, *1914.* The book was little more than a character assassination of his old enemy, Smith-Dorrien, and caused a scandal that ruined French's reputation. He died in 1925. Smith-Dorrien was a pall-bearer at his funeral.

George Barrow served as a staff officer with the Cavalry Division and I Cavalry Corps on the Western Front. In 1917 he transferred to Palestine, where he commanded the 4th Cavalry Division until the war's end. He served the remainder of his career in India and retired in 1929. He died in 1959.

John 'Johnnie' Gough served as Douglas Haig's Chief of Staff at I Corps and later at the First Army. He was selected to command a New Army division in February 1915 and decided to pay a farewell visit to the trenches held by his old comrades of the 2nd Rifle Brigade before departure. Unfortunately during the visit he was shot by a German sniper and died five days later.

Tom Bridges had an eventful war. In a famous incident on 27 August 1914 he rallied two broken British battalions at Saint-Quentin, using a tin whistle and a drum purchased from a toy shop. He subsequently commanded 19th Division between 1915 and 1917, losing his right leg to German shellfire in September 1917. He served as Governor of South Australia between 1922 and 1927. He died in 1939.

Charles à Court Repington served as military correspondent for *The Times* for the duration of the war. His reporting lay at the heart of numerous political scandals, including the 'Shell Scandal' of May 1915, which brought down Asquith's government. He died in 1925.

3

GALLIPOLI: STRATEGIC GAMBLE IN THE MEDITERRANEAN, 1915

SECTION 1
DISTANT SHORES

13 January 1915, 10 Downing Street, London

It is a cold and gloomy day in London, and the oppressive grey skies are laced with dark clouds that promise snow. A sombre mood hangs over the city as the population comes to grips with the fact that this will be a long, hard war. But there is also a sense of determination and every day new volunteers step forward to join the British army. Soon Britain will possess the largest army in its history, drawn from all ranks of society and determined to fight.

1. Lord Kitchener's famous call for volunteers

You understand this army better than anyone because you are its architect. You are Secretary of State for War ***Lord Kitchener***. In August 1914 you recognised that Britain faced a global conflict and needed a vast army to fight it. Your call for volunteers was launched through an iconic poster campaign and received an incredible response. Hundreds of thousands of men have joined the colours, leading to the formation of what the press call 'Kitchener's Army' or the 'New Army'. The success of the campaign owes much to your reputation, for you are Britain's most famous soldier, with an unbroken record of victory in colonial wars. You are a man of few words and there is an air of mystery around you, which has led to you being nick-named 'the Sphinx'. There is also some concern about your ferocity in war. Your ruthless approach to colonial warfare drew criticism from Liberal politicians; it is somewhat ironic that some of those critics now sit on the War Council and ask you for military advice.

Today's War Council meeting at 10 Downing Street is taxing all your intellect and ingenuity. At the outbreak of the war you foresaw a long struggle where France and Russia, backed by British finance and naval support, would bear the brunt of the fighting until 1917. At this point Britain's fully trained volunteer army would be ready to lead a decisive offensive and win the war. But the intense fighting of 1914 has thrown this calculation into doubt. France has suffered appalling casualties in resisting the German invasion and demands additional British troops to secure the Western Front. In the east Russia has suffered crushing defeats at the Battle of Tannenberg and the Battle of the Masurian Lakes, which have destroyed two of her best armies. The Russian situation has worsened recently as the Russians now face an offensive from the Ottoman Empire in the Caucasus mountains. Earlier this month Tsar Nicholas II asked Britain to do something against the Ottomans to relieve the pressure on Russia's southern front.

What can Britain do to help her beleaguered Allies? You know that the New Army is not ready for battle and you are reluctant to send more soldiers to France. Your colleagues agree. Chancellor of the Exchequer David Lloyd George is concerned that if it is sent to the Western Front, the New Army will be wasted on 'futile enterprises . . . against impregnable positions'. First Lord of the Admiralty Winston Churchill also cautions against sending more men to 'chew on barbed wire in Flanders'.

But finding an alternative is difficult. Today the War Council has spent many hours discussing a proposal from Field Marshal John French, the commander of the British Army in France, for a joint land and sea assault on the Belgian coast. The idea has promise, but requires a huge amount of ammunition, 'which is simply not available'. By the time this operation has been rejected, day has turned to evening, the fire that warms the council room has burned low and eyelids are beginning to droop.

But Winston Churchill, the youngest member of the council, retains his energy. You have a sense he has been waiting for this moment to reveal his proposal. Speaking with passion and precision, Churchill announces that a study led by Vice Admiral Sackville Carden has concluded that it is possible for a fleet of battleships to force their way through the Dardanelles Strait and reach the Sea of Marmara. Once there, they will threaten the Ottoman capital of Constantinople with bombardment and force the Turks to surrender.

The task will not be easy. The Dardanelles are thirty-eight miles miles long and well defended; it will require a methodical operation to push through them. Churchill explains that a fleet of battleships will

Map 1: The Dardanelles

smash the Turkish defences into rubble whilst minesweepers clear enemy mines. The operation will take several weeks, but if it is successful, then the Ottoman Empire will be defeated. Crucially, Churchill argues that the attack will be a purely naval affair, without the need for any support from the British army. Furthermore, if the straits prove impregnable, the operation can be called off with relative ease. He adds a further tantalising detail as he explains that the navy had already carried out a preliminary bombardment of the outer forts of the Dardanelles in November 1914 and shattered them with relative ease.

The mood at the War Council changes in an instant. Eyes widen, expressions brighten and fatigue vanishes. After hours of discussing the dreary vista of the Western Front, the prospects of war in the Mediterranean seem infinitely brighter.

You are impressed with the proposal, and the idea that the navy can do this alone is appealing. But the operation remains risky. The strength of the Turkish defences within the Dardanelles is unclear, and the older battleships that Churchill intends to use may not have the firepower to crush them. You are also concerned that Britain possesses only a handful of minesweepers and will have to use hastily converted trawlers for this difficult and dangerous task. Finally, even if the fleet clears the straits, there is a chance that the Ottomans will defy the battleships lying off the coast of Constantinople and simply refuse to surrender. What will happen if this occurs?

The focus on Turkey reminds you that there is another option for attacking the Ottoman Empire, which you have considered in the past – an amphibious assault on the deep-water port of Alexandretta in Syria. Alexandretta's coastal defences are feeble, and its capture would provide an excellent logistic base. Once there, British forces can advance from the port and cut the railway that links Anatolia to Arabia, breaking the Ottoman Empire in half and dealing the Turks a crippling and possibly decisive blow.

However, the Alexandretta operation will require you to deploy precious army reserves. You have the elite professional soldiers of the 29th Division in reserve, but otherwise you will be forced to rely on partially trained volunteers from Britain, Australia and New Zealand. Furthermore, you know that an assault on Alexandretta will cause trouble with

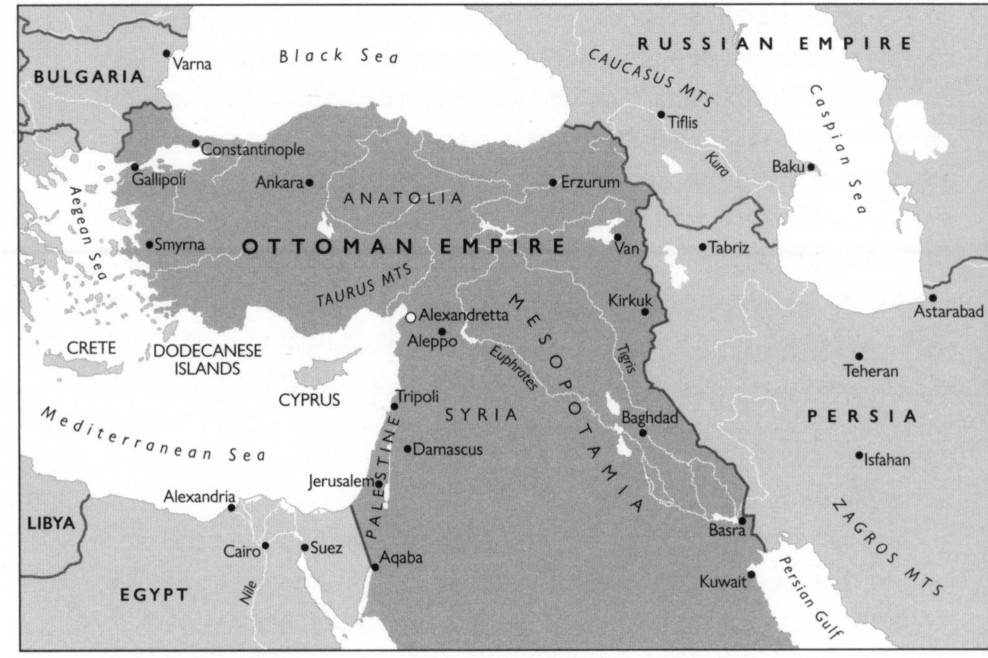

Map 2: Alexandretta and the Ottoman Empire 1914

France. The French government insists that Syria is a sphere of special interest and it will resist any attempt to land British soldiers there. You are unimpressed with this line of argument when there is a war to be won, but you know it will cause serious diplomatic headaches.

The War Council continues its discussion long into the night. Talk drifts to other subjects, although the idea of an assault on the Ottoman Empire remains at the forefront of your mind. But where should Britain attack?

AIDE-MEMOIRE

* Britain cannot afford to sit and wait until the New Army is ready. France and Russia need urgent support.
* The War Council sees no prospect of victory on the Western Front this year and fears that any troops sent there will be wasted in futile attacks.

* Churchill's plan for an attack on the Dardanelles is audacious and could defeat the Ottoman Empire in a matter of weeks. He promises that the operation can be carried out by the Royal Navy alone and that you will not need to provide any army support.
* The Dardanelles are thirty-eight miles long, and the strength of the Turkish defences is unclear. It will not be easy to force the fleet through.
* Even if the fleet clears the Dardanelles and reaches Constantinople, the Turks may simply refuse to surrender.
* An attack on Alexandretta would provide a crucial logistic base that could be used to develop further operations.
* An advance from Alexandretta could sever the railway and cut Anatolia off from the rest of the Ottoman Empire.
* A landing at the port will require you to use the last of the British army's reserves.
* The French are insistent that Syria is within their sphere of influence and will oppose any British landing.

THE DECISION

Do you authorise the naval attack on the Dardanelles, or do you order an amphibious assault against Alexandretta?

- If you believe Churchill's plan for a naval assault on the Dardanelles has merit, go to **Section 2** (p. 126).

  OR

- If you wish to pursue your own idea of an amphibious attack on Alexandretta, go to **Section 4** (p. 142).

SECTION 2
THE GREAT ASSAULT

2 p.m., 18 March 1915, HMS *Queen Elizabeth*, the Dardanelles

It is a sunny spring day and the azure waters of the Aegean Sea glisten beneath a cloudless sky. Yet the peace of this beautiful vista is shattered by the constant thunder of guns within the Dardanelles, where sixteen British and French battleships are fighting their way through the straits. Their turrets belch huge high-explosive shells that tear into the Ottoman fortifications and explode with appalling force, flinging wreckage high into the air. Royal Naval Air Service seaplanes circle overhead, directing the fall of shot and seeking out hidden enemy guns. But the Turkish defenders hold their ground and return fire from their shore batteries, surrounding the ships with a constant churn of water spouts. Several battleships receive direct hits that buckle their armour plate and cause the heavy vessels to roll and stagger.

2. John de Robeck

You stand on the bridge of your flagship, HMS *Queen Elizabeth*, with your binoculars locked onto the Turkish forts, seeking any sign that they have been silenced. You are ***Vice Admiral John de Robeck***, the commander of the largest British naval operation since the Battle of Trafalgar in 1805. You took charge of the fleet mere days ago when its original commander and the architect of the Dardanelles operation, Vice Admiral Sackville Carden, collapsed from nervous exhaustion. Until today, operations had proceeded slowly and methodically. Your fleet had silenced the outer defences, and Royal Marine shore parties had mounted several successful sorties to disable enemy batteries. But pressure from London to increase the tempo has convinced you to mount a direct assault today.

At 10.30 a.m. your battleships sailed into the straits with guns

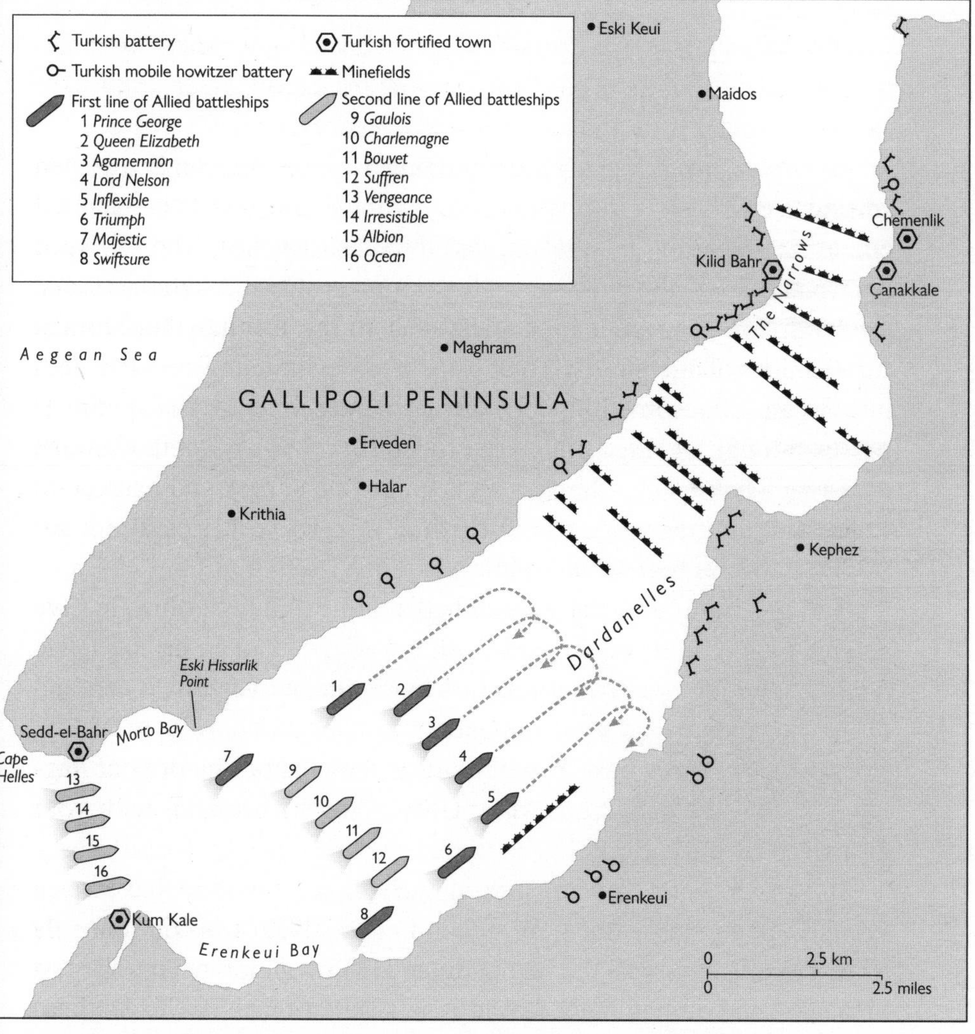

Map 3: The Allied naval attack on the Dardanelles, 18 March 1915

blazing. Each ship is preceded by a pilot boat positioned fifty yards ahead to scout for underwater mines. Further ahead a line of minesweepers struggles forward to clear the channel and enable your battleships to continue the advance. The pilot boats and minesweepers are especially vulnerable to enemy shells and are reliant on covering fire from your battleships.

You have advanced nine miles into the straits, but the waters here are narrow and in places the Dardanelles are only 8,000 yards across. The Turkish defenders blaze away at your fleet from both sides of the straits. Heavy guns focus on your battleships, whilst smaller howitzers rain fire on your minesweepers. Direct hits have set several of your battleships ablaze, but there can be no turning back. You are determined to silence the inner forts and hammer the defenders into submission.

By 2 p.m. your flagship's devastating 15-inch guns have smashed several Turkish forts into smouldering rubble and you sense that the enemy is beginning to weaken. But then disaster strikes. A cry goes up from one of the younger officers on the bridge: '*Bouvet* is in trouble!' You snap your binoculars over to the Erenköy Bay on the eastern side of the straits. Your ships have been using this bay as a turning area, but something terrible has happened to the *Bouvet* as she passes through. A huge plume of crimson smoke is pouring from the old French battleship. She may have hit a mine or received a direct hit to her ammunition magazine. British destroyers rush to her aid, but *Bouvet* capsizes before the smaller craft can reach her.

The destruction of the French battleship is a heavy blow, but the assault must continue. Several forts are silenced over the next two hours, including one that erupts in a huge plume of fire as its ammunition magazine explodes, but others remain stubbornly in action. Your minesweepers have begun to clear the channel in front of you, but it is slow and dangerous work. Only a handful of mines have been destroyed by mid-afternoon.

At 4 p.m. your forward line of warships is preparing to turn in Erenköy Bay to allow the next assault line to advance, when suddenly a huge explosion rocks the battlecruiser HMS *Inflexible.* The ship has hit a mine and immediately develops a dangerous list. The Turks sense their opportunity and rain fire upon the wounded vessel as it retreats

3. HMS *Irresistible* sinking after hitting a mine

towards the mouth of the straits. You have barely had a chance to process this loss when another disaster occurs as the battleship HMS *Irresistible* hits a mine that tears open a great hole in her hull. She is severely damaged, and you order the battleship HMS *Ocean* to assist her whilst the rest of your fleet provides covering fire.

The battle rages on for the next two hours. *Inflexible* manages to limp to the entrance of the straits, but it is soon clear that *Irresistible* is mortally wounded. HMS *Ocean* attempts to tow her to safety, but *Irresistible* is listing so badly that it proves impossible. With *Bouvet* sunk, *Irresistible* sinking and *Inflexible* seriously damaged, you reluctantly give the signal for a general withdrawal at 5.50 p.m. But your fleet has only just begun its manoeuvres when a devastating blast rocks HMS *Ocean* as she becomes the fourth ship to hit an underwater mine. The damage is catastrophic and *Ocean* sinks within an hour.

By 7.30 p.m. your ships have withdrawn from the straits, and you are left to count the cost. One-third of your fleet has been lost. *Bouvet*, *Irresistible* and *Ocean* have been sunk. *Inflexible* needs extensive repairs, whilst the French battleships *Gaulois* and *Suffren* have suffered severe damage from enemy artillery. The great assault has been repulsed and renewing the battle with your bloodied fleet will only lead to further losses.

The situation is frustrating because you are certain that the Turkish defenders have taken heavy punishment. Many forts have been smashed to pieces, and the weight of enemy fire had noticeably slackened by the end of the battle. The Ottomans may be on the brink of breaking and another determined assault could shatter their resistance.

You ponder how you might continue the offensive. One option is to request amphibious support from the British army. If the soldiers can secure the high ground, then they will be able to sweep away the enemy batteries from the landward side and allow your fleet to clear the minefields without interference. However, this approach would change the nature of the campaign completely and end Churchill's vision of a purely naval operation. You are also concerned about what might happen if the army cannot seize the high ground quickly. The bloody stalemate on the Western Front might be re-created in the Dardanelles.

The other alternative is to await naval reinforcements and attack by sea again. The Admiralty is not discouraged by your losses and replacement ships are on their way, including the British battleships *Queen*, *Implacable*, *Prince of Wales* and *London* and the French battleships *Henri IV* and *Jauréguiberry*. More destroyers and minesweepers are also promised. With these reinforcements you might be able to break through. Yet it will take time for these ships to arrive. The delay suits the Turks, who will surely use every hour to repair and improve their defences. A renewed assault might suffer even heavier losses than you have experienced today.

You face a crucial decision as darkness descends over the calm Aegean waters.

AIDE-MEMOIRE

* The assault on the straits has been repulsed with three ships lost and three severely damaged.

* You believe that the Turkish defenders were nearing collapse by the time you were forced to withdraw.
* Enemy underwater mines are a serious barrier. Mines have sunk three of your ships and severely damaged a fourth.
* Your fragile minesweepers struggle to clear the minefields whilst under fire. You need to silence the enemy shore batteries once and for all.
* An amphibious landing that secured the high ground on the western side of the Dardanelles would make the Turkish shore defences untenable. Your minesweepers would be able to clear the minefields with only fire from the eastern side.
* An amphibious landing is a major undertaking and will completely change the nature of the campaign. There is a risk it could lead to a long and bloody struggle.
* Reinforcements for your fleet are on their way and you will soon be strong enough to launch another naval assault. A renewed attack could silence the battered forts and enable you to advance.
* The Turks will be working hard to improve their defences and any fresh assault might run into even heavier opposition than you faced today.

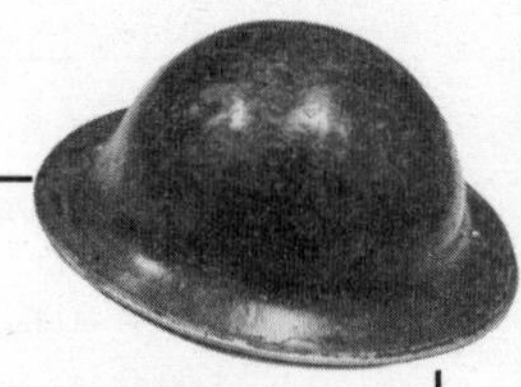

THE DECISION

Will you wait for reinforcements and attack by sea once more, or will you request that the army makes an amphibious landing to seize the Turkish forts?

- If you are convinced that the British army must be deployed to clear the Dardanelles, go to **Section 3** (p. 134).

  OR

- If you are confident that your reinforced fleet can batter its way through the straits without army support, go to **Section 5** (p. 148).

SECTION 3
A RIDGE TOO FAR?

27 July 1915, IX Corps Headquarters, Imbros

It is a brutally hot day on the Aegean island of Imbros. The unbearable humidity leaves you covered in a permanent sheen of sweat. Omnipresent flies buzz above you and your assembled commanders, their lazy turns occasionally disrupted by an irritated swat of the hand. Yet if conditions are hard for you and your officers in your tented headquarters, you can only imagine how much worse they must be in the rocky trenches at Gallipoli.

The battle for the Gallipoli peninsula has been raging for three months. British and Anzac forces landed on 25 April, but immediately encountered furious Turkish resistance. The battle to secure the beachheads cost the attackers thousands of casualties and dashed any hopes of a rapid advance. The campaign soon degenerated into a stalemate and the peninsula is now criss-crossed with trenches and strongpoints that are reminiscent of the Western Front. Neither side can break through these defences. The Ottomans are well entrenched on crucial high ground and have repulsed several Allied offensives, but Turkish attempts to drive the Allies into the sea have been defeated in turn.

The campaign has taken a bloody toll on both sides. The enervating heat exhausts the survivors and many of them are suffering from dysentery or malaria. You recently visited the British trenches and were disturbed by the ghastly conditions. No-man's-land is littered with unburied dead that seethe with colossal swarms of flies, and clean water is almost non-existent.

4. Frederick Stopford

Yet there is no prospect of calling the operation off. Lord Kitchener is 'most anxious to get through the Dardanelles this autumn' and insists that the Allies must win a victory 'somehow or the other'. You lead the force that might provide the key to unlocking the stubborn Turkish defence, for you are ***Lieutenant-General Frederick Stopford***. You are sixty-one years old and have spent almost your entire career as a staff officer. Although noted for your 'great kindliness and charm', you have never commanded troops in battle. You retired from the military in 1909 due to ill health, but the demand for officers is so great that you have been recalled and chosen to lead the men of the newly formed IX Corps, consisting of the 10th (Irish) and 11th (Northern) Divisions. These are New Army formations consisting of wartime volunteers. These men have received only limited training prior to deployment.

You have called a conference of subordinate commanders to discuss how IX Corps will be used in the coming offensive. General Ian Hamilton, the commander of the Mediterranean Expeditionary Force, is launching a new attack in the Anzac sector that aims to turn the Turkish flank. Your IX Corps is to assist this offensive by making a surprise landing at Suvla Bay, which lies to the north. Hamilton hopes that the combination of a vigorous Anzac offensive and an unexpected amphibious assault will finally unhinge the Turkish line.

Yet there is some uncertainty about your exact objectives. Hamilton believes that your landing will surprise the Turks and provide a rare window of opportunity. He has urged you to make a rapid advance and seize the Kiretch Tepe and Tekke Tepe Ridges, which dominate the north and the east respectively. British intelligence reports that these positions are practically undefended. Capturing this high ground

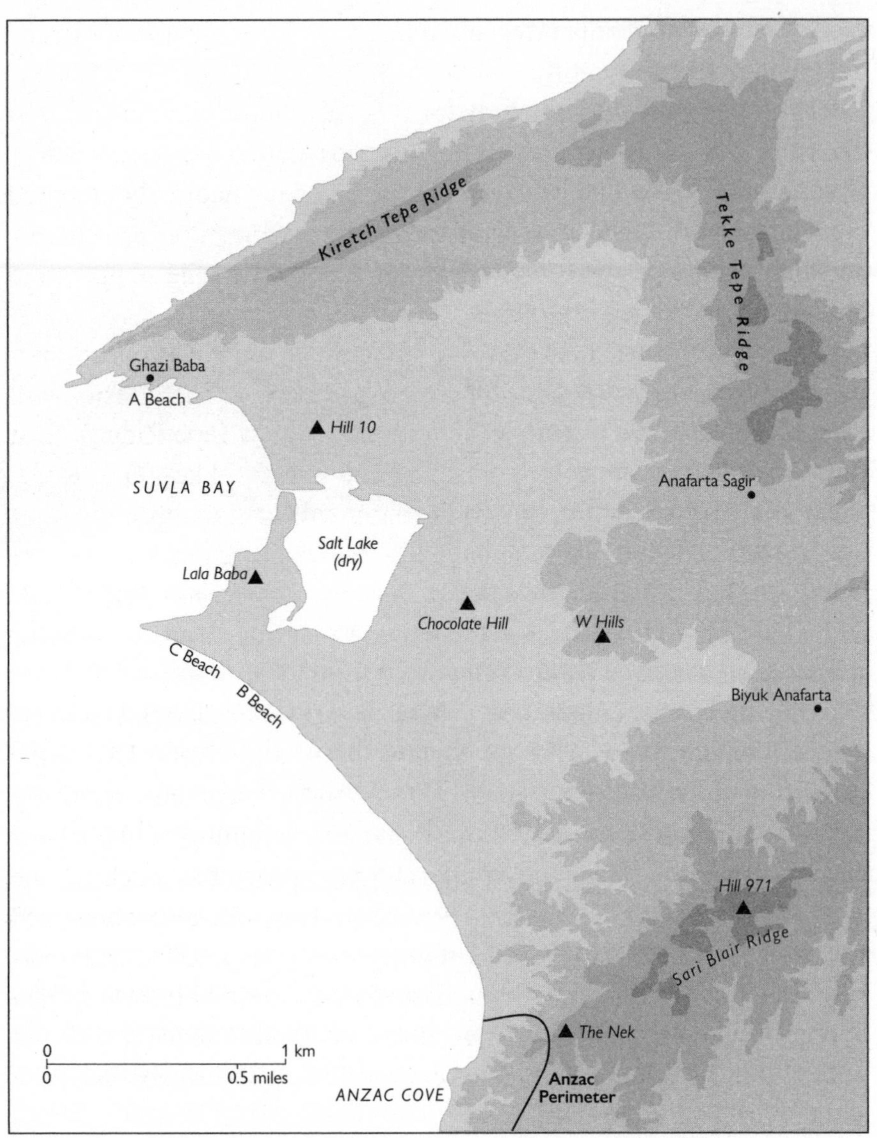

Map 4: Suvla Bay and its surrounding ridges

would be a major victory that would turn the Ottoman flank to the south and greatly assist the Anzac offensive. However, the written orders from Hamilton's Chief of Staff, Major-General Walter Braithwaite, seem to contradict these aggressive instructions. Instead they stress the need to 'seize the landing at Suvla Bay and secure it as a base of supply' and only refer to sending a 'small force' to capture the Tekke Tepe Ridge.

The ambiguity has prompted you to assemble your officers to decide whether it is practical to rush the ridges, and to assess whether the operation should be aggressive or defensive in nature. Your tented headquarters on Imbros is small and the meeting room can barely accommodate everyone. The close confines add to the temperature and the air is dense with heat.

You begin by outlining your own plan of attack. You propose landing the 11th (Northern) Division at Suvla Bay first. The division will detach a small force to gain a foothold on Kiretch Tepe Ridge whilst the remainder of the troops advance and seize Tekke Tepe Ridge. Soon afterwards the 10th (Irish) Division will land and use the foothold on Kiretch Tepe Ridge to launch an attack that captures the entire position. Once this is done, they will swing down onto Tekke Tepe Ridge and link up with the 11th Division in a pincer movement that will encircle any surviving defenders.

Your divisional commanders, Major-General Frederick Hammersley and Major-General Bryan Mahon, listen attentively despite the exhausting heat. They agree that the plan is 'clear and relatively simple', but raise concerns about the limited training of their New Army formations. The pace of advance may prove too much for the courageous but inexperienced volunteers. They are also concerned about the strength of the Turkish defences in the area. If the Ottomans really have left the positions unguarded, then there will be a golden opportunity to capture the high ground. But if intelligence reports are wrong and the enemy is already entrenched on the ridges, then the assault will end in carnage.

There is a growl of dissent from your right. The exhausting heat has shortened everyone's tempers, and this is especially true of your Chief of Staff Brigadier-General Hamilton Reed, VC. Reed is an acerbic man at the best of times and now he 'holds forth almost truculently about the folly of the plan'. Reed insists that seizing Tekke Tepe is 'too big a job' for the inexperienced IX Corps. He points out that your men will have to advance across five miles of rugged, unfamiliar terrain to reach the ridge before assaulting a Turkish garrison of unknown strength. He sneers at intelligence reports that claim the Ottomans have left Tekke Tepe undefended and reminds you of the many errors British intelligence has already made in this campaign. Drawing on his experience from the Western Front, Reed argues that the only way to capture the ridges is via step-by-step operations backed by overwhelming artillery support. It will take several days to assemble the necessary guns and ammunition, but Reed argues that this is better than rushing in blindly.

His strident assessment gives you pause for thought, and you can see from their nodding heads that it has influenced Hammersley and Mahon. Perhaps it would be better to secure Suvla Bay and then mount a methodical assault on the ridges taking place over several days, rather than risk everything by rushing them in the first hours. If the attack miscarries, then the Turks might even be able to counter-attack your disordered force and hurl it into the sea.

But this approach abandons the element of surprise. Once they know you have landed, the Turks will rush reinforcements to the area and entrench themselves on the high ground. Assaulting these forces will be no easy matter. Earlier fighting at Gallipoli suggests that the cost of gaining just a few hundred yards is measured in thousands of casualties. Would it be better to stick to your original plan and try and seize the ground whilst it is relatively undefended?

Your tropical uniform is dark with sweat and the humidity has given you a pulsating headache. The officers at the table have given their views, but the final decision rests with you. You feel the full weight of responsibility. Whatever choice you make will have a huge influence on the campaign.

AIDE-MEMOIRE

* The fighting at Gallipoli is locked in stalemate and neither side can break through the trench lines.
* British commander Ian Hamilton proposes to break the deadlock by launching a flank attack with Anzac forces and supporting

them with a surprise amphibious landing at Suvla Bay.

* Hamilton wants IX Corps to advance immediately after landing and seize the Kiretch Tepe Ridge to the north and the Tekke Tepe Ridge to the east.
* Your written orders from Chief of Staff Walter Braithwaite seem to contradict Hamilton's instructions and stress the need to secure Suvla Bay before mounting any further attack.
* You propose to follow Hamilton's concept and have suggested that 10th Division storms Tekke Tepe Ridge and 11th Division captures Kiretch Tepe Ridge.
* Your divisional commanders believe your plan is 'sensible', but are concerned about whether their inexperienced soldiers can carry it out.
* Your own Chief of Staff, Hamilton Reed, VC, is strongly against your plan and believes it may end in disaster. He suggests a methodical approach in line with Braithwaite's orders.

THE DECISION

Will you try and take advantage of surprise and seize the ridges as soon as possible, or will you assemble your forces and mount a methodical attack?

▶ If you wish to mount an immediate attack on the ridges, go to **Section 6** (p. 154).

OR

▶ If you would rather secure Suvla Bay and build up supplies before attacking, go to **Section 7** (p. 160).

SECTION 4
BREAKING THE OTTOMAN EMPIRE

18 May 1915, Alexandretta, Syria

The docks at Alexandretta are bustling with activity. Stores of all kinds are being unloaded and the port is packed with guns, ammunition and soldiers. A harassed British officer finds himself surrounded by gesticulating Arab stevedores and desperately flicks through a hastily printed language guide, searching for the correct phrase to deflect their frustration. At the waterfront an enormous line of Turkish prisoners slowly shuffles towards the transport ships that will carry them to prison camps in Egypt.

5. Winston Churchill

On any other day your arrival would have drawn attention, for you are First Lord of the Admiralty ***Winston Churchill***, one of the most famous politicians in the English-speaking world. You are forty years old, and your life has been filled with adventure and controversy. Amongst other exploits, you took part in a cavalry charge in Sudan in 1898 and escaped from a prisoner-of-war camp during the Boer War in 1899. Your political career has been just as eventful. You sensationally defected from the Conservative Party to the Liberal Party in 1904 and became the youngest minister in the government in 1908, eventually becoming First Lord of the Admiralty in 1911.

As you step onto the docks at Alexandretta, you immodestly feel that you deserve a great deal of credit for Britain's success in the Middle East. After all, it was you who saw the need to avoid entanglement in the endless barbed wire of Flanders and suggested the attack on the Dardanelles. At first you were infuriated that Kitchener preferred a landing at Alexandretta, but as the operation was explained, you saw its logic. You viewed the vast Ottoman Empire as a giant that was difficult to fell unless Britain struck at a weak point. For you, the Dardanelles represented a direct strike at the 'neck' of the empire, but you conceded that a landing at Alexandretta represented a stab to the 'armpit' and was certainly better than an advance across the Sinai Desert and into Palestine, which would be rather like attacking the giant's 'fingertips'.

The greatest barrier was political rather than military. For complex historical reasons that stretch back to the Crusades, France insisted that Syria was a sphere of special interest. British and French politicians had formally agreed on this point in 1912. Britain's sudden change of attitude made the French highly suspicious, and there was much political manoeuvring and deal-making required before the attack on Alexandretta could go ahead. Both you and Kitchener were frustrated by French intransigence and were keen to begin before the Ottomans could reinforce the vulnerable harbour, but it took until April before Paris consented to the assault. As a way of ensuring French interests were properly represented, the French army grudgingly contributed additional soldiers in the form of the *Corps expéditionnaire d'Orient*, or CEO. As you head through Alexandretta you notice that the French headquarters there occupies the largest and most impressive building in the port. An enormous tricolour flies above it, for the avoidance of any doubt.

Surprise was essential for the Alexandretta operation. If the

Ottomans reinforced the area before the Allies landed, then a disaster would soon follow. To keep the Turks guessing, the Royal Navy made a series of diversionary attacks on the Dardanelles. These were accompanied by shore-party raids and feint landings from the Royal Naval Division, which confused the defenders and locked large numbers of troops in place. Elsewhere an Anglo-Indian force began a determined advance from Basra towards Baghdad, whilst British forces in Egypt kept up an active defence of the Suez Canal to keep Ottoman attention locked on this area.

The diversions worked and the landing at Alexandretta took place on 25 April 1915. The Ottoman garrison could do little more than offer a few shots before surrendering. As the German commander Paul von Hindenburg bitterly reflected after the war, 'the protection of the Gulf of Alexandretta was entrusted to a Turkish Army which contained scarcely a single unit fit to fight'. The empire's best troops remained at Gallipoli and only the second-rate 23rd and 27th Divisions were available to oppose the Allies. Even those divisions were too far from the action to make a swift intervention: 23rd Division was eighty miles east at Aleppo and 27th Division was almost 300 miles away at Damascus. It took a fortnight for the two divisions to assemble and advance against the Allies, by which time it was far too late. A hasty Ottoman assault ran into well-prepared defences that blasted the attackers to pieces. The prisoners that you saw at the docks are some of the survivors of what the press have termed the Battle of Alexandretta.

With the port secure, Alexandretta provided the Allies with a superb logistics hub. But its real value lay in its position at a strategic hinge of the Ottoman Empire. Ottoman rail lines linking Anatolia to Arabia passed through the area, and the critical Muslimie Junction that linked all locomotive traffic from north to south lay just eighty miles east of Alexandretta. British and Indian cavalry soon set out to raid the line and cut the entire empire in half.

You arrive at the British headquarters and note how small and functional it is in comparison to the grand building occupied by the French. It is here that you find your old friend and commander of the British Mediterranean Expeditionary Force, General Ian Hamilton. He is in an ebullient mood, and you can see why from the map pinned

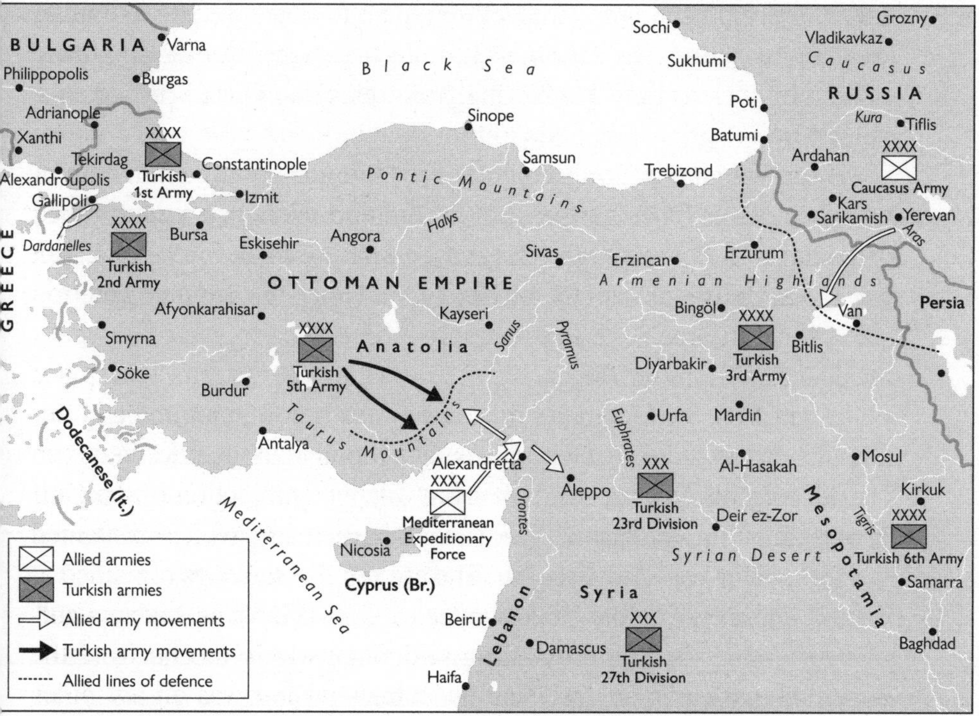

Map 5: The Alexandretta Campaign 1915

to the wall of the headquarters. Although intelligence reports that the Turks are rushing reinforcements from Gallipoli, they will take weeks to arrive. Meanwhile Hamilton's cavalry is carrying out a vigorous campaign against the rail lines to disrupt strategic communications, and Allied spearheads are racing towards Aleppo to capture Muslimie Junction and complete the dismemberment of the Ottoman Empire.

You share a cigar with Hamilton and toast his success. The war on the Western Front rumbles on, but for now your mind is filled with possibilities. Victory is in the air.

AFTERMATH

The Allied landing at Alexandretta was, as Hindenburg admitted, 'a brilliant strategic feat' that had 'a far-reaching effect on our Turkish ally'. It also 'made an enormous impression' on the neutral powers of

Italy, Greece and Bulgaria and swung them towards the Allied cause. Meanwhile, within the Ottoman Empire the successful landing provided the spark to long-simmering Arab resentments and provoked a general uprising in Syria and Arabia.

There was hard fighting to come. The Ottomans doggedly defended Aleppo, and the Allies, operating at the end of a long supply line, struggled to break through. But a combination of cavalry raids and Arab guerrilla attacks cut the rail line upon which the Turkish garrison relied for reinforcement and resupply. The defenders were forced to surrender after a brief siege.

In mid-May the Ottoman Fifth Army – the best fighting force in the Empire – began its belated journey from Gallipoli to Syria. It was too late. The Allies controlled the rail junction at Aleppo and blocked the passes through the Nur Mountains. The Turks launched several assaults to try and force their way through, but all were repulsed with heavy losses.

By August 1915 the government in Constantinople had opened secret negotiations with the Allies to bring the war to an end. A stalemate had settled in at the Nur Mountains, where the Allies were hampered by strained logistics and difficult terrain. But other dangers beset the Empire. The Ottoman Minister of War, Enver Pasha, was troubled by Russian advances in the north-east and was painfully aware that Greece and Bulgaria, although still officially neutral, were eyeing Constantinople with greedy eyes. He was willing to sacrifice the Arabian part of the Empire – which he had come to regard as a source of weakness anyway – and concentrate remaining Ottoman power in Anatolia.

After much diplomatic manoeuvring – including repeated false assurances to Berlin that the Ottoman Empire was committed to the war – a peace treaty was concluded in September 1915, hastened by rumours that Bulgaria was about to declare war and march on Constantinople. Britain and France carved up the southern Ottoman Empire, and Russia took territory in the north-east.

The defeat of the Ottoman Empire secured Allied communications through the Suez Canal and gave Britain access to the rich oilfields of Basra. But it did not end the war. The victors of Alexandretta would soon be transferred to France to face the German army in a very different campaign in 1916.

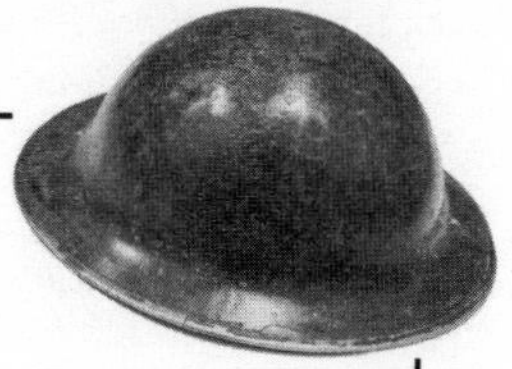

THE DECISION

▶ To follow the alternative route, go back to **Section 1** (p. 118).

OR

▶ To explore the decisions of the campaign, go to the **Historical Note** on p. 164.

SECTION 5
THE IMPREGNABLE STRAITS

28 March 1915, HMS *Euryalus*, the Dardanelles

The waters of the Dardanelles are boiling, as shell after shell plunges into the sea around the cruiser HMS *Euryalus*. The gunners in your 9.2-inch gun turrets can scarcely see a target through the constant spray of water spouts, and you and the rest of the bridge crew are soaked to the skin. The weight of Turkish fire is even greater than in your previous attack, and you can hardly believe that your ship has not been blown out of the water.

You are ***Captain Rudolf Miles Burmester*** and you have been tasked with the difficult job of leading the Allied minesweepers into the narrows. Your armoured cruiser HMS *Euryalus* is a venerable ship constructed in 1901, and you would normally expect this role to be taken by a faster and more modern light cruiser. But the battle in the straits is so intense that it is felt that *Euryalus*' heavier armour and additional firepower are essential. As the Turkish shells rain down, you wonder whether even this protection will be enough.

Yet if you feel exposed aboard your armoured cruiser, then you can only guess how the crews of the Allied minesweepers must feel. They are converted fishing trawlers and a single direct hit is enough to destroy them. The minesweepers are working feverishly to clear the enemy mines. It is work that requires 'nerve, skill and unremitting watchfulness' and is difficult at the best of times. Carrying it out under heavy Turkish fire is a Herculean task. You do everything you can to provide cover for the minesweepers. *Euryalus*' guns

6. HMS *Euryalus*

hammer away at the enemy forts, and you manoeuvre your ship to try and draw enemy fire.

Some distance behind you, the turrets of seventeen Allied battleships thunder without intermission. Every gun that can be brought to bear is in action. The shores and hillsides of the straits are churned into a mass of smoke, flames and wreckage. In the skies British aircraft, some of them operating from the world's first aircraft carrier, HMS *Ark Royal*, dive down to drop small bombs onto the Turkish defenders. Some Royal Marine landing parties have hit the beaches and are fighting their way towards enemy gun emplacements. Every effort is being made to breach the straits and win the victory that you, and every other captain, dream of.

But it is not enough. Despite the pulverising bombardment, the Turkish defenders refuse to break and maintain intense fire on the Allied fleet. Heavy shells hammer into the battleships, leaving behind vivid scars of smoke and flame. Lighter guns rain fire onto you and

7. A Turkish heavy artillery emplacement in the Dardanelles

the minesweepers. For a while your luck holds and the shells plunge into the sea around you, but it is only a matter of time before the enemy finds the correct range. The first hit shatters a funnel; the second knocks out your rear 9.2-inch turret; the third hits on the waterline and rips a dangerous hole in the hull. Yet although she is listing, ablaze and riddled with shell splinters, *Euryalus* stays in the fight.

But the minesweepers are not so sturdy. Direct hits wreck several of the trawlers, and the remainder clear the fields at an agonisingly slow pace. You continue to provide covering fire from your surviving turret, but the situation is becoming desperate by mid-afternoon. Most of the battleships have been hit, several of the minesweepers have been destroyed and only the most determined efforts of your crew are keeping *Euryalus* afloat.

In a desperate attempt to silence the enemy forts, several battleships move dangerously close to the minefields so that they can bring their rapid-firing secondary guns to bear. HMS *Vengeance* leads the way, with HMS *Albion* and HMS *Majestic* close behind. Your sailors cheer at the sight of these heavy, battle-scarred ships, and for a moment you hope they will turn the tide.

The hope lasts until *Albion* is shaken by an underwater explosion as she hits a mine. Your heart sinks. The minefields are simply too dense, and your brave but crude minesweepers cannot clear them. Turkish shells rain down as *Albion* develops a fatal list. You are manoeuvring *Euryalus* to assist the stricken battleship when suddenly there is a deafening explosion on your starboard side that shakes every rivet. A heavy Turkish shell has found its mark, and seawater pours into your breached hull. Your gallant cruiser has finally met its end and all you can do is give the order to abandon ship.

AFTERMATH

After almost eight hours of intense combat, the assault on 28 March ended in bitter defeat. The Allies had done their best to learn the lessons of 18 March and had supplemented the firepower of the battleships with air attacks and Royal Marine landing parties. But the Turks had learned too. The defenders had repaired their damaged forts, stockpiled ammunition and laid additional minefields to stop the Allied advance.

Vice Admiral John de Robeck pushed his fleet as hard as he could. He was not discouraged by the loss of *Albion* and *Euryalus* and pressed forward in the belief that the Turks were on the brink of collapse. It was a vain hope. *Vengeance* and *Majestic* struck mines and sank, whilst the aged French battleship *Henri IV* was reduced to a burning wreck by accurate Turkish gunnery before she turned turtle and sank. By the end of the day the attackers had lost four battleships, an armoured cruiser and several minesweepers. Every surviving Allied battleship was damaged, many of them seriously. Even de Robeck's flagship, the modern and heavily armoured *Queen Elizabeth*, was left dented and battered.

It was clear that the straits were impregnable to a naval attack. The battleships could not silence the forts, and the minefields could not be cleared under heavy fire. The assault ended in disappointment and a grudging realisation that, if the campaign were to be continued, it would require army support.

In London there was a moment of hesitation. The War Council was divided on whether to continue the campaign. De Robeck reported that the Turks were on the brink of collapse, but the loss of eight battleships in ten days suggested otherwise. Churchill backed the Admiral, arguing that the Turks must have expended a vast amount of ammunition and suffered heavy casualties. But Kitchener had doubts. He reminded Churchill of the promise that the attack could be called off in the event of defeat, and questioned whether an amphibious landing would make any difference against such tenacious defenders.

After a series of tempestuous meetings, the decision was made: there would be no landings at Gallipoli and the campaign was called off. The Ottomans celebrated their victory and strengthened their defences while the Royal Navy retreated to lick its wounds.

The guns had fallen silent in the Dardanelles, but a political battle of unprecedented ferocity broke out in London. Churchill was enraged that the operation had been called off, and the rest of the War Council were dispirited at the thought of sending the army to the Western Front after all. The British press were furious and, whipped up by Churchill, turned their anger against Kitchener. The Secretary of State for War was accused of abandoning the campaign when victory lay within his grasp. Surely a determined attack from the army would have swung the tide? The criticism grew even louder after a series of British offensives on the Western Front in May and June 1915 ended in bloody disaster.

Kitchener's reputation plummeted, and by August he was removed from the government under the guise of promotion to command the Egyptian Expeditionary Force stationed on the Suez Canal. Winston Churchill agitated to be his replacement, but Prime Minister Asquith thought better of it and kept the youngest member of the War Cabinet at the Admiralty.

The war on the Western Front would grind on throughout 1915, and the spiralling casualties made the premature abandonment of the Dardanelles campaign ever more painful. It would become one of the great 'what if' questions of British military history.

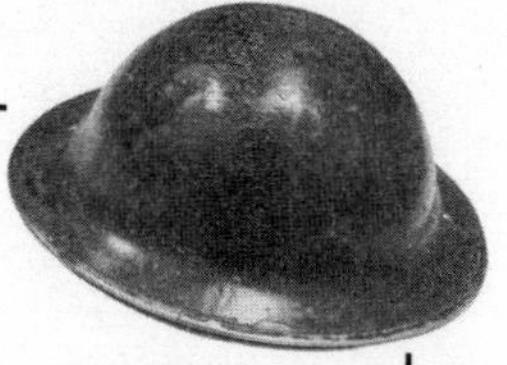

THE DECISION

- To follow the alternative route, go back to **Section 2** (p. 126).

OR

- To explore the decisions of the campaign, go to the **Historical Note** on p. 164.

SECTION 6
THE BATTLE OF TEKKE TEPE RIDGE

9 August 1915, Tekke Tepe Ridge

The thunder of rifles and machine guns echoes amongst the russet boulders on the Tekke Tepe Ridge. Turkish artillery fire and shells from offshore British battleships scream overhead and plunge into the valleys. British officers, their throats bone-dry from want of water, try to make themselves heard over the din of combat.

You are in the hottest part of this inferno, for you are ***Lieutenant-Colonel Henry Glanville Allen Moore***, commanding officer of the 6th East Yorkshire Battalion. Although you are fifty years old, you are tremendously fit and believe in leading from the front. Yesterday you personally led your soldiers up the rugged slopes of Tekke Tepe Ridge. The climb took place under a remorseless Aegean sun that sapped the strength of men half your age. But you knew how important it was to seize the high ground and pushed your soldiers on, with the exhortation that 'sweat now will save blood later'. Your footsore battalion eventually crested the ridge at around midday on 8 August; the men were sunburned, glassy-eyed and exhausted, but they had won the race to the summit and reaped their reward, for the ridge was almost completely undefended. The small Turkish garrison was soon driven off.

Your weary men had little time to rest. You knew that the Turks would launch an immediate counter-attack to try and reclaim the high ground and you busied yourself organising your defences. The work was complicated by the lack of fresh water, because incompetent administration on the beaches of Suvla Bay meant that water supplies had been unloaded late. Nevertheless, you urged your men to 'dig dig dig', in the knowledge that their foxholes would mean the difference between life and death in the battle that would soon erupt.

The Turkish counter-attack came on 9 August as the Ottoman 7th and 12th Divisions stormed up the slopes of Tekke Tepe Ridge. These formations included many tough veterans, seasoned in heavy fighting elsewhere at Gallipoli. They advanced with skill and determination and were well supported by artillery fire. But they were even wearier than your men. They had been resting in reserve when IX Corps landed at Suvla Bay and had marched more than thirty miles to reach the Tekke Tepe Ridge.

The fighting rages throughout the day, and advantages are won and lost on both sides. In some places inexperienced British soldiers, 'tired out, hungry, thirsty and a little cowed', are driven back by Turkish assaults. Yet the climb up the slope leaves the attackers 'exhausted in the extreme' and they are unable to hold their ground. Other Turkish formations find themselves under blistering rifle and machine-gun fire and are repulsed, with 'incredible losses'. You are at the heart of the action and the 6th East Yorkshires repel several determined attacks. At times the fighting is so intense that the men's rifles become too hot to hold and, in desperation, some soldiers resort to throwing sharp stones. But somehow the British line holds throughout the day and into the night.

At first light on 10 August there is a sudden cheer from behind your lines as the British 53rd and 54th Divisions arrive to reinforce your position. The newcomers can scarcely believe the state of your bloodied and battered battalion. Your gaunt survivors 'look like ghosts'. Many are wounded, and all are utterly exhausted. Yet as you hand over your trenches to the reinforcements and lead your weary men to the reserve area, you have a sense that something remarkable has been achieved. The Suvla Bay landings have turned the Turkish flank and the campaign is about to enter a new phase.

AFTERMATH

The Battle of Tekke Tepe Ridge was a trial of endurance that would become legendary for both the British and Ottoman forces. But the fact that the British 10th and 11th Divisions held the high ground ultimately gave them a decisive advantage. The Turkish 7th and 12th Divisions fought valiantly and suffered heavy losses, but could not reclaim the summit.

Stopford was lauded for his determination to seize the ridges, overriding the objections of Hamilton Reed, VC, and assuaging the doubts of his divisional commanders. The advance from Suvla Bay was undertaken in exhausting heat over a maze of broken ground, but Stopford's clear and unambiguous instructions made sure that IX Corps pushed on.

The capture of Tekke Tepe Ridge did not immediately unhinge the Turkish position to the south, but the British soon emplaced artillery on the high ground, which could interdict communication routes and fire into the Turkish rear areas with devastating effect. Worse was to come for the Ottomans. After a period of consolidation, Hamilton secretly redeployed the elite 29th Division to Suvla and used it to spearhead a flank attack on the Turks while Anzac forces advanced from their beachheads. The fighting was confused and bitter, but the Ottomans were forced to withdraw to avoid encirclement. By 24 August the British and Anzacs had secured the Sari Bair Ridge and made their largest advance since the campaign began.

After months of bloody stalemate, news of the victory sparked jubilation in the government in London. No one benefited more than Winston Churchill, who had been blamed for the failure of the naval assault in March and had languished in the political wilderness ever since. Suddenly his policies seemed vindicated, and he began to speak of capturing Constantinople by Christmas 1915. Even the normally stoic Kitchener was enthused, despatching reinforcements to Gallipoli and urging Ian Hamilton to win the campaign by the end of the year.

But although the Battle of Tekke Tepe had dealt a heavy blow to the Turks, it did not break their will to resist. The Ottomans fell back and reorganised on the next defensible positions. The Turks anchored their defences on the Kilid Bahr Plateau, a natural stronghold that could only be approached through a maze of ridges, spurs and depressions. Its name aptly translates as 'key of the sea' and while the Ottomans held this position, the straits remained impregnable.

As the euphoria of victory faded away, the British and Anzacs

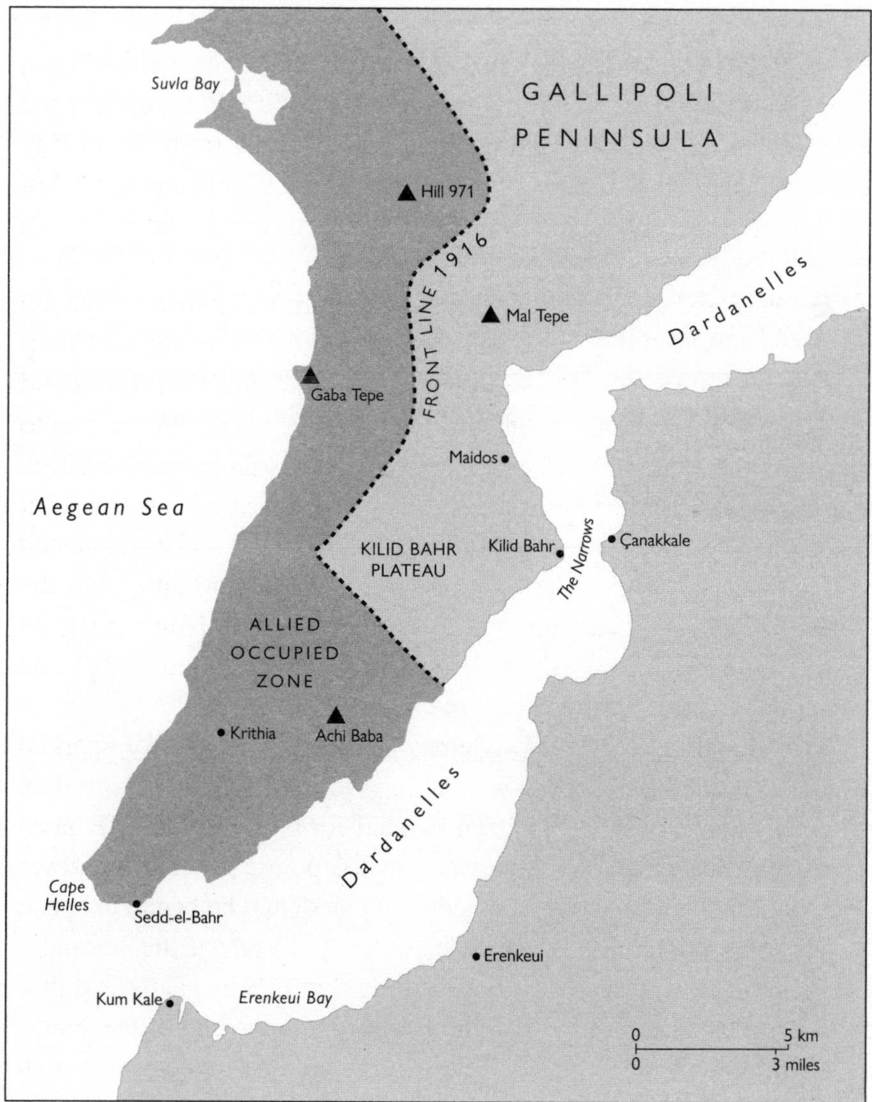

Map 6: The Gallipoli Front 1916

realised they faced another grave task to capture this citadel. The fighting for the Kilid Bahr Plateau would be prolonged and bitter, raging throughout September and October until freezing winter temperatures brought operations to a halt.

But the British government was not dissuaded. The taste of victory at Suvla Bay had convinced them that the campaign could be won. Gallipoli would be the focus of the British war effort throughout 1916. It was a controversial decision, and the lack of direct support for the French on the Western Front strained inter-Allied relations to breaking point.

The campaign at Gallipoli would prove to be as bloody and attritional as the war in France and Flanders. Every Allied assault required 'long and careful preparations and the expenditure of an enormous amount of High Explosive Gun ammunition'. The fighting was, as Hamilton admitted, 'a question of who can slog longest and hardest'.

Events elsewhere would eventually decide the Gallipoli campaign. By mid-1916 the unbearable pressure on the French at the Battle of Verdun prompted the British government to rush reinforcements to the Western Front to assist her bloodied ally. But this left Hamilton's operations at Gallipoli short of resources and removed even the faint prospect of a breakthrough.

8. Anzac gunners enduring icy conditions at Gallipoli

Even though it was clear that dreams of capturing Constantinople were long gone, the British government insisted on retaining its foothold at Gallipoli. The campaign settled into a stalemate amidst the bullet-scarred rocks and scorched scrub. The army clung on, sweltering in the summer and freezing in the winter, in a campaign that one officer described as 'another Crimea'. The soldiers grimly commented that the GF – officially the Gallipoli Front – stood for 'God Forsaken'. The British and Anzacs would still be there, barely ten miles further forward than they had been in April 1915, when the war finally came to an end in 1918.

THE DECISION

▶ To follow the alternative route, go back to **Section 3** (p. 134).

OR

▶ To explore the decisions of the campaign, go to the **Historical Note** on p. 164.

SECTION 7
DAMN THE DARDANELLES

8 January 1916, HMS *Lord Nelson*, Cape Helles

A razor-sharp wind howls across the deck of the venerable battleship HMS *Lord Nelson*, swirling the snow that fills the air. You take a moment to wipe the flakes from the lenses of your binoculars and peer nervously into the early-morning gloom. Under the cover of darkness, the last British soldiers are being evacuated from the Gallipoli peninsula. Every effort has been made to conceal the evacuation from the Ottomans, but you are desperately anxious that the enemy might perceive what is happening and launch a sudden attack that drives the survivors into the sea.

9. William Birdwood

The operation is complicated by the abysmal weather. A storm has blown up from the southwest and the wind speed has risen to forty knots. You are painfully aware of the pitch and roll of the sea as you stand aboard the *Lord Nelson* and can only guess at how much worse the conditions are for the fleet of small boats that are ferrying the soldiers from the beaches to their evacuation vessels.

You are ***Lieutenant-General William Birdwood*** and you command what is now called the Dardanelles Army. You replaced your former chief, General Ian Hamilton, after he was recalled to London to answer for the failure of the operation. Overseeing the evacuation is a particularly emotional moment for you. You landed on Gallipoli with the Anzacs on the first day of the campaign and have seen the battle ebb and flow for almost eight months.

It was you who first proposed the Suvla Bay landings, intended to turn the Turkish flank and support your Anzac forces as they tried to break out of the beachhead where they had been stuck since April. But Stopford had dawdled at Suvla Bay and wasted a golden opportunity to capture key positions whilst they were undefended. By the time IX Corps was ready to attack, the Turks had entrenched themselves atop the high ground and the British assault was stopped dead in its tracks. Stopford was sacked just nine days after the landing.

Despite the failure of the Suvla Bay operation, you never lost faith in the campaign and were the only senior commander who opposed the decision to withdraw. Yet now you are watching the last soldiers and stores leave Gallipoli for good and you must acknowledge that the operation has ended in complete failure.

It is a fraught night on the bridge of *Lord Nelson.* You expect a Turkish assault at almost any second, and every minute seems to last an eternity. But the Royal Navy carries out its job with calm professionalism. The evacuation boats brave the gale-force winds and rising seas and, as dawn approaches, you are relieved to receive a message informing you that all the men are safely aboard the fleet. Incredibly, there has not been a single casualty.

As dawn breaks, you cast a final look at the beaches. The abandoned trenches are empty and forlorn. A handful of obsolete artillery pieces have been left behind with their barrels pointing skywards. The front line is eerily silent and there is no sign of any Turkish advance. You breathe a sigh of relief and, as *Lord Nelson* turns to lead the fleet to Imbros, you reflect that you are 'now again a free man with no anxieties – but just a little done up, though only for a day or so'.

AFTERMATH

The final evacuation was completed almost exactly a year after Winston Churchill proposed the attack on the Dardanelles to the War Council. The campaign had been an almost unmitigated disaster for the Allies, characterised by ignorance, incompetence and inexperience. A naval assault that was intended to last a matter of weeks had turned into a combined-arms operation that lasted twelve months and cost the Allies approximately 188,000 men killed, wounded and missing, with thousands more falling sick.

The architects of the operation became political casualties. Churchill's reputation plummeted after the naval assault failed, and he was soon demoted from First Lord of the Admiralty to Chancellor of the Duchy of Lancaster. In November 1915, deeply depressed and with his political career ruined, he abandoned politics and went to the Western Front to serve as the commander of the 6th Royal Scots Fusiliers.

Kitchener's reputation was also ruined by the disaster at Gallipoli. His secrecy, inability to delegate and tendency to be swayed by so-called 'strategic entrepreneurs' such as Churchill eroded his authority. His public stature was too great for the government to sack him, but he was relegated to an advisory role until his death in June 1916. He was drowned aboard HMS *Hampshire* when she struck a mine and sank off the coast of Scotland.

In July 1916 the British government announced an official inquiry into the Gallipoli campaign. The Dardanelles Commission would be marred by controversy and delays, and it did not produce its final report until 1917. Its conclusions savaged the government for its overconfidence in authorising the operation, its lack of oversight and its failure to provide sufficient artillery and ammunition. General Ian Hamilton escaped with moderate criticism that focused on his over-optimism and his deference to Lord Kitchener. The greatest censure fell on Frederick Stopford, who was condemned for his poor performance at Suvla Bay.

On the other side of the line, the Turks had suffered 186,000 killed, wounded and missing, but had won a decisive victory. The Dardanelles had been held, the Allies had been defeated and the threat to Constantinople had passed. The Ottoman Empire seemed unassailable. The Turkish army now turned its focus on Mesopotamia, where it would win another great victory over an Anglo-Indian force at the Siege of Kut in April 1916.

Gallipoli forced Britain to change its strategic focus. The Turkish army had proved itself to be a formidable fighting force, and there was no appetite for major operations against the Ottoman Empire. Britain's strategists stoked the fires of the incipient Arab Revolt to keep Turkish forces occupied, but otherwise turned their attention to the Western Front. The situation that Churchill and Kitchener had tried to avoid in January 1915 had come to pass, and the inexperienced divisions of the New Army would endure a baptism of fire against the Germans at the Somme in 1916.

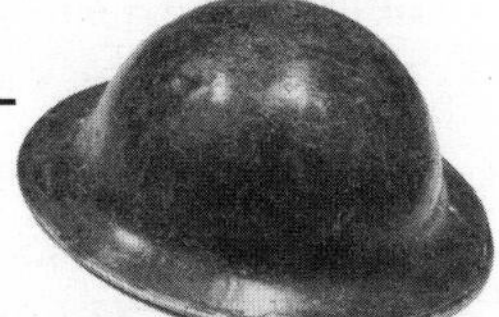

THE DECISION

- To follow the alternative route, go back to **Section 3** (p. 134).

OR

- To explore the decisions of the campaign, go to the **Historical Note** on p. 164.

HISTORICAL NOTE

Gallipoli is one of the most famous campaigns of the First World War. The battle is enshrined in national memory by Anzac Day in Australia and New Zealand and occupies an important place in the historical identity of modern Turkey.

It is also a campaign replete with endless controversy and 'what ifs'. Was it a foolhardy expedition that was always destined to fail, or was it a strategic masterstroke undone by inept execution? Winston Churchill expended much ink arguing the latter, most notably in *The World Crisis*, his entertaining but unreliable history of the First World War. Churchill's reputation was permanently scarred by the Dardanelles, and he was determined to restore it by showing that his plan could have worked. In *The World Crisis* he identified several turning points where the campaign might have been won. One was Vice Admiral de Robeck's decision to call off the naval attack after his defeat on 18 March. Churchill argued that this was a grave mistake, as the Turks were exhausted and short of ammunition. Another was Lieutenant-General Frederick Stopford's dismal performance at Suvla Bay, which robbed the army of a golden opportunity to turn the Ottoman flank. This chapter gives you an opportunity to explore both of these controversies.

The historical route begins with the decision to attack the Dardanelles by sea (Section 1 to Section 2). Churchill's concept was based on the false belief that the guns of battleships could destroy shore defences with relative ease. It also ignored many practical difficulties, not least what might happen if the fleet reached Constantinople. Nevertheless, in the gloomy atmosphere of January 1915 it seemed better to take what seemed to be a relatively low-risk, high-reward gamble rather than commit more soldiers to the deadlocked Western Front.

The next decision comes after the failure of the naval attack on 18 March. The Turkish minefields wrought havoc on the fleet, but Vice Admiral John de Robeck believed he had inflicted heavy losses on the Ottoman defenders in return. Nevertheless, the inability of British minesweepers to clear mines under heavy fire led to the decision to deploy the army to capture the enemy guns from the landward side (Section 2 to Section 3). This was a fateful decision that changed the campaign, from a relatively low-risk naval assault that could be called off at any time to a prolonged ground operation that would take weeks, if not months. The landings on 25 April were a near-disaster, redeemed only by the courage and determination of British and Anzac forces (French forces made a successful diversionary landing on the Asiatic side of the Dardanelles), and stalemate soon set in.

In August the Allies made a final attempt to restart the stalled campaign. Anzac forces launched a major attack from their beachhead, and British IX Corps landed to the north at Suvla Bay. The planning for Suvla Bay was confused; Hamilton wanted IX Corps to seize the ridges, but his Chief of Staff, Walter Braithwaite, had little faith in the plan and wanted the attackers to concentrate on securing the bay. This left IX Corps' commander, Frederick Stopford, in an ambiguous position. In the event he focused on Suvla Bay itself rather than on the ridges (Section 3 to Section 7) and thereby lost a golden opportunity to capture crucial high ground. By the time the advance began, the Turks had secured the ridges. The 6th East Yorkshires advanced the furthest of any Stopford's battalions and almost reached the summit of Tekke Tepe Ridge, but were eventually repelled with heavy losses.

The failure of the August offensive doomed the campaign. By October 1915 it was clear that the Allies could not breach the Turkish defences, and in December the decision was finally made to evacuate the Gallipoli peninsula. This was no easy matter, and Kitchener feared that it could end in a bloody disaster if the Turks attacked whilst the evacuation was under way. But the withdrawal was perhaps the only aspect of the campaign that went well; British and Anzac forces withdrew without a single fatality.

But what if other options had been chosen? One of the most intriguing possibilities is an attack on Alexandretta (now İskenderun in Turkey) in early 1915. Kitchener had long harboured ambitions to seize this vital port and use it as a launch pad for an offensive to break the Ottoman Empire in two. Historically, stubborn French political opposition rendered it an impossibility, but the text allows you to see what might have happened (Section 1 to Section 4). It is likely that the attack would have worked. The quotes from Hindenburg in this section are real ones, taken from his post-war autobiography; and no less an authority than Lawrence of Arabia thought the failure to attack Alexandretta was the worst strategic mistake of the entire war in the Middle East. Alexandretta was essentially undefended (and largely indefensible from an attack from the sea). Allied forces could have used it as a base to cut Ottoman communications and break the empire in two. In these circumstances, it is likely that Enver Pasha would have made peace rather than risk the Allies invading Anatolia from several directions.

Another option, and one that especially intrigued Churchill, was renewing the naval attack after 18 March (Section 2 to Section 5). Churchill argued in *The World Crisis* that the Ottomans were exhausted and short on ammunition. But the information available to him at the time was misleading. In fact the defenders were confident, after sinking three Allied battleships, and were still well supplied with heavy shells. A renewed attack would have run into intense resistance and dense minefields. It would have ended in defeat.

Finally, what might have happened if Stopford had prioritised the ridges at the Suvla Bay landings (Section 3 to Section 6)? A stronger-willed commander could have pushed the inexperienced 10th and 11th Divisions onto the ridges much earlier. Possession of the high ground would have given them a huge advantage against the Ottoman counter-attack, and it is likely they would have been able to hold the position. From there it is possible that renewed attacks to the south could have unhinged the Turkish line in front of the Anzac beachhead. This victory would not have ended the campaign – the Turks would have fought on from the remaining ridges rather than surrender the peninsula – but it would have encouraged the British government to provide additional resources. The campaign would have ground on indefinitely, without either side being able to break through the inhospitable terrain.

Lord Kitchener found his reputation in steep decline in 1915. He was blamed for the bloody deadlock at Gallipoli and the serious shortage of artillery ammunition in France, and by the end of the year he was quietly replaced as Britain's primary strategist by Chief of the Imperial General Staff, William Robertson. He died in June 1916 when HMS *Hampshire*, the ship carrying him on a diplomatic mission to Russia, struck a German mine and sank off the Orkney Islands.

John de Robeck commanded the naval forces at Gallipoli throughout the campaign. He became commander of the 2nd Battle Squadron of the Grand Fleet in November 1916, flying his flag above HMS *King George V*. In a somewhat ironic twist, he served as High Commissioner of Constantinople after the war.

Frederick Stopford was unceremoniously sacked just nine days after the Suvla Bay landings. The Dardanelles Commission was highly critical of Stopford's conduct, and he felt that he had been scapegoated to protect the reputations of other failed commanders. He retired in 1920 and lived out the remainder of his life in relative obscurity.

Winston Churchill was humiliated by the failure at Gallipoli and left politics to serve on the Western Front as the commander of the 6th Royal Scots Fusiliers. He survived this trial by fire and returned to politics in mid-1916. He would find political redemption in 1917 when he became Minister of Munitions – the largest civilian ministry in the British Empire. Nevertheless he would be haunted by the ghosts of Gallipoli for years to come, and hecklers often yelled, 'What about the Dardanelles?' at him during public events in the 1920s and 1930s.

Rudolf Miles Burmester served in the Mediterranean for the whole war, eventually rising to become Chief of Staff of the Mediterranean Fleet. He continued to serve in the inter-war years and commanded naval forces based at Swansea in the Second World War. He retired after the war with the rank of admiral.

Henry Glanville Allen Moore met a tragic end. On 8 August patrols from the 6th East Yorkshire Battalion scouted towards Tekke Tepe Ridge and found it largely undefended. He led an ad-hoc group to seize it on 9 August, but by now it was too late and the Ottomans had arrived in strength. The British attack was repulsed; Moore stayed behind to organise a rearguard to cover the retreat, but was surrounded and forced to surrender. After being taken prisoner, he was bayoneted to death by his captors.

William Birdwood was one of the few officers to emerge from Gallipoli with his reputation relatively intact. He commanded I Anzac Corps on the Western Front in 1916 and the Australian Corps in 1917. He commanded the Australians through several bloody and controversial battles, but was popular with the troops and was held in high regard by his peers. By mid-1918 he rose to command the Fifth Army and led it during the war, winning Hundred Days Offensive. He ended his career as a Field Marshal.

4

JUTLAND:

CLASH OF STEEL IN THE NORTH SEA, 1916

SECTION 1
ENEMY IN SIGHT

2.20 p.m., 31 May 1916, HMS *Barham*, the North Sea

Map 1: The Royal Navy's route across the North Sea

It has been an uneventful afternoon aboard the battleship HMS *Barham* and you are starting to suspect that the Royal Navy is on yet another wild goose chase. The disappointment is keener as the day had begun with such excitement. The previous evening an intelligence report from the code-breakers at Room 40 had revealed that the German High Seas Fleet was preparing to sortie from its fortified lair at Wilhelmshaven on 31 May. The British Grand Fleet – the most powerful force of warships in the history of the world – had set sail in the early hours to intercept it. Since the outbreak of the war the Royal Navy has longed to get to grips with its elusive foe and win a victory to rank alongside the Battle of Trafalgar 1805. Yet there is no sign of the enemy as the clock slowly ticks into mid-afternoon.

You are ***Rear Admiral Hugh Evan-Thomas***. You joined the Royal Navy in 1875 at the age of thirteen and have spent more years at sea than you have on land. You are serious-minded, intensely professional, and curiously old-fashioned, earning the nickname 'Old Voice' while you were a cadet. Despite your experience at sea, you have not seen action and your most famous role was serving aboard the rigged corvette HMS *Bacchante* alongside the royal teenagers Prince Albert and Prince George during their world tour between 1880 and 1882.

You are far away from sails and masts today, for now you command the 5th Battle Squadron, consisting of the battleships *Barham*, *Valiant*, *Warspite* and *Malaya.* These *Queen Elizabeth*-class ships are the most powerful in the world. Their modern oil-fuelled engines give them much greater speed than coal-powered warships and they are armed with massive 15-inch guns. Fast, heavily armed and well armoured, they are described as a 'ship that can do everything'.

1. Hugh Evan-Thomas

The squadron needs its speed, for today it is attached to the Battlecruiser Fleet under the command of Rear Admiral David Beatty. The Royal Navy's battlecruisers combine the firepower of a battleship with the speed of a cruiser, but these strengths have come at the cost of their armour, and they are lightly protected for their size. Your squadron has been assigned to Beatty to give his force extra punch.

You and Beatty are quite different characters. Unlike you, the commander of the Battlecruiser Fleet revels in the limelight. As well as being the talk of high society, Beatty has won naval victories against the Germans at the Battle of Heligoland Bight (27 August 1914) and the Battle of Dogger Bank (24 January 1915). The latter might have ended in a decisive triumph, but a series of signalling blunders aboard Beatty's flagship HMS *Lion* allowed the enemy to escape with the loss of only one ship. The admiral has been itching for another chance to face the Germans ever since.

But it does not seem that the rematch will take place today. Your squadron is five miles to the north-west of Beatty's Battlecruiser Fleet and is currently on a north-westerly course, away from the probable location of the enemy. Your mind is beginning to turn to the thought of afternoon tea when there is a sudden flurry of activity on *Barham*'s bridge as a message arrives from your telegraphist. It is a decoded signal from the light cruiser HMS *Galatea*:

URGENT. TWO CRUISERS, PROBABLY HOSTILE,
IN SIGHT BEARING ESE, COURSE UNKNOWN.
MY POSITION LAT 56° 48'N, LONG 5° 21'E.

The message is an encouraging one – but no more than that. Light cruisers are the eyes and ears of the fleet and often skirmish with enemy ships. It does not mean a fleet action is imminent.

But then something else begins to happen. Five miles to the south-east the battlecruisers start to manoeuvre. Gazing through your binoculars, you can see that Beatty's flagship, HMS *Lion*, and the five ships of the Battlecruiser Fleet are changing course and turning to the south-east. The manoeuvre is unmistakable, even though the ships are obscured by dense clouds of coal smoke.

This change of course puzzles you. What is Beatty doing? Does he want you to follow him? If so, he would surely have sent you a signal to do so – most readily by hoisting signal flags or through a searchlight message. You snap the binoculars back to your eyes and study the Battlecruiser Fleet once more. It is now sailing directly away from your squadron and, judging by the smoke pouring from their funnels, the battlecruisers are increasing their speed. But there is no signal of any kind to indicate what you are supposed to do.

You lower the binoculars and rub your chin as you consider your options. All your training tells you that you should wait for a signal before turning your battleships. The sheer size of the Grand Fleet means that precise control is essential, to avoid collisions between vessels. Surely Beatty will send you an order if he wishes you to turn?

Yet you also know that Beatty handles his Battlecruiser Fleet differently from the other squadrons of the Grand Fleet. His approach to regulations is flexible – some would say lax – and he lauds the initiative that defined Nelson's band of brothers at Trafalgar. It may be that he expects you to follow him, even without direct orders.

The staff on the bridge await your command. You must decide how to steer *Barham* and your squadron of battleships.

AIDE-MEMOIRE

* You command 5th Battle Squadron, consisting of the most powerful battleships in the world. Whatever decision you make will have profound consequences.
* Your training and experience have given you immense respect for Royal Navy regulations. These are clear that you should wait for a signal from your commanding officer before undertaking a major change of course.
* You know that Beatty's Battlecruiser Fleet operates to a looser set of regulations.

You are not familiar with these, but it may be that Beatty expects you conform to his movements without a signal.

* Your squadron has been attached to the Battlecruiser Fleet to give the lightly armoured battlecruisers more punch. Surely you should stay close to them to ensure that you can fulfil this role?
* Manoeuvring a 30,000-ton battleship is no easy matter and collisions can be fatal. If Beatty wanted you to follow him, surely he would have sent you a signal?
* Such a drastic manoeuvre might be acceptable in battle, but it is not clear that the German fleet is even at sea.
* The scouting report from HMS *Galatea* suggests that at least some enemy vessels are in the area.

THE DECISION

Do you stay on your course and await a signal from Beatty or take the initiative and turn your ships immediately?

▶ If you believe it is correct to wait for a direct order to change course, go to **Section 2** (p. 176).

OR

▶ If you feel that you are justified in turning and following Beatty without instructions, go to **Section 4** (p. 188).

SECTION 2
TORPEDOES IN THE WATER

7.15 p.m., 31 May 1916, HMS *Iron Duke*, the North Sea

The 13.5-inch guns of HMS *Iron Duke* bellow once more. Through the lenses of your powerful binoculars their target appears as a small black silhouette on the horizon, but even at this distance you can see huge water spouts surround the enemy vessel as your shells plunge all around her, and a sudden yellow flash of flame as a shot strikes home. You smile grimly. Finally you have the German High Seas Fleet exactly where you want it.

You are ***Admiral John Jellicoe***. You joined the Royal Navy as a midshipman at the age of twelve and have enjoyed a stellar career ever

2. HMS *Iron Duke*

since. You have seen action on land, including fierce fighting in the Boxer Rebellion of 1900, where you were severely wounded, but you are best known for your mastery of the intricacies of naval gunnery. Your technical skills, impeccable record of service and cool professionalism have elevated you to command the entire Grand Fleet. Now you lead it in its first full-scale battle.

3. John Jellicoe

The battle did not start as you would have liked. Responding to HMS *Galatea*'s sighting report, Beatty's Battlecruiser Fleet raced after the German battlecruisers of the First Scouting Group. But in his eagerness to engage, Beatty failed to order the 5th Squadron to join him and left his most powerful ships trailing several miles behind. The absence of these battleships was keenly felt in the fighting that followed. Superior German gunnery took its toll and the battlecruisers HMS *Indefatigable* and HMS *Queen Mary* were blown apart by enemy shells that tore through their fragile armour and detonated their ammunition magazines. It was only the belated intervention of HMS *Barham* and her sister ships that saved Beatty's fleet from further punishment.

Yet Beatty played his role, despite these losses. At around 4.30 p.m. his scouts spotted the main body of the German High Seas Fleet approaching from the south. Beatty turned his Battlecruiser Fleet north to lure them to you, although there was another signalling error as he failed to order Evan-Thomas to follow him once more, forcing 5th Squadron to endure a harrowing pursuit under heavy fire. Nevertheless, by 6.20 p.m. the Germans had been lured far enough north that a full-scale fleet battle was imminent.

You carefully timed your fleet deployment and positioned your huge battlefleet to 'cross the T' of the enemy, so that your ships could pour broadsides into the vanguard of the German High Seas Fleet. For about ten minutes your ships rained shells on the stunned Germans before the enemy retreated into the early-evening gloom, masked by a mixture of smoke from their funnels and the fires that raged aboard the damaged vessels.

You held a southerly course, hoping to encounter the enemy again. You did not have long to wait. At around 7 p.m. the vanguard of the High Seas Fleet emerged from the mist to your west like a herd of mammoths from a snowstorm. Once more you 'crossed the T', and this time the position was a decisive one. The enemy was silhouetted on the horizon, making them perfect targets, while your ships were hidden in the haze. Even more importantly, you blocked the enemy's line of retreat to Wilhelmshaven. They would have to fight their way through you if they wished to escape.

Through your binoculars you can see that the enemy fleet is in a state of pandemonium. The German formation is completely disorganised, and battleships are lurching wildly to avoid collisions. The Grand Fleet's salvoes add to the chaos. *Iron Duke*'s guns roar again, and your target is wreathed in flames as your huge shells strike home.

But you suddenly discern new movement through the smoke and mist. The much-battered German battlecruisers of First Scouting Group are heading directly towards your fleet. Around them swarm massed flotillas of German torpedo boats, and you realise with alarm that the enemy is launching a do-or-die torpedo attack on your battlefleet.

Iron Duke's secondary gun batteries thunder into action and the entire length of the battleship is soon wreathed with muzzle flashes. But the German torpedo boats are small, fast and difficult to hit. They surge onwards through the hail of shells to unleash their deadly torpedoes.

This is a scenario that you have always dreaded. Your battleships are well protected against gunfire, but are much more vulnerable to underwater weapons. A single torpedo has the potential to sink even

4. A German torpedo boat

the mightiest of your battleships. You must manoeuvre swiftly to deal with this attack.

The standard approach is to order your fleet to turn away from the oncoming torpedoes. By opening the range, you make your ships harder to hit and some of the torpedoes will simply run out of fuel before they reach your line. It also gives individual ships more time and space to manoeuvre to avoid any oncoming torpedoes. But if you do this, you will be forced to break contact with the enemy battlefleet and it will escape into the evening mists.

A riskier approach is to turn your fleet *towards* the torpedo attack. A bow-on battleship presents a narrow target that will be difficult to hit and, by closing the range, your secondary batteries will be able to inflict more damage on the torpedo boats. It also ensures that you maintain visual contact with the High Seas Fleet and will prevent them escaping into the dusky gloom. Yet this decision comes with extreme risks. Individual ships will not have the time or space to manoeuvre to avoid torpedoes and must trust to their armour to survive. There is the potential for a complete disaster if several of your battleships are hit and sunk.

Another thought arcs through your mind. The Royal Navy is vital to Britain's war effort. It protects the British Isles from invasion and ensures that supplies can arrive from around the globe. If your fleet suffers heavy casualties, then the consequences will be fatal.

The first telltale bubble trails of torpedoes are streaking towards your fleet. You must give a crucial order.

AIDE-MEMOIRE

* After almost two years of waiting, you finally have the High Seas Fleet where you want it and are on the cusp of winning a decisive victory.
* The enemy is making a desperate attempt to escape by launching a massed torpedo attack to give its battleships time to retreat.
* Torpedoes pose a special danger. Your ships are well armoured against shellfire, but are vulnerable below the waterline. A single torpedo can sink even the mightiest battleship.
* The safest procedure for dealing with a massed torpedo attack is to turn your fleet away from it – but this will enable the High Seas Fleet to escape.
* It is possible to turn into the torpedo attack and stay in contact with the enemy – but this increases the risk that your own battleships will be hit.
* The Royal Navy is vital to the safety of the British Isles. If it is destroyed or heavily damaged, the entire war might be lost.

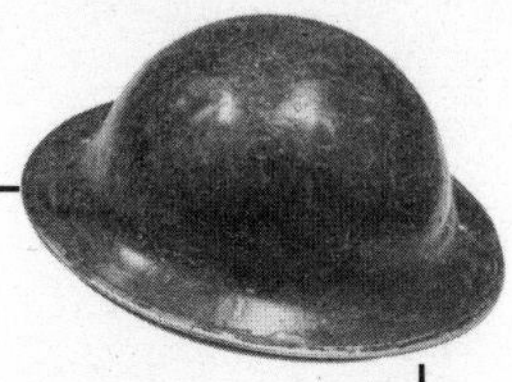

THE DECISION

Do you turn away from the torpedo attack to ensure the safety of fleet or turn into the torpedoes to prevent the enemy from escaping?

- If you wish to order your fleet to turn away from the oncoming torpedoes, go to **Section 3** (p. 182).

OR

- If you prefer to turn to face the torpedo attack head-on, go to **Section 4** (p. 188).

SECTION 3
MANOEUVRES IN THE DARK

12.45 a.m., 1 June 1916, HMS *Malaya*, the North Sea

There is something eerie about the silence of the night after a day filled with fire and fury. You stand with your officers on the bridge of HMS *Malaya*, one of the *Queen Elizabeth*-class battleships of Rear Admiral Evan-Thomas' 5th Battle Squadron and take a moment to enjoy a welcome mug of hot cocoa.

You are ***Captain Algernon Boyle***. You are the son of Henry Boyle, 5th Earl of Shannon. Your father wanted you to follow in the family

5. HMS *Malaya*

tradition and join the British army, but from an early age your heart was set on joining the Royal Navy. You began your cadet training at the age of twelve and you have enjoyed an excellent career, marked by your expertise in gunnery and love of history. Yet none of your studies could fully prepare you for the intensity of today's battle.

Malaya and her crew have endured a baptism of fire. The 5th Battle Squadron was left behind when the Battlecruiser Fleet suddenly turned to investigate HMS *Galatea*'s sighting report. Once the error was realised, the battleships strained their engines to join the fight, but had only just brought their powerful guns into range when the full might of the German High Seas Fleet emerged from the mist ahead.

Beatty turned his Battlecruiser Fleet about to lure the enemy north, but there was another signalling error that almost ended in disaster. The signal flags aboard HMS *Lion* ordered 5th Battle Squadron to turn north when they were hauled down, but in the chaos of battle they were left flying for far too long. As a result, 5th Battle Squadron sailed dangerously close to the German fleet and by the time the battleships turned, they were already under fire from dozens of enemy guns.

A harrowing chase followed, and 5th Battle Squadron needed all its speed and armour to survive as the four ships came under intense fire from the enemy fleet. Every bolt and rivet of *Malaya* shook as heavy shells hammered into her. One shell tore through a secondary gun battery and ignited stored ammunition. A potentially fatal explosion was prevented only by the chief gunner and a crew member hurling themselves onto burning cordite and extinguishing the flames with their own bodies. Both men were severely burned, but their courage saved the ship. Mere minutes later, another shell smashed through the hull just below the waterline, giving your ship an ominous four-degree list to starboard and causing her to lose speed. It was a moment of the utmost crisis, and it was only the skill of your stokers that kept the engines running and prevented you from being caught and destroyed.

It is testament to the fighting power of the *Queen Elizabeth*-class battleships that not only did *Malaya* survive this ordeal, but also stayed in action. Her 15-inch guns returned fire throughout the chase and the fleet action that followed. Now your damage-control parties are working feverishly to prepare her for a renewal of battle in the morning. *Malaya* remains a formidable battleship, despite her scorched, holed and dented appearance.

You have seen no sign of the enemy since Admiral Jellicoe ordered the fleet to turn away from the massed torpedo attack five hours ago. The manoeuvre was perfectly executed. Not a single torpedo struck home, and the Grand Fleet soon swung back onto its southerly course. But turning away ensured that the Germans escaped into the mist and the day's fighting ended.

The Grand Fleet hopes to renew the battle at dawn, and Jellicoe has ordered the fleet to head south towards Horn's Reef to cut off the German retreat to Wilhelmshaven. If the Royal Navy can catch the High Seas Fleet here, then it will be able to finish the job it began at Jutland.

But first the hours of darkness must be endured. The ships of the Grand Fleet have little training in night-fighting and for now the fleet has adopted a defensive formation to protect it from torpedo-boat attacks. Although your crew remains alert for any sign of the enemy, you do not expect any action before daylight.

After the stress of the day, the hot chocolate you are drinking acts as a tonic. You are making small talk with the officers on the bridge when suddenly the horizon behind you explodes with dozens of gun flashes. Your drink is instantly forgotten, and your binoculars snap onto the pyrotechnics. Amid the flashes you can see that a flotilla of British destroyers are making a daring torpedo attack against a line of German battleships. The excitement on the bridge is palpable and there is a cry of 'Hun!' from one of your younger officers.

For a moment you are transfixed by the action. Gouts of fire burst from guns, and German searchlights sweep through the darkness to find targets. One of the British destroyers receives a fatal hit, and a crimson fireball erupts into the night sky. The explosion clearly illuminates an enemy battleship, and you recognise it as a *Nassau*-class dreadnought.

Then, as suddenly as it began, the action ends. The firing ceases and the Germans switch off their searchlights. Silence settles over the sea once more.

You lower your binoculars and consider the situation. The Grand Fleet is steaming south, on the assumption that the enemy is steaming to the west and parallel to your position. But after the sudden night action, you are certain that at least part of the German High Seas Fleet is directly behind you. The enemy may be trying to slip around behind the Royal Navy and escape.

You must report this at once. You dictate a short report for your telegraphist to transmit to your squadron commander, Rear Admiral Evan-Thomas. But then you pause. Should you also transmit the information to Admiral Jellicoe directly?

The sighting report will surely be of great interest to the Grand Fleet's commander and will enable him to change course to prevent the Germans slipping behind the Royal Navy. Yet you are conscious that transmitting this message will break the chain of command and go against regulations. You have sent the information to Rear Admiral Evan-Thomas, and it is his duty to decide whether it should be passed on to Admiral Jellicoe, not yours. It would be impertinent to do otherwise.

The officers on the bridge look at you expectantly. You must decide how to transmit your report.

AIDE-MEMOIRE

* The German High Seas Fleet escaped into the mist after the torpedo attack and the Grand Fleet is now cruising south to cut off its retreat.
* The fleet's cruising formation assumes that the enemy fleet is cruising on a parallel course to the west. If this is the case, then the Royal Navy will cut the Germans off from their home port and re-engage them at first light.
* The night action has shown that enemy battleships are directly behind you, rather than to the west. This suggests

that the enemy may be attempting to slip behind you and make a dash for safety in Wilhelmshaven.

* This information is crucial. It will be necessary to redirect the fleet to cut off this escape route.
* Regulations state that you should report this sighting to your squadron commander, who will decide whether to pass it further up the chain of command. Surely Evan-Thomas will pass on the information if he deems it valuable?
* This report is vital. Surely you are justified in sending it directly to Admiral Jellicoe too?

THE DECISION

Do you follow regulations and send your report to Evan-Thomas alone or disobey them and send the information directly to Jellicoe?

▶ If you believe that regulations are there for a reason and send the report to Rear Admiral Evan-Thomas only, go to **Section 7** (p. 204).

OR

▶ If you think that Admiral Jellicoe should see your information immediately, even if it means disobeying regulations, go to **Section 6** (p. 198).

SECTION 4
THE BATTLECRUISER DUEL

4.25 p.m., 31 May 1916, HMS *Lion*, the North Sea

A German salvo howls over HMS *Lion* and plunges into the sea fifty yards beyond the battlecruiser. Huge white plumes of water are flung high into the air where the shells land and, even at this distance, the concussion rocks your ship. But you pay no attention to this near-miss and keep your binoculars locked on your target. The enemy is within your grasp, and you are determined to press your advantage.

6. David Beatty

You are ***Rear Admiral David Beatty***, commander of the Battlecruiser Fleet. Handsome, dashing and daring, you became the talk of high society in 1901 when you married Ethel Tree, a wealthy American divorcee, following a passionate affair. Your marriage has given you immense wealth, which has encouraged your daredevil attitude. You demand aggression from the captains of your Battlecruiser Fleet, but critics claim this had led to sloppy discipline and careless errors.

You are stung by this criticism, especially as the Germans were able to escape from your clutches at the Battle of Dogger Bank in January 1915 due to signalling errors.

But now you have a chance to erase this black mark on your record. Your six battlecruisers – *Lion*, *Princess Royal*, *Tiger*, *Queen Mary*, *New Zealand* and *Indefatigable* – are locked in a running fight with the five battlecruisers of the German First Scouting Group, *Lützow*, *Derfflinger*, *Seydlitz*, *Moltke* and *Von der Tann*. It has been a tough battle. The enemy is a crack squadron boasting some of the finest gunnery in the entire German navy. *Lion* has felt the force of the enemy's fire, and one of her 13.5-inch gun turrets is smashed and ablaze after suffering a direct hit.

But you have a crucial advantage in this fight, for your battlecruisers are supported by the dreadnoughts of 5th Battle Squadron. At the beginning of the action you turned your fleet south, expecting these ships to join you. Evan-Thomas understood your intentions and ordered his huge battleships to follow in your wake. It means that you can pit ten ships against five opponents.

You clamp your binoculars to your eyes once more. The enemy is wreathed in waterspouts as your salvoes plunge around them. A shell hits the enemy flagship *Lützow*, detonating in a plume of flame that hurls wreckage high into the air.

The German battlecruisers are fighting hard, but the sheer weight of fire from your fleet takes its toll. As you watch the action you can see that the enemy is zigzagging to try and throw off the aim of your gunners, but is reducing its own accuracy in the process. German salvoes sail over your flagship, but your guns – especially the colossal 15-inch guns of 5th Battle Squadron – find their targets. It is testament to the sheer toughness of the German ships that the enemy battlecruisers remain in the fight.

You are wondering how much more punishment your opponent can endure when an urgent signal arrives on the bridge from your advance light-cruiser screen. 'Have sighted enemy battlefleet SE. Enemy course north.' The main body of the High Seas Fleet is on the way. Now is the time for you to turn your fleet and lure the enemy into the waiting arms of Admiral Jellicoe and the Grand Fleet.

AFTERMATH

The fierce running battle between the Battlecruiser Fleet and First Scouting Group would become known as the 'Run to the South'. Outnumbered two-to-one and severely outgunned, the German battlecruisers suffered heavy punishment that left all five ships battered and burning.

Nevertheless, the arrival of the main High Seas Fleet presented the Germans with a chance to even the score. The Germans now had the numerical advantage and doggedly pursued Beatty's and Evan-Thomas' squadrons north. It was to prove a fatal mistake.

At around 6.20 p.m. the Grand Fleet emerged from the mist to the north and engaged the head of the High Seas Fleet. For ten terrifying minutes British salvoes pummelled the leading elements of the German fleet. But then the Germans executed a skilful *Gefechtskehrtwendung* – a sudden, simultaneous turn-away – and retreated into the darkening mists.

The battle might have ended here, had it not been for a terrible error by German Admiral Reinhard Scheer. As the firing died down, he reasoned that if he were to reverse course again, then he could pass in the wake of the Grand Fleet and slip behind them while the British fruitlessly cruised south, searching for targets. This done, he would be able to escape into the dusk and retreat to safer waters.

It was a fatal miscalculation. Instead of passing behind the Grand Fleet, he mistimed his turn and led his ships right into the middle of the southbound British line. This time the situation was even worse than the initial encounter. Visibility decisively favoured the British, while the German fleet was damaged and disorganised. A tornado of shells tore through the High Seas Fleet, ripping through armoured compartments, smashing gun turrets and blasting away funnels.

In desperation, Admiral Scheer ordered the battered battlecruisers of First Scouting Group to make a do-or-die charge at the head of a mass of torpedo boats to delay the British long enough for the High Seas Fleet to retreat. But the damage suffered in the earlier 'Run to the South' now told. The First Scouting Group bravely set course for the Grand Fleet, but immediately ran into a perfect storm of shells. *Lützow* was soon sinking after suffering mortal damage below the waterline. Repeated hits had set *Seydlitz* ablaze from stem to stern, and she suddenly vanished in a towering explosion as the fires reached her ammunition magazines. A British shell wrecked the engine room of *Derfflinger* and brought her to a dead stop. Unable to manoeuvre and under remorseless fire, she soon capsized and sank. Only *Moltke* and *Von der Tann* survived the inferno, retreating into the mist, concealed by smoke from the uncontrolled fires that raged aboard.

The massed torpedo attack forced Jellicoe to break contact with the High Seas Fleet. Although the British pursued the Germans throughout the night, there would be no renewed contact. The Battle of Jutland was effectively over. While not a decisive clash in the style of Trafalgar, Jutland was a clear British victory. Three modern German battlecruisers had been sunk and many other capital ships had been severely damaged. In return the British had suffered casualties among the Royal Navy's light forces, but had not lost a single major vessel.

The close cooperation between Beatty and Evan-Thomas was key to the victory. The damage they had inflicted on the First Scouting Group doomed the German battlecruisers and ensured their later destruction at the hands of the Grand Fleet. There were some inevitable mutterings that the battle might have ended in an even more decisive victory, but overall the Royal Navy could be proud of its achievements.

THE DECISION

- To follow the alternative route, go back to **Section 1** (p. 170).

OR

- To explore the decisions of the battle, go to the **Historical Note** (p. 208).

SECTION 5
ENGAGE THE ENEMY MORE CLOSELY

7.25 p.m., 31 May, HMS *Marlborough*, the North Sea

The North Sea is a vision of Armageddon as the British Grand Fleet and the German High Seas Fleet fight to the bitter end. The early evening air is thick with smoke and is illuminated by gun flashes and explosions. The thunder of guns is continuous and deafening. Then, from the inferno, bursts a wave of small German torpedo boats, racing forward at top speed to deliver a desperate do-or-die attack against the British battle line.

7. Cecil Burney

Your battleship, HMS *Marlborough*, is at the heart of this maelstrom, for you are ***Vice Admiral Cecil Burney***. You have enjoyed a stellar career, which has included action ashore in the Anglo-Egyptian War of 1882 and delicate political work in the First Balkan War of 1913. You are known for being a stern disciplinarian and are severe on those who perform poorly, for you demand the highest standards of professionalism from your officers and men.

HMS *Marlborough* has needed every ounce of skill from its crew today. While following the retreating Germans after the initial clash of battlefleets, *Marlborough* encountered the crippled light cruiser *Wiesbaden*. Your guns poured shells into this lame duck, expecting to finish it off with ease, but it turned out that the wounded ship still had teeth. *Wiesbaden* fired two torpedoes as you sailed past. The evening mist and smoke from your guns masked their approach until it was too late, and at 6.45 p.m. there was an almighty explosion on *Marlborough*'s starboard side as one of the torpedoes hit home. The blast tore a 28-foot hole in the battleship's hull, and seawater poured through the breach. *Marlborough* developed an alarming eight-degree list while the crew, many of them up to their knees in icy water, worked feverishly to control the flooding. It is testament to their skill and determination that the ship not only remains afloat, but holds its place in the battle line.

Having already felt the force of an enemy torpedo, you scowl as you see the oncoming torpedo-boat attack. You are about to bark out instructions for evasive manoeuvres when orders arrive straight from Admiral Jellicoe aboard *Iron Duke*. The Grand Fleet is to turn towards the attack, presenting a narrow target for the enemy and keeping in contact with the High Seas Fleet. If there were any lingering doubts as to Jellicoe's intentions, they are dispelled as another instruction is issued: ENGAGE THE ENEMY MORE CLOSELY. Every sailor in the Royal Navy knows Nelson's famous instruction from the Battle of Trafalgar 1805 and it stirs your blood. This daring manoeuvre could lead to a victory to rank alongside Britain's most famous sea battle.

Marlborough swiftly complies with the order and the vast 30,000-ton battleship turns towards the swarm of torpedo boats. Twenty-eight huge British battleships turn to face their much smaller tormentors, like a herd of elephants dispersing a pack of hyenas. But these hyenas have a vicious bite, and within moments the sea is filled with bubble trails as torpedoes streak towards your line. There is no time or space for evasive manoeuvres. You must trust to your luck and your ship's armour.

Your face remains emotionless, but your jaw is tightly clamped. *Marlborough* is already wounded below the waterline and a second torpedo hit will be fatal. Guns continue to thunder and crash as your forward turrets engage the enemy, but over the din of gunfire comes the piercing alarm cry 'TORPEDOES!'

A spread of three torpedoes is racing towards *Marlborough*. You quickly calculate that two will pass on either side of you, but the third is coming straight for your battleship. You briefly consider turning to try and avoid it, but quickly realise there is no time. You simply must trust your luck. The white bubble trail streaks beneath your ship and you silently brace yourself for impact.

But there is no explosion. After what seems like an eternity, the torpedo emerges from beneath the stern of your ship and races away into the empty sea. It must have run too deep and has passed harmlessly beneath *Marlborough*. You allow yourself a small sigh of relief before turning your attention back to the enemy High Seas Fleet. The Germans will not be allowed to escape so easily.

AFTERMATH

Jellicoe's turn towards the torpedoes was decisive, but it was not without its cost. HMS *Agincourt* and HMS *Hercules* were both hit and heavily damaged, while HMS *Colossus* was lucky when she was hit by a dud torpedo that bounced off her hull. Yet despite the damage, *Agincourt* and *Hercules* stayed in action and continued to pour salvoes into the battered High Seas Fleet.

Jellicoe's turn had brought him closer to the German fleet and prevented it escaping into the mist. The enemy torpedo boats scattered in the face of the oncoming Grand Fleet, leaving the enemy battlecruisers and battleships dangerously exposed. Visibility favoured the British and the sun would not set for another sixty minutes. It was to be an hour of agony for the High Seas Fleet.

The battlecruisers of the First Scouting Group had already suffered plenty of punishment and were now subjected to an irresistible hail of fire. *Lützow* was soon wrecked from end to end and sinking. As the Scouting Group's flagship disappeared beneath the grey waves, British attention turned to *Seydlitz* and *Derfflinger.* Shell after shell smashed into the German battlecruisers until both were reduced to crippled, burning hulks. The oldest of the battlecruisers, *Von der Tann*, received a direct hit to a forward ammunition magazine that blew the bow of the ship clean off and condemned her to sink within scant minutes. Only *Moltke* managed to escape the inferno by retreating, covered by the smoke from her burning sister ships.

The main body of the High Seas Fleet fared no better. *König* was targeted by several British battleships and suffered a hail of hits from 15-inch and 13.5-inch guns. A shell smashed into the armoured bridge compartment and killed or wounded all the officers stationed there. Another hit blew out a secondary battery and started a fire that filled the interior of the ship with toxic smoke. Finally, a plunging shell smashed into *König*'s propellors and brought the battleship to a juddering halt. Unable to escape, the unlucky ship was soon smothered with shells and vanished beneath the waves with a final groan of tearing metal and collapsing bulkheads.

Other German ships also suffered. The flagship of the High Seas Fleet, *Grosser Kurfürst*, took a hit on the waterline that gave her such a severe list that her main guns were unable to elevate sufficiently to engage the enemy. *Markgraf* was set ablaze in several places and could barely keep a single gun in action. *Kaiser* had a funnel shot away, and a 15-inch hit to her hull gave her a drunken list. *Helgoland*'s steering gear was shattered by British fire and she struggled to maintain a straight course.

It was only the onset of darkness that saved the High Seas Fleet from complete destruction. Firing gradually petered out as the sun disappeared beneath the horizon. Jellicoe assumed a cruising formation and headed south, with the intention of intercepting the enemy at first light.

Meanwhile, the ramshackle High Seas Fleet reeled through the night like a punch-drunk boxer. The seas grew heavier as the night wore on and the swell proved too much for the mortally wounded *Grosser Kurfürst.* Desperate efforts to keep her afloat could only delay the inevitable. At 2 a.m. the crew were evacuated and the German flagship was scuttled.

Somehow the High Seas Fleet managed to slip behind Jellicoe and were able to limp into Wilhelmshaven in the early hours of 1 June. It was a depressing homecoming and there was no way to disguise the defeat they had suffered. Four battlecruisers and two battleships had been lost, as well as several smaller vessels caught between the clash of giants. It was a shattering blow to German morale and effectively ended the High Sea Fleet's war. The fleet would never set sail again, and its battleships would suffer the ignominy of having their heavy guns removed and sent to support the army.

By contrast, the Grand Fleet returned home to a hero's welcome. The Royal Navy had lost three battlecruisers – *Indefatigable*, *Queen Mary* and *Invincible* – but this was considered an acceptable price for victory. Although the High Seas Fleet had not been annihilated, it had received a blow from which it would never recover. Jellicoe would become a national hero for his decision to 'engage the enemy more closely' at a crucial moment.

With no prospect of breaking the Royal Navy's blockade, Germany would turn to its U-boats to impose a counter-blockade. This decision was taken just a few weeks after the defeat at Jutland and would have the disastrous effect of bringing the United States into the war on the side of the Allies.

THE DECISION

- To follow the alternative route, go back to **Section 2** (p. 176).

OR

- To explore the decisions of the battle, go to the **Historical Note** on p. 208.

SECTION 6
ENCOUNTER AT HORN'S REEF

2.45 a.m., 1 June 1916, HMS *Benbow*, the North Sea

The first rays of dawn are breaking over the North Sea, but they illuminate only a blanket of dense mist. Weary lookouts rub their tired eyes and peer through the gloom in the hope of sighting German ships. Few of your crew have been able to snatch more than an hour or two of sleep, but as a new day begins everyone is confident that the battle will soon be resumed.

8. Doveton Sturdee

One of the reasons for this optimism is the change of course that Admiral Jellicoe ordered at 1 a.m. He must clearly have received vital information and he has swung his ships further to the east. Your tactical sense tells you that he must have learned that the Germans were attempting to pass behind the Grand Fleet before bolting for home. You know much about naval tactics, for you are ***Vice Admiral Doveton Sturdee***. You are one of the Royal Navy's foremost tacticians and are one of the few captains who has had the chance to prove your theories in combat. You won a decisive victory at the Battle of the Falklands (8 December 1914) when you crushed the fearsome German East Asia Squadron without losing a single ship. Your triumph earned you fame and promotion, but it also stoked your sizeable ego, and your enemies whisper that you are the most conceited man in the entire navy.

You have had little opportunity to put your tactics into use at the current battle. HMS *Benbow*'s 13.5-inch guns were in action in the early-evening engagement, but a combination of smoke and mist – not to mention the enormous number of water spouts being produced by the combined fire of the Grand Fleet – meant that you cannot be sure your ship scored any significant hits.

Today's early-morning mist is particularly thick. Visibility is barely 4,000 yards, meaning that any encounter will be at point-blank range for a battleship capable of firing at 20,000 yards. Your eyes comb the fog, searching for the telltale outline of an enemy vessel. In the distance there is a sudden eruption of gunfire, and you recognise the distinctive sound of 4-inch guns, which indicates that British destroyers are in action. But it is impossible to see the source of the action in the fog, and the firing soon dies away.

You silently curse the mist. If it would only clear for a moment, you feel sure it would reveal the location of the High Seas Fleet. They must be here somewhere, but it will require a chance encounter to find them.

You are on the point of abandoning the search when the shadow of a large, dark ship emerges from the mist to the east. Your binoculars snap onto the newcomer, but it is obscured by rolling banks of fog. Agonising seconds tick by as you and your lookouts strain your eyes trying to identify whether the ship is friend or foe. Proper identification is crucial as there is a real risk of a friendly-fire incident, but if the ship is an enemy, then every second that passes gives it a chance to either escape or to identify you in turn – and at this point-blank range whoever fires first will surely triumph.

The fog parts for a few precious seconds and you finally get a good look at the mysterious vessel. It is the German battlecruiser *Seydlitz*, but she is almost unrecognisable from the trim fighting ship that is pictured in your identification books. The forward turret looks as if it has been crushed by a giant hand, and its guns point haphazardly into the air. The hull is scorched and scarred, and you can see the evidence of hasty repairs in many places. The ship's bow sits unusually low, which is a telltale indicator that she must have suffered severe flooding below the waterline. There is something about the sight of this ruined vessel that reminds you of the legend of the ghost ship, the *Flying Dutchman*, cursed to sail the world for ever and yet never reach port.

One thing is certainly the same, for you have no intention of letting this wounded enemy ship make it home. You snarl the order to open fire, and *Benbow*'s guns answer. At this range, both *Benbow*'s 13.5-inch main guns and her 6-inch secondary batteries can be brought into action and your ship is soon studded with gun flashes. Your target stands no chance against this hail of shells. Your first salvo strikes home with appalling force, turning *Seydlitz*'s remaining superstructure into twisted wreckage and wreathing the ship in flames. The enemy battlecruiser is defiant to the last and valiantly returns fire from its few remaining guns, but they are soon smashed into silence. The engagement is over within minutes as the German vessel capsizes under the weight of your broadsides.

Silence descends across the misty sea once more as your lookouts search for additional targets. But this is to be the only action this morning. The mist thickens and the visibility drops to barely 2,000 yards. The Grand Fleet is drawing dangerously close to the German coastline and there is a risk of running into hidden minefields or being ambushed by prowling U-boats. It is little surprise when orders arrive from Admiral Jellicoe instructing the fleet to turn north and return to the British Isles. The Battle of Jutland is over.

AFTERMATH

The heavy fog on the morning of 1 June saved the High Seas Fleet from annihilation. Jellicoe had responded quickly to the message from *Malaya* indicating that the Germans were passing behind the

Grand Fleet and had repositioned his ships to intercept their retreat. By 2.30 a.m. the two fleets were within touching distance, but neither side could see the other through the dense mists.

Seydlitz was unlucky. She had become separated from the rest of the High Seas Fleet in the night and was making her own course home. Severely damaged and desperate to make it to the safety of port, she had the misfortune to run into *Benbow*. The resilient German battle-cruiser could neither run nor fight, and her fate was sealed the moment she was spotted.

There were some sharp actions in places where the fog was thinner. At around 2.40 a.m. the British 11th Destroyer Flotilla was shocked when a line of German battleships emerged from the mists ahead of them. The nimble destroyers reacted quickly and made an immediate attack. HMS *Mons* led the charge and one of her torpedoes scored a direct hit on *Kaiser*. The damage was severe and could have proved fatal, had *Kaiser* not been able to retreat into the mist. She managed to limp home, but her flooded engines gave out on the approach to Wilhelmshaven and she had to be towed into port.

But these engagements were the exception. The two fleets passed one another without realising how close they were. It was a lucky escape for the damaged and disorganised High Seas Fleet, for its ships were in no condition to survive a renewed battle.

By 4 a.m. Admiral Jellicoe understood that the Germans must have eluded him in the fog. This hunch was soon confirmed by Room 40 intelligence, which reported that the German flagship *Grosser Kurfürst* had returned to harbour. The Grand Fleet had no reason for remaining at sea and Jellicoe was forced to order his ships home.

Jutland would come to be seen as a lost opportunity for the Royal Navy. Most of the criticism fell on Beatty, for his failure to keep 5th Battle Squadron close in the early part of the battle. Jellicoe was castigated for his decision to turn away from the torpedo attack rather than into it, but he also received praise for the way he had outmanoeuvred the High Seas Fleet, and even his strongest critics acknowledged that he had been unlucky that the sea was blanketed with mist on 1 June. Had the weather cooperated, then a decisive victory could have been won.

THE DECISION

▶ To follow the alternative route, go back to **Section 3** (p. 182).

OR

▶ To explore the decisions of the battle, go to the **Historical Note** on p. 208.

SECTION 7
COUNTING THE COST

4.15 a.m., 1 June, HMS *New Zealand*, the North Sea

The grey giants of the Grand Fleet pass solemnly through the wreckage of the previous day's battle. The evidence of intense fighting floats all around you. Shoals of dead fish, killed by the concussion from shell blasts, line the surface. Wooden planks from shattered decks mingle with pieces of uniform that are carried along by the waves, and oil slicks paint the sea in dark iridescent patterns. Drowned sailors float among the detritus and you recognise uniforms from both the Grand Fleet and the High Seas Fleet. Your lookouts search for survivors among the wreckage, and smaller vessels move to investigate rafts and chains of men in life-rings, but most have succumbed to the chill waters of the North Sea. There are terribly few survivors from the inferno of the previous day.

You are grateful that your own ship has survived unscathed. You are ***Captain John Green***, the skipper of the battlecruiser HMS *New Zealand.* Although you are a consummate professional, your crew whisper that you are a 'Jonah' – a person who brings bad luck to a ship. Your career has been dogged by small but repeated incidents of ill fortune, culminating in 1913 when your ship, HMS *Natal*, crashed into a fishing boat and sank it.

Yet your unlucky streak has been broken at Jutland. HMS *New Zealand* fought hard alongside the Battlecruiser Fleet throughout the battle. Every ship in the fleet was hit and *Indefatigable* and *Queen*

9. HMS *New Zealand*

Mary were destroyed by German shells. But somehow *New Zealand* emerged from the maelstrom intact and with just two men wounded.

This good fortune might be attributed to the blessings that your ship received when it visited New Zealand in 1913. A Maori chieftain presented the vessel with a unique steering wheel, carved from indigenous wood and engraved with the war cry '*Ake, Ake, Ake, Kia Kaha!*' ('Fight on, fight on, fight on, for ever!'). The chief also gave the ship a *piupiu* – a traditional waist garment – and a *hei tiki* greenstone pendant, with the promise that *New Zealand* would be invincible in battle as long as the captain wore these items.

At Jutland you donned the *hei tiki* but, true to your own bad luck, found that you were too stout to wear the *piupiu* comfortably around your waist. Nevertheless, you kept it close to hand, in case the situation became truly desperate. In the superstitious world of the navy, such actions have power and, whatever the cause, you are grateful that *New Zealand* survived the battle without losing a single man.

The sweep for survivors takes up most of the morning before the Grand Fleet turns for home. As the day wears into evening, the Battlecruiser Fleet reduces speed and lowers its flags to half-mast as it prepares to carry out burial at sea for those who were killed in action. Your crew turns out on deck as a mark of respect for the fallen on your sister ships. The sun is slowly setting, the swell has grown and the air is thick with the tang of salt. In the distance the haunting strains of the 'Last Post' can be heard playing on bugles as the dead are committed to the deep.

The Battlecruiser Fleet arrives home in the early hours of 2 June. Despite the exertions of the previous twenty-four hours there is no time for rest, and your ship immediately commences re-coaling in anticipation of another sortie against the Germans. Surely the next one will be decisive?

AFTERMATH

The controversy over the Battle of Jutland began before the Grand Fleet had even reached home. The Germans were quick to issue a press release describing the battle, claiming to have sunk four British battlecruisers and battleships and proclaiming a decisive victory over the invincible Royal Navy. In fact they had sunk three battlecruisers – *Indefatigable*, *Queen Mary* and *Invincible* – plus several smaller vessels. These were bitter casualties for the Royal Navy, but they were also ones that Britain could afford, for even with these losses the Grand Fleet retained a significant numerical advantage over its German opponents.

The High Seas Fleet had suffered fewer casualties at the battle. They had lost one battlecruiser, *Lützow*, plus the obsolete battleship *Pommern*, which had been torpedoed by British destroyers during the night. *Seydlitz* and *Derfflinger* had survived, but had suffered horrendous damage that would take months to repair. These losses could not easily be replaced. Germany's industry was committed to supplying the army, and most of its shipbuilding capacity was being used to construct U-boats. A handful of new warships were under construction, but none would be ready until late 1917.

After the initial euphoria of the triumphant press release had faded, a deep sense of gloom settled over the High Seas Fleet. A sober analysis showed that the fleet had been lucky to survive its bruising encounter and there was little appetite for a rematch. German Admiral Scheer mounted a cautious sortie on 19 August, screened by Zeppelin reconnaissance. Once again British code-breakers alerted the Grand Fleet, and Jellicoe put to sea to intercept the enemy. But as the fleets manoeuvred, one of the German airships misidentified British light cruisers and destroyers as battleships, spooking Scheer and prompting him to retreat to Wilhelmshaven before the fleets made contact. Another German sortie on 18 October was abandoned just a few hours after the High Seas Fleet had left port, when a torpedo from British submarine *E38* severely damaged the battleship *München*.

Bloodied and chastened, the High Seas Fleet abandoned the idea of seeking battle in the North Sea. The power of the Grand Fleet was overwhelming, and the prospects of German victory were slim. With the surface fleet neutralised, German admirals were forced to turn to the U-boats to win victory at sea. But this came at a terrible strategic price, for the resumption of all-out U-boat warfare enraged the United States and brought her into the war on the side of the Allies.

The once-proud High Seas Fleet would become a bystander, rusting in harbour while the morale of its sailors steadily sank. When it was finally ordered to sea in a do-or-die sortie in October 1918, the weary crews mutinied and refused to sail. In many ways its heart had been broken at Jutland.

Yet in Britain the strategic importance of the Battle of Jutland was not immediately understood. To most British officers, the battle felt like a missed opportunity. The Germans had been able to escape from the Grand Fleet and had inflicted heavier casualties than they had received. This was a bitter pill to swallow for a navy steeped in the legend of Lord Nelson and the Battle of Trafalgar.

Emotions ran high and a bitter feud developed between supporters of Beatty and those of Jellicoe. Beatty blamed restrictive Royal Navy regulations and Jellicoe's lack of daring, while Jellicoe criticised Beatty's reckless handling of the Battlecruiser Fleet and his error of judgement in leaving 5th Battle Squadron behind when the engagement began. The arguments raged right up to the outbreak of the Second World War.

Yet the controversy masked the fact that the Battle of Jutland had achieved its objective. Although the High Seas Fleet had not been destroyed, it had been neutralised. It would cease to be a threat to Britain and contented itself with minor operations in the Baltic for the rest of the war. The outcome was decisive, even if the manner of victory was not.

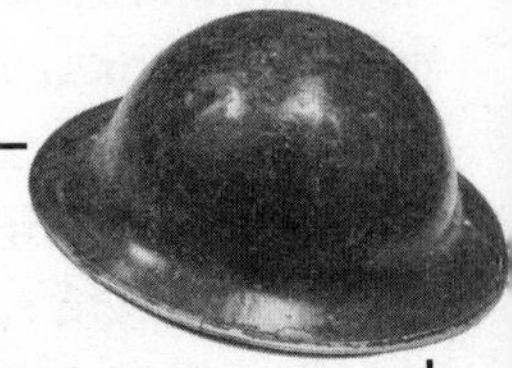

THE DECISION

- To follow the alternative route, go back to **Section 3** (p. 182).

OR

- To explore the decisions of the battle, see the **Historical Note** below.

HISTORICAL NOTE

The Battle of Jutland was the only major fleet battle of the First World War. It is this uniqueness that makes it such a fascinating and controversial subject. This chapter enables you to explore some of the most prominent 'what ifs' from this clash of steel.

The historical route begins with Rear Admiral Hugh Evan-Thomas and whether he follows Beatty or awaits a signal. Historically, Evan-Thomas chose to wait for instructions (Section 1 to Section 2). This decision has been much criticised, but defenders of Evan-Thomas are right to point out that it was Beatty's responsibility to ensure that 5th Squadron followed him. The signalling arrangements aboard HMS *Lion* were poor and had caused problems at the Battle of Dogger Bank in January 1915, yet nothing seems to have been done to improve them. Beatty's failure to concentrate his forces would cost the Battlecruiser Fleet dearly. *Indefatigable* was overwhelmed by shells and blown apart, and *Queen Mary* was destroyed when a direct hit plunged into her ammunition magazine and set it ablaze.

Nevertheless, despite these casualties Beatty was able to lure the High Seas Fleet north towards Jellicoe. The second clash of battlefleets at 7.15 p.m. had the potential to be decisive. The Grand Fleet had a dominant position and blocked the High Seas Fleet from escaping. There was still roughly an hour of daylight left and there was the possibility of a conclusive battle. In desperation, Admiral Scheer committed his battlecruisers and torpedo boats to rush the British line to buy time for his battleships to escape. Historically, Jellicoe chose to prioritise safety and turn away from the torpedo attack (Section 2 to Section 3). This preserved the Grand Fleet but allowed the enemy to escape.

The main battle had ended, but the two fleets skirmished with one another in the darkness. Several British captains saw the German battlefleet trying to slip behind the Grand Fleet, but none of them reported this information to Jellicoe. Captain Boyle of HMS *Malaya* had the clearest sighting of the enemy, but stuck to regulations and passed the information only to his squadron commander (Section 3 to Section 7). The failure to report German movements meant that the High Seas Fleet managed to pass in the wake of the Grand Fleet en route to the safety of Wilhelmshaven.

What if things had been done differently? If Evan-Thomas had chosen to follow Beatty without orders (Section 1 to Section 4), then the 'Run to the South' would have turned out very differently: 5th Battle Squadron's huge 15-inch guns and excellent gunnery would have inflicted heavy punishment on the German First Scouting Group. The battle would have played out in a contrasting way, and *Indefatigable* and *Queen Mary* would probably have survived. Furthermore, the damage to the German battlecruisers would have meant they were unlikely to survive the clash of battlefleets at 7.15 p.m. In this scenario *Lützow*, *Seydlitz* and *Derfflinger* are all destroyed.

Another option to explore is what might have happened if Jellicoe had turned towards the torpedo attack rather than away from it (Section 2 to Section 5). This was a high-risk manoeuvre, but one that could have had decisive results. The Germans fired thirty-one torpedoes at the Grand Fleet in their covering attack, but they were difficult to aim, and it is unlikely that more than 10 per cent of them would have struck home. Furthermore, dreadnought battleships were surprisingly resilient to torpedo hits and unless a ship was struck twice, it is unlikely that it would be sunk. In this alternative the turn-towards proves decisive and the High Seas Fleet is crushed.

The final alternative relates to Boyle's sighting of the German fleet shortly after midnight. If he had communicated this information directly to Jellicoe, then the Grand Fleet could have repositioned itself further east to block the retreat to Wilhelmshaven (Section 3 to Section 6). This is an intriguing possibility, but the heavy fog that covered the area on 1 June meant that a decisive engagement was all but impossible. However, the two fleets would have been remarkably close to one another, and this might have led to sudden encounters, such as that described between *Benbow* and *Seydlitz*.

Hugh Evan-Thomas commanded 5th Battle Squadron until October 1918. But after the war his reputation was relentlessly attacked by Beatty and his supporters, who blamed Evan-Thomas for failing to follow the Battlecruiser Fleet at Jutland. This caused him immense stress and his health collapsed in the 1920s. He died in 1928.

John Jellicoe was promoted to First Sea Lord in November 1916. He was not a success in this role. He struggled to direct the Royal Navy to counter the renewed U-boat campaign throughout 1917 and was dismissed from the post in December. He held no military command for the remainder of the war, and served as Governor-General of New Zealand in the 1920s. He and his supporters would spend much of the post-war period locked in a vicious battle of reputations with Beatty. He died in 1935.

Algernon Boyle served as captain of HMS *Malaya* until January 1918, at which point he became Chief of Staff for the Dover Patrol. After the war he served as aide-de-camp to King George V and was Fourth Sea Lord from 1920 to 1924. He died in 1949.

David Beatty succeeded Jellicoe to command the Grand Fleet in November 1916. He would never have a chance to see action again, and he would not see the High Seas Fleet until November 1918, when the Grand Fleet escorted the defeated German navy to internment at

Scapa Flow. After the war he and his supporters sustained a long-running feud with Jellicoe and his defenders. Nevertheless, Beatty insisted on being a pall-bearer at Jellicoe's funeral in 1935, despite his own ill health. He died in 1936.

Cecil Burney became Second Sea Lord in November 1916, but proved unpopular with the War Cabinet, which regarded him as too old (he was fifty-nine) and too deferential towards Jellicoe. He was removed from post in September 1917 and held various administrative roles until his official retirement in 1924. He died in 1929.

Doveton Sturdee commanded 4th Battle Squadron from HMS *Benbow* until February 1918. Always a keen student of history, after the war he became President of the Society for Nautical Research and dedicated his energy to the renovation and preservation of HMS *Victory.* He died in 1925.

John Green served as captain of HMS *New Zealand* until September 1917. His strange run of bad luck continued and in 1925 he was involved in a bizarre incident on a hunting trip when he accidentally shot Admiral Sir Henry Oliver. Oliver was not seriously injured and remarked drily that it was not the first time Green had accidentally shot someone, and that in fact he had a reputation for it! Green died in 1948.

5

BATTLE OF THE SOMME:

THE WESTERN FRONT, 1916

SECTION 1
THE BIG PUSH

April 1916, Fourth Army Headquarters, Querrieu, France

The chateau at Querrieu is a hive of activity as dozens of staff officers work to prepare the British army for its greatest offensive of the war. The building is unrecognisable from its pre-war heyday. The medieval tapestries that once adorned the walls have been replaced by vast maps of the Western Front, and antique tables now groan beneath the weight of reports and documents. The low rumble of conversation echoes through every room and mingles with the sound of typewriters chattering and ringing.

1. Henry Rawlinson

You sit at the heart of this nerve centre, for you are ***General Sir Henry Rawlinson***, the commander of the Fourth Army. You are experienced, intelligent and famously debonair, but you are also a devious schemer determined to advance your career at all costs. These traits have earned you the double-edged nickname of 'The Fox' – attractive and clever, but also sly and untrustworthy. You deserved to be sacked in March 1915 when you were caught attempting to scapegoat a subordinate for your own mistakes. You were saved only by the direct intervention of General Sir Douglas Haig and now feel a certain obligation towards him. Yet despite this misstep, you have steadily risen in rank and reputation. You commanded IV Corps in the bitter battles of 1915, including Neuve Chapelle (10–12 March), Aubers Ridge (9 May) and Loos (25 September–8 October). You are now the most experienced battlefield commander in the British Expeditionary Force.

You will need all your experience for the current task. The British army must launch the largest attack in its history as part of its contribution to the Allied General Offensive, a series of coordinated assaults to be mounted by Britain, France, Russia and Italy in summer 1916. The General Offensive is designed to overstretch the Central Powers of Germany and Austro-Hungary by forcing them to fight on three fronts simultaneously, and it is hoped that the relentless pressure will crush the enemy.

The General Offensive on the Western Front was to take the form of an Anglo-French attack astride the River Somme. Although the French army suffered terrible losses in 1914–15, it has emerged from this brutal period with hard-won lessons. In the original plan, the battle-hardened French would provide the spearhead of the attack, with the courageous but inexperienced BEF playing an important supporting role.

But the Germans had other ideas. On 21 February 1916 they launched a massive offensive against the fortress city of Verdun, which is a potent symbol of courage in the French national psyche, and the Germans know that it will be defended at all costs. The German offensive is designed to trap the French army in an attritional battle that they hope will 'bleed France white' and force her to surrender.

The intense fighting at Verdun has derailed the Allied plans. The murderous battle has drawn in vast numbers of French troops, reducing their commitment to the Somme offensive. Furthermore, with the French fighting for their lives at Verdun, the attack on the Somme has taken on immense significance. The BEF must make a major assault to relieve the pressure on her beleaguered ally.

You survey the detailed reports that sit atop your desk. The long

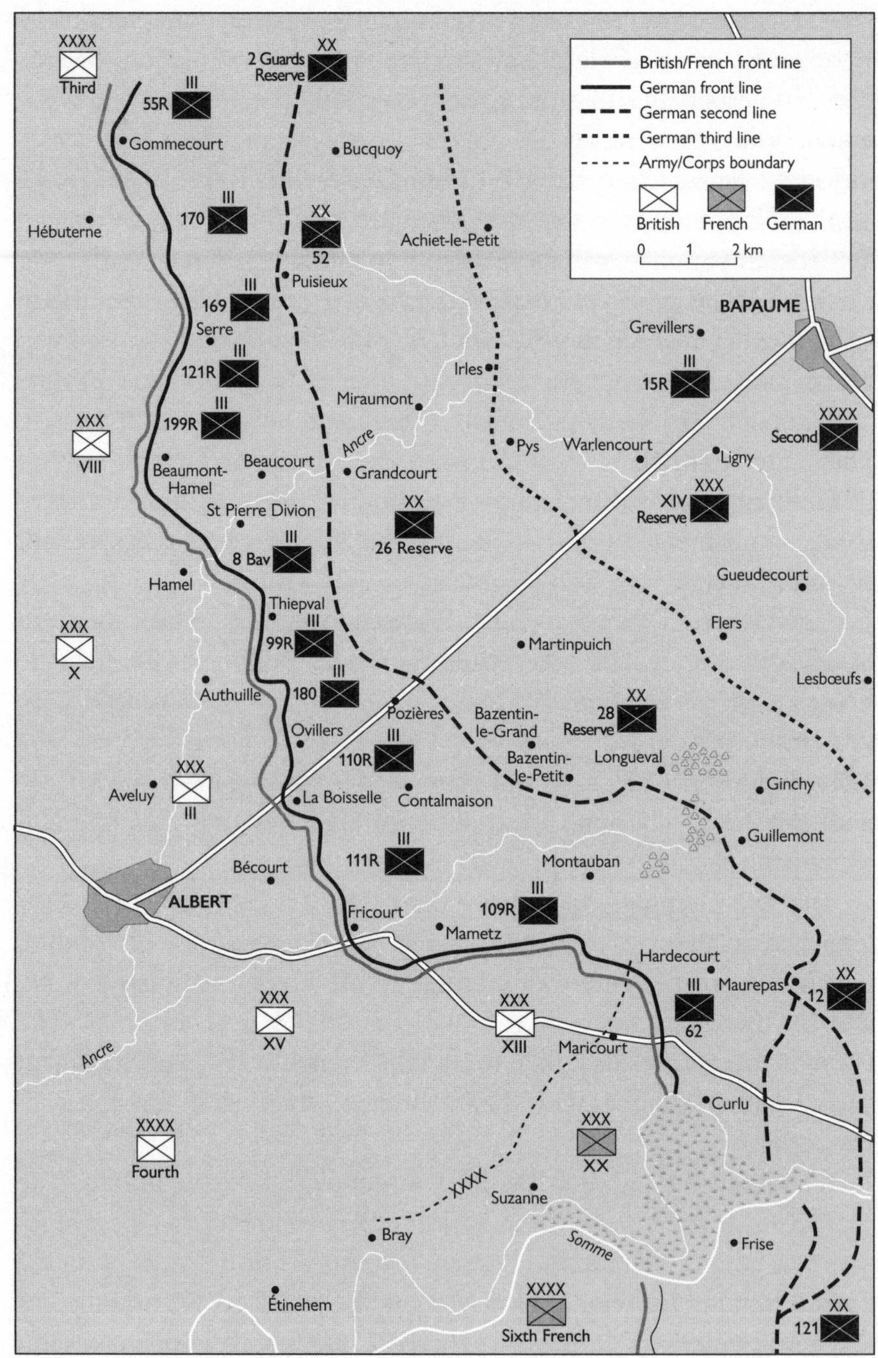

Map 1: The German defences at the Somme

lists of corps and divisions reminds you of the strength of your army. Swelled by volunteers and armed by the industry of the British Empire, the BEF now numbers 1.5 million men and is highly motivated and eager for action. But the scale and speed of the army's wartime expansion have meant that training has been limited. Many of your units are ill-trained and you worry about their capabilities.

You are also concerned about the strength of the German defences on the Somme. You ponder the maps of the area that are pinned to the chateau wall, tracing your finger along the dark lines that represent enemy trenches. The Somme has been a quiet sector since 1914 and the Germans have used the lull to construct some of the most formidable defences on the entire Western Front.

A series of aerial reconnaissance photographs are pinned next to the maps. They show that the German position consists of two distinct defensive lines, linked by a network of communication trenches and protected by dense belts of barbed wire. A third line is also under construction. These daunting defences are anchored on a chain of fortified villages, including Thiepval, Serre and Beaumont-Hamel. The once-picturesque hamlets have been turned into imposing fortresses bristling with machine guns and surrounded by an impenetrable maze of barbed wire.

You know that the Royal Artillery is the key to crushing these defences and you have assembled more than 1,400 guns and howitzers for the task. The question is how best to employ them. Your experience in 1915 has shown that the artillery can inflict severe damage on the German front line, but lacks the range to hit the second line with the same force. This contributed to the many disasters of that bloody year. British infantry could often capture the German first line, but attempts to press on and storm the largely intact second line ended in disaster.

These setbacks prompted you to outline a methodical, step-by-step attack doctrine under the shorthand term of 'bite and hold'. The concept is simple. The BEF will launch a carefully managed assault to capture the German front line, but rather than advancing further, your troops will halt and consolidate their position. The Germans will launch a counter-attack to retake their lost position, but your men and

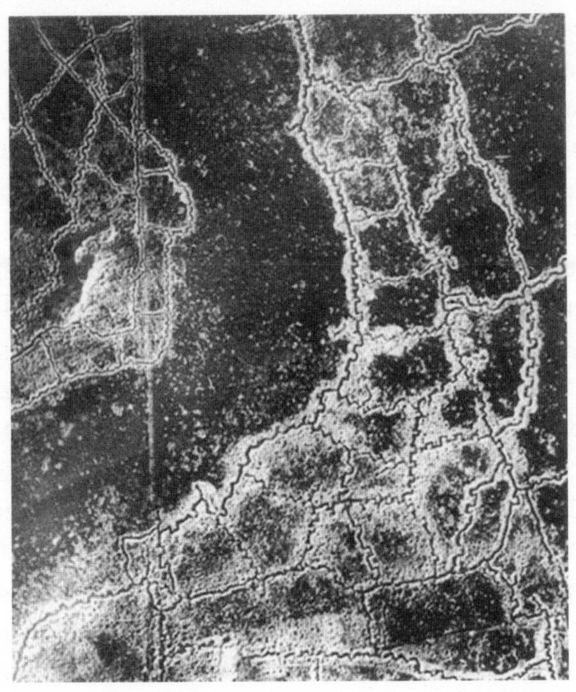

2. German trenches as seen from the air

artillery will be ready and waiting for them. They will destroy the enemy counter-attack and inflict heavy losses. Then, after a pause of two or three days, the process will be repeated.

Another glance at the aerial photographs reminds you of the daunting strength of the German defences. A 'bite and hold' attack could take this position one bite at a time. It will be a slow, grinding battle, but it will also inflict heavy losses on the enemy while minimising your own. You jot down in your notes, 'It does not appear to me that the gain of 2 or 3 more kilometres of ground is worth much consequence . . . Our object rather seems to be to kill as many Germans as possible with the least loss to ourselves.'

But there is a problem with your plan. In March you submitted your concept to the BEF's Commander-in-Chief, General Sir Douglas Haig. He was unimpressed and thinks you are being overly cautious. Whereas you believe that the attackers should halt and consolidate after taking their first objective, Haig believes that the key to victory is exploiting their momentum and pushing on. He feels that the Germans will be shaken after the loss of their front line and argues that a swift advance can overwhelm the second line before the stunned defenders can be reinforced. In this way the entire German defensive system can be broken in one mighty heave.

Haig has reasons for optimism. The General Offensive is hammering the Central Powers on all fronts. The Italians are pushing the Austro-Hungarians back in the Alps, the Battle of Verdun is inflicting terrible losses on the German army, and in June a new Russian offensive dealt a massive blow to the Central Powers on the Eastern Front. Intelligence reports indicate that German morale is low and that they are short of reserves. The British army may have a rare opportunity to make a decisive attack, and perhaps even to end the war.

Haig wants the German first and second lines to be captured on the opening day of the battle. You anticipated this argument, jotting in your diary, 'I daresay I shall have a tussle with him over the limited objective for I hear he is inclined to favour the unlimited with the chance of breaking the German line.' But does your artillery have sufficient firepower to breach the first *and* second German lines, as Haig demands? There is a risk that you will dilute your fire so much that neither position will be sufficiently damaged. If this happens, the consequences for your infantry will be fatal. Yet you also recognise that your cautious attack cannot win a decisive victory. You will be committing the BEF to a relentless attritional battle, akin to that which is raging at Verdun. A final concern lingers at the edge of your mind. You are painfully conscious that Haig saved your career in 1915 and you must carefully judge how and when to argue with him, lest he withdraw his favour.

You look at the map of the Somme once more. You must make a critical decision.

AIDE-MEMOIRE

* The German defences on the Somme are some of the most formidable on the entire Western Front. You will need every gun at your disposal to break them down. Surely

it is better to concentrate your fire on the first line to ensure that it is captured?

* The Germans are under pressure on every front and their morale seems to be ebbing away. A heavy blow from the BEF could prove decisive.
* The BEF is courageous, but inexperienced. A carefully controlled 'bite and hold' attack minimises the battlefield chaos and compensates for its lack of training.
* Haig's plan seeks to take advantage of the chaos. After seizing the German front line, the enemy's second line may be there for the taking. If this opportunity is not seized immediately, then the Germans will bring in reinforcements and the second line must be assaulted in subsequent days – at a heavy cost in lives.
* The French are locked in a do-or-die struggle at Verdun and expect a major contribution from the BEF. Is a limited 'bite and hold' attack enough to satisfy your allies?
* An ill-prepared charge against the German defences will surely result in disaster for your infantry. Will you be aiding the Allied cause by fruitlessly smashing the BEF against the German barbed wire?
* You owe your career to Haig's patronage. Do you dare argue with your Commander-in-Chief?

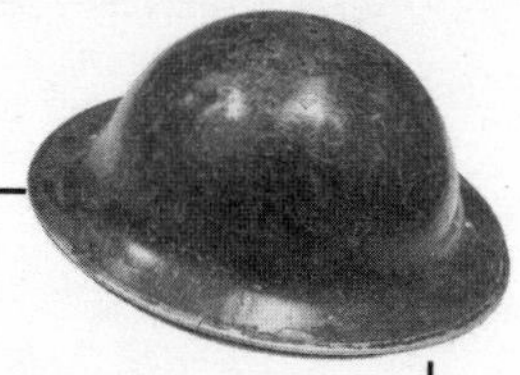

THE DECISION

Do you insist on your original 'bite and hold' approach or revise your plan to match Haig's ambitions?

- If you wish to alter your plan to match Haig's vision, and assault the German first and second lines on the same day, go to **Section 2** (p. 222).

OR

- If you are convinced that your 'bite and hold' approach is correct and wish to reject Haig's demands, go to **Section 3** (p. 226).

SECTION 2
THE RESERVES

June 1916, Fourth Army Headquarters, Querrieu, France

Preparations are under way for the massive British offensive on the Somme. The ground behind the front line is packed with men, guns and stores. Aircraft of the Royal Flying Corps drone overhead as they carry out reconnaissance patrols, the dull thump of artillery fire can be heard in the distance as the Royal Artillery registers its weapons on their targets, and the strains of 'Tipperary' echo along the roads as your infantry marches towards the front.

3. Archibald Montgomery

You are ***Major-General Archibald Montgomery***, currently serving as the Chief of Staff to Henry Rawlinson at the Fourth Army. You are an Anglo-Irish soldier who began his career in the Royal Artillery in 1891 and who has served with distinction ever since. You fought bravely in the Anglo-Boer War (1899–1902), but your real talents lie in staff work. You have served as a staff officer with the British Expeditionary Force since 1914 and have established a reputation for meticulous attention to detail. You have planned several great offensives on the Western Front and have learned hard lessons about the realities of trench warfare.

You have been anxious all month. You have grave doubts about Haig's desire to attack the German first and second lines in a single day but, to your surprise, Rawlinson did not argue against the idea, instead stating, 'It is clear that D. H. [Douglas Haig] would like us to do the whole thing in one rush and I am quite game to try but it certainly does involve considerable risks . . . It will be difficult unless we start a panic.' This change of opinion may owe something to Rawlinson's reluctance to argue with the man who saved his career in 1915. But now another key question has emerged: how should you position your reserves to support the assault and exploit any breakthroughs?

Your impeccably tidy desk includes several letters from Haig on this matter. Haig is a cavalryman and favours using mounted troops. A letter from him notes, 'Opportunities to use cavalry, supported by guns, machine-guns, etc. and infantry, should be sought for, both during the early stages of the attack and subsequently.' He has assigned two cavalry divisions from GHQ Reserve to the Fourth Army, as well as forming a new Reserve Army under the command of Lieutenant-General Hubert Gough. The Reserve Army is primarily a cavalry force, and Haig hopes that their speed will allow them to burst through any breach in the German lines. He also hopes that breakthroughs will occur elsewhere, and he adds an instruction to Rawlinson to 'impress on his Corps Commanders the use of their Corps Cavalry and mounted troops, and if necessary supplement them with regular cavalry units . . . it is better to prepare to advance beyond the Enemy's last line of trenches, because we are then in a position to take advantage of any breakdown in the enemy's defence . . . if no preparations for an advance are made till next morning we might lose a golden opportunity.'

Every officer in the BEF longs for the day when the trenches are broken and open warfare is restored, although you cannot help but reflect that opportunities to commit reserves are rare. You remember how, in early 1915, Haig insisted on having cavalry on hand to exploit breakthroughs – but no opportunity for the horsemen ever arose and they were left sitting idle.

Your thoughts are broken as Rawlinson arrives in your office. The normally cheerful 'Fox' seems weighed down by the responsibility of commanding the battle. He confesses to you that he is uncertain how to use Fourth Army's reserves. He seems ambivalent about the prospects of a breakthrough and prefers to use reserves for consolidation rather than exploitation. Gough's Reserve Army is positioned to the north of the battlefield, but otherwise Haig's instructions have been ignored.

You discuss the possibility of a breakthrough elsewhere. As you study the maps, reconnaissance photographs and intelligence reports, you notice that the southern sector of the battlefield seems particularly suitable for a breakthrough. The German line is weak here and there seem to be few reserves behind it. If the forward position can be taken, then there may be an opportunity to push through cavalry and burst into the open ground beyond. You outline your ideas to Rawlinson and see a flicker of interest in his eyes. He trusts your judgement and will listen to your advice. What do you recommend?

AIDE-MEMOIRE

* Haig believes there may be opportunities to advance through the enemy position. Surely it is right to prepare for them in case they arise?

* If the German second line falls, then there is a chance to advance into the open country beyond. Fast-moving cavalry could burst through and cause havoc behind the German lines.

* Is the prospect of a breakthrough a realistic one? The lessons of 1915 suggest that opportunities for cavalry in trench warfare are almost non-existent.

* Can your inexperienced forces be trusted to recognise fleeting opportunities? If

not, they run the risk of launching rushed attacks that will suffer heavy losses.

* If opportunities to advance are not seized on the first day, then the Germans will reinforce their defences and make any subsequent attacks far more costly.
* The Germans will launch ferocious counter-attacks to reclaim captured positions. It is important to consolidate captured ground to resist these assaults.

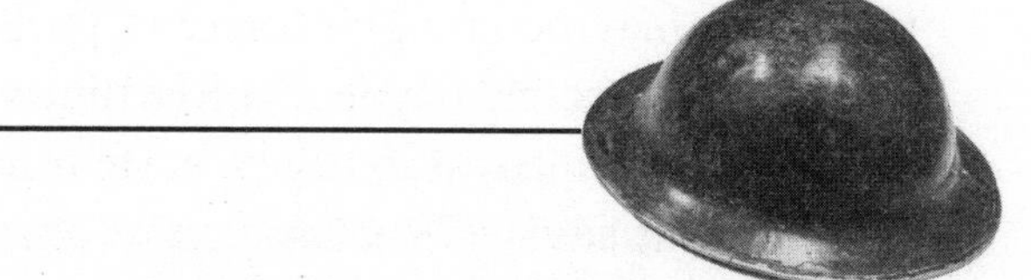

THE DECISION

Do you advise Rawlinson to prepare the reserves to exploit a breakthrough? Or do you suggest that he uses them defensively and focuses on consolidating captured ground?

▶ If you believe the Fourth Army should position its reserves to exploit potential breakthroughs, go to **Section 5** (p. 238).

OR

▶ If you feel that the reserves are best used to consolidate captured positions, go to **Section 4** (p. 232).

SECTION 3
BITE AND HOLD

1 July 1916, VIII Corps Headquarters, France

Weeks of preparation have led you to this moment. The guns and howitzers of the Royal Artillery have systematically obliterated the German defences over the past seven days. Your gunners have fired more than 1.5 million shells and have turned the front line into a pockmarked wilderness.

The barbed wire has been torn asunder and the enemy's trenches reduced to muddy ruins. The fortified villages of Beaumont-Hamel, Thiepval, Ovillers, La Boisselle, Fricourt and Mametz have been smashed into smoking rubble. German infantry sought shelter from the inferno in deep dugouts buried beneath the trenches. Although this gave them physical protection from the ceaseless rain of shells, the psychological strain was almost unbearable. Captured Germans tell you that the period has been termed *die Leidenswoche* – 'the week of suffering'.

4. Aylmer Hunter-Weston

You are ***Lieutenant-General Aylmer Hunter-Weston***, the commander of VIII Corps. You are an eccentric Scottish officer with a controversial reputation. Your skilful leadership of 11th Brigade in 1914 marked you out as a rising star in the BEF and you were promoted to command 29th Division at Gallipoli. But your performance here was dismal, and your soldiers paid a high price for your incompetence. Nevertheless, the inexperienced BEF is in dire need of battle-hardened commanders and you have been promoted to command VIII Corps in France. In a curious twist of fate, 29th Division is part of your corps and falls under your command once more.

You anxiously await news at your headquarters. In the final minutes before Zero Hour the German position is swept by a howling storm of flame, smoke and metal. Although you are some distance from the front line, you can feel the ground shake as the bombardment reaches its terrifying crescendo. Then, at 7.30 a.m., the bombardment lifts and the shrill sound of whistles echoes across no-man's-land as British infantry clamber from their trenches and surge forward. It seems impossible that anyone could have survived the crushing bombardment. Yet almost immediately there is the zip of rifle bullets and

5. British soldiers going over the top at the Battle of the Somme

the chatter of machine guns. The German defenders are battered and their positions are all but annihilated, but the survivors are determined to fight.

The first messenger pigeon flutters into your headquarters soon after the attack begins. A note attached to the bird's ankle informs you that the attack is progressing well in the north and that your troops have gained a precious foothold in the fortified village of Serre. Your staff officers update the maps as more information arrives, carried by pigeons, runners, or sometimes relayed through crackling telephone conversations. By midday your corps has overrun the ruined German trenches and is locked in deadly combat in Serre.

The surviving defenders cling doggedly to their positions, and your men are forced to clear them out with grenades, bayonets and rifle butts. The fighting for the ruins rages long into the night, with the village illuminated by the ghostly light of descending flares and punctuated by muzzle flashes, shell bursts and tongues of fire from flamethrowers.

Nevertheless, as dawn breaks on 2 July it is clear that the Germans have been dealt a severe blow. Your neighbouring formations have all achieved successes. To the south, X Corps battered its way into the fortress of Thiepval, although fighting continues to rage in the ruins. III Corps managed to take Ovillers and La Boisselle after intense grenade fighting, while XV Corps and XIII Corps captured Fricourt and Montauban respectively.

Your staff update the maps, and you nod with satisfaction as you see that the first attack has bitten off a great chunk of the German line. Although bitter fighting is raging at the strongpoints of Serre, Thiepval and Beaumont-Hamel, most of the German front-line system has been taken and their counter-attacks have been defeated. Total British casualties are estimated at around 30,000 men. You reflect that while these are heavy, they are certainly lower than the losses suffered by the Germans.

AFTERMATH

The attack shook the German army to its core. Chief of the General Staff, Erich von Falkenhayn, immediately ceased offensive action at

Verdun and rushed reserves to the threatened Somme sector. Murderous fighting raged along the front as the British snuffed out the last pockets of resistance and the Germans launched counter-attacks to reclaim lost ground.

Haig was pleased with the results of the first day and urged Rawlinson to press the advantage. But the original timetable was disrupted by the prolonged and bloody fighting to secure the captured front line, not to mention the need to drag artillery to new positions and register the guns on fresh targets. Rawlinson's original plan to launch an attack on the second line within two to three days proved impossible. Meanwhile, the fighting for the strongpoints of Serre and Thiepval took a bloody toll on the inexperienced British infantry. The villages had been reduced to labyrinths of rubble, barbed wire and shell holes, and progress was costly and slow.

The bitter struggle for the fortified villages delayed the next major offensive and it was not until mid-July that the Fourth Army was in position to make a second great 'bite' against part of the German second line. The attack, supported by an even heavier bombardment than that which preceded 1 July, simply blew away the enemy positions. Yet this victory was followed by another hard fight to consolidate the gains, straighten the line and prepare for the next attack.

The slow progress frustrated Haig. He believed that the German army was on the brink of complete collapse and demanded that Rawlinson increase the tempo of battle. But 'The Fox' refused to be rushed and insisted that his approach was reaping results. German doctrine demanded swift counter-attacks to retake lost ground, and this meant that they were locked into an attritional battle that was being fought on British terms. As per Rawlinson's original 'bite and hold' concept, the BEF's short advances baited the Germans into launching a counter-attack. British infantry would consolidate their position and await the assault, while Royal Flying Corps aircraft would locate the enemy as they prepared to attack and direct artillery fire upon them the moment they began to advance. Any Germans who survived this shelling would find themselves facing entrenched British soldiers who greeted them with a hail of bullets. This 'bite and hold' method was brutally effective and German counter-attacks suffered severe casualties.

The Germans struggled to find a countermeasure to this approach. The front line could not resist the sheer weight of artillery that the British rained down upon it, and the constant counter-attacks to retake lost ground were bleeding the army to death. The only alternative was to withdraw, but this was politically and military unacceptable. The German army was locked into an attritional struggle from which it could not escape.

The BEF relentlessly chewed its way forward over the coming weeks. The fortified villages were finally cleared by the end of July and the battle intensified as the summer wore on. Yet to some observers, the ammunition expended and the lives lost did not seem proportionate to the objectives gained. Rawlinson defended the approach on the grounds that the battle was killing Germans at a higher rate than it was killing British soldiers.

The British army continued to make great bites throughout August and September. As the autumn wore on, Germany found herself facing the worst crisis of the war. The German army could not find an answer to 'bite and hold' and had suffered horrendous casualties on the Somme. The relentless battle at Verdun, the continued Russian attacks in the east and the declaration of war by Romania in August 1916 were piling further pressure on her overstretched forces. There were almost no reserves left to plug the gaps and morale plummeted to an all-time low. There were whispers that the Kaiser would be forced to beg for peace to save his empire from ruin.

It was the weather that kept Germany from defeat. Temperatures fell in September and torrential rain fell throughout October. The British advance got bogged down in the mud and they could not maintain the pressure. By the time heavy snow brought the battle to an end in November, the British had captured the German first and second lines. More important to Rawlinson were the appalling casualties that had been inflicted on the German army. German insistence on holding the ground at all costs and on counter-attacking to retake lost positions had played directly into the hands of the wily 'Fox'.

Worse still for Germany was the realisation that they had no answer to the methodical, step-by-step approach that the BEF had perfected. In early 1917, fearing a renewed offensive on the Somme, the Germans fell back to the specially prepared Hindenburg Line and waited grimly for the British to take their first bite.

The Battle of the Somme was a clear Allied victory, but it was not without its controversies. It had been a bloody and gruelling engagement, which cost the British army some 325,000 casualties for an advance of just six miles. Haig was frustrated that opportunities to move faster had not been taken, and politicians in the United Kingdom were horrified by the casualty figures, especially as the battle seemed to lack any strategic objective except killing Germans.

Rawlinson was unfazed by the criticism. His 'bite and hold' approach had proved its worth. Its methods would be refined and employed with ruthless effectiveness in 1917. Alongside the French, who adopted a similar approach, termed *grignoter* (nibbling), the Allies would slowly but surely devour the German army over the coming year.

THE DECISION

- To follow the alternative route, go back to **Section 1** (p. 214).

OR

- To explore the decisions of the campaign, go to the **Historical Note** on p. 257.

SECTION 4
THE TANKS

2.30 p.m., 26 August 1916, Saint-Riquier, France

It has been six weeks since the bloodbath of 1 July 1916. Your decision to attack the first and second German lines in a single day meant that the fire of the Royal Artillery was fatally diluted. The week-long bombardment inflicted some damage, but there were simply not enough guns to engage all the targets required. Enemy strongpoints remained standing, barbed wire was uncut and German artillery was barely engaged. The moment your infantry left their trenches, they were flayed by bullets and swept by shrapnel. They pressed the attack with immense courage, but it was not enough against the storm of steel. By the end of the day the BEF had suffered a staggering 57,470 casualties – the bloodiest day in the history of the British army.

6. Douglas Haig

But the battle did not end on 1 July. Although violently repulsed in the north, your men had achieved success in the south, where the German first line had been overwhelmed. You immediately switched the axis of your attack here, and your forces have been slowly advancing in this sector throughout July and August. The Germans have fought ferociously, and it has been a punishing campaign where advances are measured in hundreds of yards but casualties are recorded in thousands of lives.

You are ***General Sir Douglas Haig***, Commander-in-Chief of the British Expeditionary Force. You went to war as a corps commander in 1914, but soon became the heir apparent to the erratic Field Marshal Sir John French. In late 1915 you secretly used your political connections to outmanoeuvre French and replace him as Commander-in-Chief. Despite the repeated setbacks at the Battle of the Somme, you are convinced that the Germans are weakening and that a breakthrough is still possible.

The demonstration that you are attending today might provide the key to unlocking the enemy defences. You are leading a high-ranking observation party consisting of your Chief of Staff, Lieutenant-General Sir Launcelot Kiggell, plus your army commanders Henry Rawlinson (Fourth Army) and Hubert Gough (Fifth Army, previously known as the Reserve Army). It is a sunny afternoon at a training ground near Yvrench, behind British lines on the Somme. The Royal Engineers have built accurate re-creations of German trenches and have even converted a patch of woodland into a replica strongpoint.

The demonstration begins at 3 p.m. as five bulky vehicles rumble onto the training ground. This is the first time you have seen 'tanks' in

7. A Mark I tank in training

France – given this bland name to trick German intelligence into believing they are water tanks – and you are keen to see their capabilities. Their 105-horsepower engines wheeze and groan under the strain of driving the metal monsters forward, but their progress is relentless. You can imagine how the clattering of their tracks and the fire from their guns will terrify the enemy. Soldiers of the 7th Middlesex follow close behind them to simulate a combined-arms attack. The tanks will flatten the barbed wire and destroy enemy strongpoints, enabling the infantry to mop up the survivors and secure the ground.

The demonstration is an encouraging one. The tanks smash their way through the replica trenches 'with the greatest ease', grinding through barbed wire and crushing breastworks beneath their tracks. One tank even simulates an attack into the woodland strongpoint, where it demolishes log barricades and 'easily walked over fair sized trees'.

As the exercise concludes you feel a surge of optimism. These machines are slow and mechanically temperamental, but you can see their immense potential. Bulletproof, heavily armed and able to crush enemy defences beneath their tracks, they can form a powerful vanguard that might prove irresistible. You are eager to use them at the Somme.

You discuss the tanks with Rawlinson and Gough. They are cautiously optimistic about the new vehicles, but express concern about using them too soon. The technology is novel and the crews need more training. There are few tanks available and although more are on their way, they will not arrive in significant numbers until early 1917. Finally there is also the question of your allies. The French are developing their own tanks, but are months away from being able to deploy them. They have asked you to hold your armour in reserve until they are able to launch a simultaneous tank attack. They believe that a massive tank assault will shock the Germans and win a decisive victory. But if the tanks are deployed prematurely, the surprise value will be lost and the enemy is sure to develop countermeasures.

You ponder these questions on your return to your headquarters. If you hold your tanks in reserve, then they will not see action until spring 1917 at the very earliest. This will please the French and will give your crews valuable training time, but the thought of holding back this innovative new weapon troubles you. You are confident that the Germans on the Somme are close to breaking point, and the appearance of the tanks could push them over edge. Surely it is better to use every weapon at your disposal *now* to ensure victory? Holding back the tanks also runs the risk that German intelligence will learn of the new weapon and be ready for it in 1917. You must make a difficult decision.

AIDE-MEMOIRE

* The Battle of the Somme has been raging for six weeks and a breakthrough remains elusive. The tanks could turn the tide.
* The tanks are a completely novel weapon. Although they look impressive in demonstrations, how they will perform in battle remains unknown.
* The appearance of dozens of metal fighting machines on the battlefield will come as a huge shock to the Germans and could lead to a decisive victory.
* The tank crews have had little time to train, and your infantry has no experience of working with them. A premature deployment could end in disaster.
* You believe the Germans on the Somme are near breaking point. One last great heave could finally break their defences. The tanks can play a key role in this final offensive.
* The French are developing their own tanks and have asked you to wait until an Anglo-French tank attack can be launched in early 1917. Such an attack would achieve maximum surprise.

THE DECISION

Will you deploy the tanks immediately to try and win victory on the Somme or will you keep the machines in reserve until you have enough for an all-out attack in 1917?

- If you wish to deploy your tanks as soon as possible in an attempt to win a decisive victory at the Somme, go to **Section 6** (p. 244).

  OR

- If you prefer to hold your tanks in reserve and wait until you can use them in a large-scale attack in 1917, go to **Section 7** (p. 252).

SECTION 5
BREAKTHROUGH!

12.00 p.m., 1 July 1916, XIII Corps Headquarters, Chipilly, France

The voice on the other end of the telephone is masked by static and almost drowned out by the thunder of artillery fire, but the message is clear. 'Sir, I am pleased to report that the German first and second line have been captured. The enemy are retreating and our cavalry is in pursuit.' The soldiers of XIII Corps have won one of the British army's greatest victories.

8. Walter Congreve, VC

As you return the receiver to the cradle you allow yourself a small smile of satisfaction. You are ***Lieutenant-General Walter Congreve, VC***, and you are not given to great displays of emotion. You hail from one of the most famous military families in Britain. One of your relatives, William Congreve, was the inventor of the Congreve Rockets used in the Napoleonic Wars and was immortalised in the American national anthem. Famed for your courage and toughness, you won the Victoria Cross in the Boer War at the Battle of Colenso in December 1899. You are a supporter of 'bite and hold' methods, but some of your colleagues think you are overly slow and cautious, contributing to your nickname of 'Old Concrete'.

When preparing for the Battle of the Somme, even Rawlinson – the army's main proponent of 'bite and hold' – criticised you for your caution. He encouraged you to be more ambitious and assigned you the 1st Indian and 2nd Indian Cavalry Divisions to exploit any breakthroughs. 'The Fox' used all his charm to convince you to take an optimistic view of the coming offensive. You eventually agreed, trusting to the high standard of your soldiers to carry you to victory. You are a great believer in the value of training, and your soldiers spent more days in training than any other corps in the British army.

You also took a great interest in your artillery preparations, even boarding a Royal Flying Corps aircraft for a personal reconnaissance flight to study the damage inflicted on the German defences. The bombardment in this sector was devastating. Local geography forced the Germans to build their trenches on a forward slope, which could be observed from British lines. This enabled the gunners to hammer it with accurate and remorseless fire. Your guns were supported by several batteries of French artillery, including sixteen monstrous 220mm mortars capable of turning even the most formidable strongpoints to smouldering ruins. Soon the German front line was reduced to 'sand dunes, enormous mounds and holes of earth, absolutely untenable', while the fortified village of Montauban 'was all wreck and ruin, a monstrous heap of rubble stinking of death, brick-dust and high-explosive', with its garrison buried alive beneath the wreckage.

Although you betrayed no emotion at Zero Hour on 1 July, you were confident of success. Information trickled into your headquarters and you watched as your staff updated the vast maps that line the walls. Then came the news you had been waiting for. The highly trained soldiers of the 18th and 30th Divisions had broken through the enemy line, encircling the surviving defenders and spreading panic throughout the German position.

By midday, XIII Corps had seized all its objectives. British soldiers in the ruins of Montauban reported that they could see hundreds of German soldiers 'fleeing backwards in hopeless confusion', throwing away their equipment and abandoning their guns. You could sense the optimism in your headquarters as you read this powerful message. Now was the time to strike.

Shortly after 12 p.m. you gave the order for the cavalry to advance. Your men were ready to seize the opportunity. The 1st and 2nd Indian Cavalry Divisions were trained to a peak of perfection and were supported by the infantry of the elite 9th (Scottish) Division. The victorious soldiers of 18th and 30th Divisions cheered wildly at the sight of the Indian cavalry cantering through the ruins of the German front line.

The cavalry mounted a ruthless pursuit of the shattered defenders. The sight of the Indian lancers racing through the fields beyond Montauban terrified the surviving Germans. Many surrendered, and those who did not were soon ridden down. The cavalry thundered over Willow Stream and turned the enemy retreat into a full-scale rout. Behind them came the infantry of 9th (Scottish) Division, who secured key positions, notably Mametz Wood and Longueval. You have won a victory worthy of any in British army history.

9. Indian cavalry preparing to advance on 1 July 1916

AFTERMATH

The breakthrough at Montauban unhinged the German line. On your left, the German defenders in front of XV Corps realised that their flank was turned and fell back in disorder, while on your right, French soldiers of the battle-hardened XX Corps stormed the enemy line singing '*La Marseillaise*'.

Haig immediately saw the opportunity and sent all available reserves to exploit the victory. Further gains were made in the subsequent days as the Germans reeled from your blows. For a time, the enemy seemed powerless to stem your attack and a sense of despair began to settle over the German high command. In mid-July the Chief of the German General Staff, Erich von Falkenhayn, was unceremoniously sacked and replaced by the ruthless duo of Paul von Hindenburg and Erich Ludendorff. The two men immediately decided that the original Somme defences had to be abandoned or else the German line would be rolled up from the south. Work began on a fall-back

10. A German machine gun waits for its next target

position, employing thousands of forced labourers from the occupied territories, but until then the line had to be held at all costs to prevent a complete collapse.

Savage fighting raged throughout the summer as the Allies pressed their advantage and the Germans fought to buy precious time. Casualties on both sides were very heavy. Haig believed that victory was at hand and pressured Rawlinson and Gough to seize the opportunity. But German defences were solidifying as reinforcements reached the Somme, and the momentum of those first heady days could not be maintained. The British learned this the hard way as hasty, ill-prepared attacks were mown down in a hail of machine-gun fire.

The glimpse of open warfare seen on 1 July turned out to be an illusion. The battle would settle into a grinding attritional struggle as the British battered their way forward and the Germans fought to hold their line at all costs. Nevertheless, the Allied gains in the south gave the attackers some crucial advantages. Control of high ground here enabled the Royal Artillery to pour fire into the flank and rear of German positions to the north.

Slowly but surely the British prised open the German line, and by September the defenders were facing a crisis. Containing the British breakthrough in the south had cost the Germans dearly and had overstretched their defences. The position to the north, anchored on Thiepval, had crumbled by the end of the month. There were almost no reserves left to plug the gap and there was a real risk that the entire German position might collapse.

Haig pushed his commanders to seize the opportunity. Unfortunately for the BEF, the weather was turning. October was cold and extremely wet, and the battlefield became a sodden swamp. British attacks floundered in the mud and gave the Germans precious time to recover. The battered defenders held on until November snow froze the battle lines in place.

The Battle of the Somme ended in frustration for Haig and the BEF. The breakthrough on 1 July would be remembered as one of the British army's greatest victories, but it led to a prolonged and bloody attritional battle that was marred by controversy. The German line had buckled, but the advance could not be maintained. Critics damned

Haig for hammering away at the same point long after the chance for a decisive victory had passed. Yet the Germans could take little comfort from the battle, either. The German army had suffered heavy losses in its last-ditch attempt to halt the Allied advance and had eventually been forced to abandon ground that it had fought so hard to hold. Neither Hindenburg nor Ludendorff would countenance the idea of peace, but even they were forced to admit that the Somme had been the 'muddy grave of the German army'.

THE DECISION

- To follow the alternative route, go back to **Section 2** (p. 222).

OR

- To explore the decisions of the campaign, go to the **Historical Note** on p. 257.

SECTION 6
ARMOURED WARFARE

10.00 a.m., 2 March 1917, War Office, London

It is a frigid day at the War Office in London. Frost coats the window-panes and the roaring fire in the meeting room does little to dispel the cold. Yet there is an atmosphere of excitement and anticipation at this remarkable gathering that warms your blood. Tank experts from Britain and France have been gathered to discuss their plans for the coming offensive.

You are the foremost of these experts, for you are ***Colonel Hugh Elles***. You began your career in the Royal Engineers, but soon established a reputation as an excellent staff officer. You were wounded at the Second Battle of Ypres in April 1915 and, while recovering from your injuries, you were sent to observe early trials of innovative 'caterpillar' vehicles – the forerunners of the tank – under development in Britain. You became one of the army's leading experts on the new weapon, and in September 1916 you were appointed as overall commander of British tank forces on the Western Front, now named the Heavy Branch, Machine Gun Corps.

11. Hugh Elles

As you take your seat, you reflect

on how far the Heavy Branch has come in such a brief time. A steady trickle of tanks has flowed into France and your force can deploy 150 Mark I tanks and fifty slightly upgraded Mark II tanks. Tanks come in a 'male' variant, armed with two six-pounder guns in their side sponsons, or a 'female' version where the heavy guns are replaced by additional machine guns. The two variants are intended to work side-by-side. The 'males' will destroy strongpoints with their six-pounders while the 'females' will scourge enemy trenches with their machine guns.

Preparing the Heavy Branch for action has taxed your imagination and ingenuity. The tanks attract immense interest from generals, politicians and other assorted VIPs, and at times your training areas resemble a circus, where the Heavy Branch is expected to perform stunts for the amusement of the audience. You have had to ruffle feathers to banish these freeloaders and give your crews time to train.

Over the winter months you put your men through intensive training and learned much about the strengths and weaknesses of the tanks. This was a gruelling process for all involved. Temperatures inside the cramped confines of a tank are almost unbearable, and the carbon-monoxide fumes from the engine leave crews nauseous and light-headed. The machines suffer frequent breakdowns, and weary mechanics spend many cold nights labouring to repair them for the next day's training. Yet the potential of the new weapon is clear. The machines are bulletproof, can crush barbed wire with ease and deliver a hail of fire from their own guns. Furthermore the weeks of hard training have created a powerful *esprit de corps* among the tank crews.

You explain your preparations to the assembled officers at the meeting. A stocky, cheerful French officer across the table nods in agreement, and you recognise him as Général de Division Jean-Baptiste Eugène Estienne, who commands the French armoured branch, the *Artillerie spéciale*, and is eager to put his new machines into action. The French have designed two tanks, the compact Schneider CA1 and its larger and more heavily armed cousin, the Saint-Chamond. They possess fewer tanks than the Heavy Branch, but Estienne assures you that they will make up for their limited numbers with surprise.

With Estienne on your side, you present a powerful argument that tanks should be used in the largest numbers possible, but you caution

12. Schneider CA1 tank

13. Saint-Chamond tanks

that a surprise attack that relies on tanks alone is unwise, for the machines are still untested in battle. Instead, you argue for a conventional attack, in which the Heavy Branch and the *Artillerie spéciale* will form the vanguard. The British will mount an offensive around Arras, and the French will strike on the River Aisne. If a breakthrough can be achieved, then a huge portion of the German line on the Western Front will be encircled.

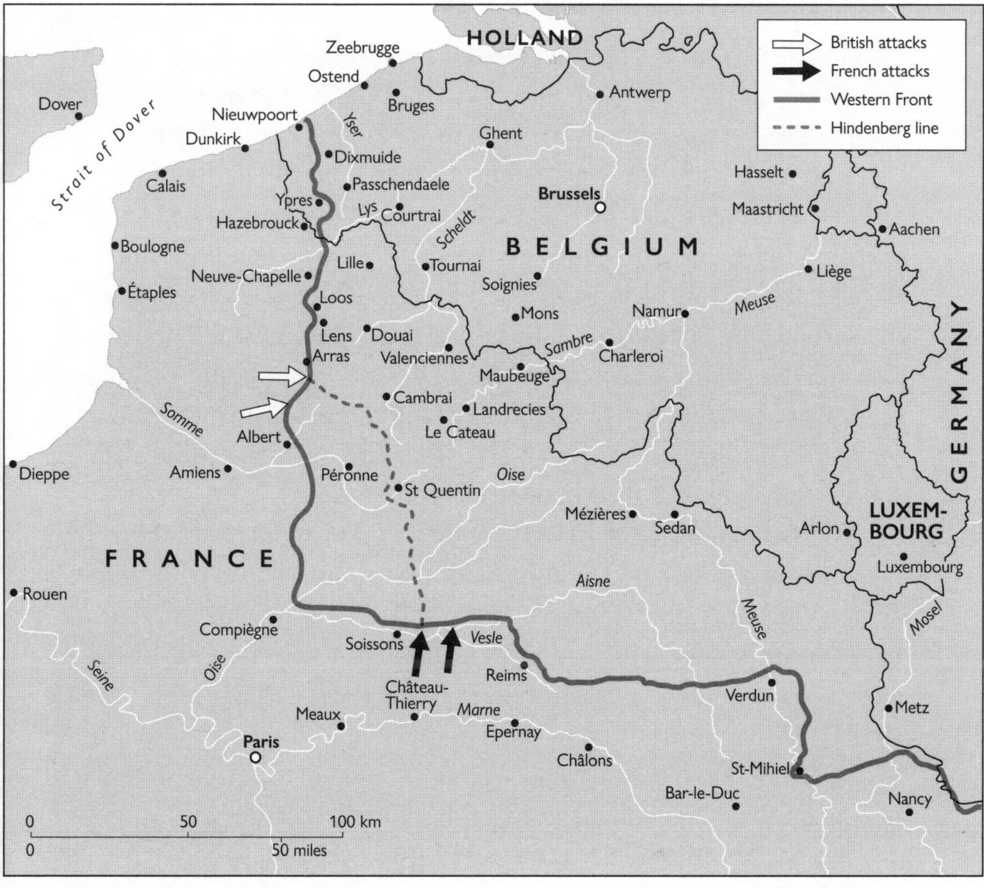

Map 2: The Allied tank offensive, 1917

Following the meeting, you return to France to prepare the Heavy Branch for its baptism of fire. The last days before the attack at Arras are spent in feverish preparation. Tanks are secretly moved into position behind the lines, attack routes are reconnoitred and final mechanical checks are carried out. You are meant to remain behind the lines and direct operations, but you have no intention of missing the first tank action in history. Instead you will lead the Heavy Branch into its first action in your own tank, H1 *Hilda*.

At Zero Hour on 9 April the British bombardment lifts and the trench whistles shriek once more. Yet this time they are joined by a different noise – the deep, throaty sound of 150 tanks starting their engines.

The mechanical monsters lumber from their lairs on rattling tracks and grind their way across no-man's-land. Some vehicles stall as their drivers mishandle the gears and others become bogged down in waterlogged shell holes, but many more press on towards the German front line.

Your tank leads the way across no-man's-land. The interior of H1 *Hilda* is deafening and the roar of the engine shakes every surface. Your vehicle pitches and rolls through the shell holes as you peer anxiously through the narrow vision slit. There is a satisfying crunch as you crush the barbed wire beneath your tracks and then, looming out of the smoke, you see the enemy trenches for the first time. Somewhere off to your flank there is a distinctive coughing chatter as a German machine gun opens fire. Bullets hammer into H1 *Hilda* and the tank echoes with the sound of ricochets as they bounce off your armour.

You bellow, 'OPEN FIRE!' with all your might. Somehow your crew hear the order and the noise within the tank reaches painful levels as your machine guns hammer away and your six-pounders roar into life. Within seconds the enemy machine-gun nest takes a direct hit from a six-pounder shell and burning wreckage is flung high into the air. H1 *Hilda* crashes across the enemy trench line and, through the vision slit, you can see German soldiers fleeing in terror. Prisoners will later describe the attack as 'not war, but bloody butchery'.

You feel a surge of elevation as H1 *Hilda* presses on and harries the retreating enemy. British infantry swarms around you to clear any last pockets of resistance. The Heavy Branch has proved its worth and you are in the vanguard. But your own advance does not last much longer. The tank's tortured engine gives a final wheeze and gives out completely. No amount of effort can coax it back into life, and you are forced to temporarily abandon your tank. Other tanks pass you by and you urge them on as they continue the advance deep into German territory.

AFTERMATH

The surprise tank attack on 9 April was a stunning success. Unfortunately the dramatic progress made on the first day of the battle could not be maintained. Only about 50 per cent of your tanks were available for action on the second day of the offensive. Mechanical failures and bogging down accounted for most of the losses, while some tanks were knocked out by direct hits from German artillery. The number of available tanks continued to fall and by the end of the third day you were forced to withdraw the Heavy Branch for rest and refit. Your crews were exhausted by stress, heat and carbon-monoxide poisoning, but they took pride in their victory.

With the aid of the tanks, the Allies had made the biggest advance since trench warfare began. Further advances were made over the coming days, before the arrival of German reinforcements turned the battle into an attritional struggle that was grimly familiar to both armies. Yet the success of the new armoured vehicles was clear. These crude first-generation machines had shattered the front line and sown panic among the enemy. For you and Estienne, it was a vindication of the power of tanks and a testament to the courage and determination of your crews.

The French army was revitalised by the success of the tanks. French soldiers had suffered terrible losses between 1914 and 1916 and there were whispers that they were close to exhaustion, but the victory on the Aisne provided a crucial morale boost and restored hope that the war might be won by the end of the year. French industry worked tirelessly to design and construct new tanks, including the revolutionary Renault FT – the first tank to have a revolving turret.

In Britain the success of the tanks prompted church bells to be rung to celebrate a victory, for the first time since the war had begun. The Heavy Branch was rewarded by being granted the title of the Royal Tank Corps. Minister of Munitions Winston Churchill, an early supporter of the tank, promised that British industry would 'strain every nerve and sinew' to provide vehicles to the new corps and that a 'Thousand Tank Army' would be available by 1918. The superior Mark IV tank poured into France in mid-1917 and became the backbone of the Royal Tank Corps.

The tanks delivered a crushing blow to German morale. This reinforced their impression that the Allies fought with steel and fire while the Germans fought with flesh and blood. There was a rush to introduce countermeasures, including armour-piercing bullets and improvised anti-tank guns – German 77mm artillery pieces dragged into the front line – but even these could not lift the sense of despair at the front.

Further tank offensives followed in 1917, including a surprise British 'tank raid' at Ypres in the summer and a renewed French offensive near the River Aisne. The mechanical weaknesses of the tanks still limited their overall effectiveness, but wherever infantry, artillery and armour attacked in combination they won victories. The Royal Tank Corps would be in the vanguard of all future British offensives until victory was finally won in 1918.

THE DECISION

- To follow the alternative route, go back to **Section 4** (p. 232).

OR

- To explore the decisions of the campaign, go to the **Historical Note** on p. 257.

SECTION 7
THE ENDLESS BATTLE

November 1916, Fifth Army Headquarters, Toutencourt, France

It is bitterly cold in France and you are grateful for the roaring fire in the chateau that serves as your headquarters. Your meteorologists have warned you that this will be the coldest winter in decades. A glance out of the window reveals frozen ground and water-filled shell holes capped with a thick crust of ice. In the distance you watch a shivering supply column struggling towards the distant front line, its progress punctuated by the heavy puffs of white breath from the horses. The Battle of the Somme has become a struggle against nature as well as a fight against the Germans.

14. Hubert Gough

You are ***Lieutenant-General Sir Hubert Gough***, the commander of the Fifth Army on the Somme. You come from a legendary Anglo-Irish military family – your great-uncle Hugh, your father Charles and your younger brother John were all awarded the Victoria Cross for bravery. At forty-six years old, you are the youngest army commander in the BEF and certainly its most controversial. You disdain 'bite and hold' tactics and have a reputation as an aggressive 'thruster' who likes to strike the enemy head-on.

Your aggression on the battlefield is reflected in your command style, and you are notorious for bullying your subordinates. Despite these flaws, you have enjoyed a meteoric rise from a cavalry brigadier in 1914 to a full army commander in 1916. Your career owes much to Haig's unstinting support. The Commander-in-Chief admires your aggressive spirit, but your rivals whisper that you are little more than his 'pet'.

At the beginning of the Battle of the Somme you commanded the Reserve Army, which Haig hoped might be used to exploit the expected breakthrough. The disaster of 1 July dashed these hopes and your formation, soon to be renamed the Fifth Army, was used to relieve the mauled divisions of the Fourth Army on the northern part of the front. Over the coming months you fought a bloody campaign along the Pozières Ridge to outflank the German position in the fortified village of Thiepval. Your forces slowly battled their way through stubborn German defences until Thiepval – a first-day objective – finally fell at the end of September. Earlier that month the Fourth Army won an important victory at Fleurs in the south, with the aid of the new tanks. Although only a handful were available and their performance was limited, their potential is clear and more will soon be on their way.

The victories in September raised hopes that the Germans might be on the brink of collapse. It proved to be a false dawn. The weather worsened throughout October, and the Somme became a chilly wilderness of shell-scarred ridges overlooking valleys that had been reduced to corpse-filled swamps. Simply surviving in these appalling conditions is a challenge and morale on both sides has plummeted. Your assaults against the German-held ridges on the Ancre Heights have made little progress, and no amount of hectoring your subordinates has improved the situation.

The icy conditions in November have magnified the suffering of your soldiers, but the cold has also frozen the mud and given you a window of opportunity for another attack. Haig is determined that the BEF wins a final victory before winter brings the campaign to an end. He believes this will be an important psychological boost for weary British soldiers and a heavy blow to the morale of the German defenders. You also suspect he needs a triumph to silence a growing chorus of criticism from politicians in the United Kingdom, who are appalled by the cost of the battle.

You are determined that the new assault will succeed. As you study the maps of your objective, you are struck by the grim echoes of 1 July. Some of your objectives – notably Serre and Beaumont-Hamel – were meant to have been captured on the very first day of the battle, and your soldiers will be advancing over the bones of those who fell in earlier attempts.

In the distance you can hear the dull thump of heavy artillery as your guns begin to soften up the enemy. The sound makes you reflect on how much the BEF has evolved. Your gunners have told you that the bombardment at the Ancre Heights is twice as heavy as that which preceded the initial assault in July. There are also new weapons at your disposal, including a handful of tanks, while tactics that were considered novel in July, such as creeping barrages, are now standard practice. There is no doubt that the BEF has learned much – but it has paid for its lessons in blood.

The attack is set for 13 November. Thick fog blankets the front line at dawn and no-man's-land echoes with the thunder of artillery as your infantry and tanks slog through the icy mud. Information trickles through to your headquarters at an agonisingly slow pace, but the news is encouraging. The bombardment has breached the enemy barbed wire, and your troops slowly but surely fight their way through the German trenches.

The battle rages for the next five days in sub-zero temperatures. At the end of the fighting the Fifth Army has taken almost all its objectives, at a cost of 22,000 casualties. Beaumont-Hamel and several other important targets are captured, along with 7,000 German prisoners. To your frustration and disappointment, Serre resists your attack and remains in German hands. Nevertheless, the battle feels like a victory. The Germans have been driven from strong positions and your soldiers are proud of what they have achieved.

You are studying your maps on 18 November and are considering the possibility of a renewed attack on Serre when you notice that the

15. British soldiers in the snow near Beaumont Hamel

first snow is falling. By the end of the day the battlefield is buried beneath deep drifts that make movement impossible. Your soldiers can do nothing except try to stay warm in the freezing conditions. The Battle of the Somme is over.

AFTERMATH

The winter of 1916–17 was the coldest of the First World War (and one of the worst of the entire twentieth century). Military operations were impossible in the arctic conditions and the Allied General Offensive shivered to a halt. It had achieved some of its objectives. The Austro-Hungarians received a series of devastating blows on the Eastern Front and the German army suffered dreadful casualties – perhaps as many as 850,000 in total – at Verdun and the Somme.

Yet the Allies were not able to win a decisive victory and their armies paid dearly for their efforts. The Russian army suffered appalling losses in 1916 – at least 500,000 men and perhaps as many as one million – and was left teetering on the edge of complete collapse. The

French army held its ground at Verdun, but only at the cost of some 377,000 casualties. At the Somme, 420,000 British and 200,000 French soldiers fell.

The Allies could afford these losses under the grim metrics of attritional warfare. Allied commanders proposed a second General Offensive in 1917, and Haig and the French commander Joseph Joffre intended to renew the Battle of the Somme as soon as possible. Yet events elsewhere were moving fast. The massive casualties suffered in 1916 sent political shockwaves through Britain and France. French Prime Minister Aristide Briand reorganised his Cabinet and decided to install a new commander for the French army. He replaced Joseph Joffre, an iconic figure since his victory at the Battle of the Marne in 1914, with Robert Nivelle, who was young, charismatic and a hero of Verdun – but also arrogant and severely misguided. He seduced French and British politicians with his promise of a new offensive that would break open the Western Front in a mere forty-eight hours. His plan would translate into the Battle of the Aisne, a bitter defeat that prompted a mutiny in the French army.

There would be no renewal of the Battle of the Somme. In March 1917 the Germans skilfully withdrew to a new position called the *Siegfriedstellung* (Siegfried Position) – termed the Hindenburg Line by the British. The Germans now occupied formidable new defences rather than clinging to the shattered ruins of the Somme, and the overall length of the Western Front was reduced by twenty-five miles, which eased the pressure on German reserves. Yet the withdrawal was also the first major German retreat since trench warfare began and gave grudging acknowledgement that the army could not afford a second Somme.

The war would rage on through 1917. The Central Powers were bloodied, but far from broken. The Allies continued their offensives, but the spiralling cost of the war would soon send Russia tumbling into revolution and plunge the French army into mutiny. Britain was forced to shoulder the burden of the war, and the BEF would instead find itself locked in a harrowing campaign at Passchendaele.

THE DECISION

- ▶ To follow the alternative route, go back to **Section 3** (p. 226).

  OR

- ▶ To explore the decisions of the campaign, see the **Historical Note** below.

HISTORICAL NOTE

The first day of the Battle of the Somme was the bloodiest day in the history of the British army. Despite this disaster, the BEF continued the offensive for the next five months. By the end of the campaign the army had suffered at least 420,000 casualties and had advanced just six miles.

The origins of the disaster on the opening day lay in the confused planning process. Rawlinson believed that a methodical 'bite and hold' attack was the best method for an assault at the Somme, but the optimistic Haig wanted a more ambitious offensive that might produce a breakthrough. Mindful of his obligation to the man who had saved his career, Rawlinson acquiesced to Haig's demands. Yet 'The Fox' never really believed in Haig's ideas and gave almost no thought as to how he might position his reserves or exploit any breakthroughs. The final plan was an unhappy compromise of Haig and Rawlinson's visions. The BEF aimed for distant objectives and diluted its artillery fire, leading to complete disaster in the northern half of the battlefield. Yet in the south, where a breakthrough was tantalisingly possible, there were no reserves on hand to exploit the opportunity. Although a truly decisive victory at the Somme was unlikely, a firm commitment to either Haig's vision or Rawlinson's plan might have led to a vastly different outcome.

Another controversial decision, made later in the battle, was the decision to deploy Britain's first tanks in September 1916. The wisdom of this remains hotly debated. It infuriated the French, and Winston Churchill considered it one of the greatest mistakes of the entire war, but others have argued that it provided the armoured branch with crucial combat experience, which helped them improve their equipment, training and tactics.

The historical route leads you through these controversies. Rawlinson expected to clash with Haig over his 'bite and hold' plan, and yet he made almost no attempt to argue his case and accepted Haig's ambitious vision instead (Section 1 to Section 2). Having agreed to attack the German first and second lines in one day, Rawlinson then largely ignored Haig's instructions to prepare to exploit a breakthrough with cavalry and mobile troops (Section 2 to Section 4). The action then moves forward to August 1916 and the decision over whether to use tanks immediately or hold them back until 1917 (Section 4 to Section 7).

The scenario provides the opportunity to change history and stick to Rawlinson's 'bite and hold' attack (Section 1 to Section 3). This method had much to recommend it, and it would be employed with ruthless effectiveness at the Third Battle of Ypres in 1917. It would probably have proved effective in 1916. Concentrated fire on the German first line would have enabled the British assault to get into the trenches and fortified villages rather than being mown down in no-man's-land. German doctrine demanded that the front line be held at all costs and reclaimed if it were lost, which would have led to severe fighting in the aftermath of the initial assault. Historically, the Battle of the Somme cost the German army dearly, and a BEF 'bite and hold' attack would have inflicted even heavier casualties upon it.

Another option was to adopt Haig's aggressive plan and ensure that reserves were on hand to exploit any victories (Section 3 to Section 5). In reality XIII Corps had a single reserve infantry division and used it to consolidate its gains. What if there had been cavalry and infantry on hand to widen the breach? This would have led to a deep advance and the capture of key positions, such as Mametz Wood. It would have unhinged the line and created real problems for the Germans.

The final decision revolves around the tanks. What if they had been held back for a massed tank assault in early 1917 (Section 4 to Section 6)? The Heavy Branch and the French *Artillerie spéciale* might have been able to achieve something spectacular in April 1917, although the limitations of their machines and the effects of carbon monoxide on tank crews would have prevented a truly decisive victory. However, a successful large-scale deployment of tanks would have stunned the Germans and given powerful impetus to develop the armoured branch further. Furthermore, a clear victory at the Aisne in 1917 would have prevented the mutinies that rocked the French army that year.

Henry Rawlinson was sidelined after the Battle of the Somme and saw no action in 1917. He was recalled in 1918 and took command of a reformed Fourth Army. His army won a decisive victory at the Battle of the Amiens on 8 August 1918 and broke the Hindenburg Line in September 1918. After the war he served as Commander-in-Chief, India. He died in 1925.

Archibald Montgomery served as a staff officer for the remainder of the war. He was reunited with Rawlinson in 1918 when the Fourth Army was re-formed. In 1926 he incorporated his wife's name into his own and became Archibald Montgomery-Massingberd. In 1933 he was appointed Chief of the Imperial General Staff and organised the mechanisation of Britain's cavalry regiments. He died in 1947.

Aylmer Hunter-Weston commanded VIII Corps for the remainder of the war and became a Member of Parliament in October 1916. He left the army in 1919, but remained in Parliament until his retirement in 1935. He died in peculiar circumstances in 1940 when he fell from a turret at his ancestral home in Scotland during his morning exercise.

Douglas Haig commanded the BEF for the remainder of the war. He fought the mud-stricken Third Battle of Ypres in 1917, struggled against the German Spring Offensive in 1918 and led the BEF in the decisive Hundred Days Offensive in the same year. The cost of these battles made him a deeply controversial figure. After the war he campaigned for the welfare of ex-servicemen, and his Haig Fund would eventually become the British Legion's Poppy Appeal. He died in 1928.

Walter Congreve, VC, had a hard war. His beloved son William was killed on the Somme in July 1916. William received a posthumous Victoria Cross, making the Congreves the last father and son to win this award. Walter lost his left hand to German shellfire in 1917 and was in such poor health by 1918 that he was recalled to the United Kingdom. After the war he served as Governor of Malta. He died in 1927.

Hugh Elles commanded the Royal Tank Corps throughout the war and saw the force grow from a handful of crude machines in 1916 to a powerful fighting force of hundreds of tanks by 1918. At the Battle of Cambrai in November 1917 he led the Corps into action in his tank, H1 *Hilda*. After the war he held various army roles related to armoured warfare. He died in 1945.

Hubert Gough commanded the Fifth Army throughout 1917 and 1918. His disastrous attack at Bullecourt and bloody setbacks at the Third Battle of Ypres tarnished his already-controversial reputation. He commanded his army well when it was struck by the German Spring Offensive in 1918, but it was not enough to save him from the wrath of Prime Minister David Lloyd George and he was sacked later that year. He died in 1963.

6

LAWRENCE OF ARABIA:

THE ARAB REVOLT, 1916–17

SECTION 1
THE ARAB REVOLT

January 1916, Savoy Hotel, Cairo

The suites at the Savoy Hotel in Cairo ooze opulence. Cool, airy and exquisitely decorated, each suite boasts a four-poster bed, a magnificent oak writing desk, a gleaming marble bathroom and a selection of fine Persian rugs. In happier times this suite would have hosted the rich and famous of the British Empire, but now it has been turned over to a peculiar intelligence department, officially known as the Arab Bureau, but nicknamed 'The Intrusive' due to its tendency to ask difficult questions. It is an eclectic team of explorers, academics and

1. The Savoy Hotel, Cairo

experts selected for their knowledge of the Middle East and tasked with providing independent advice to the British government.

2. Gertrude Bell

You are one of the Arab Bureau's most notable members, for you are ***Gertrude Bell***, famed author, explorer, linguist and archaeologist. Your globe-trotting adventures are the stuff of legend. You have mapped the mountains of Switzerland, translated medieval Persian poetry into English and excavated Byzantine ruins in Turkey. You have spent years travelling in the Middle East and are one of the world's foremost experts on the area. You feel a special affinity with the Arabs and are proud that they refer to you as a 'daughter of the desert'.

Today you are far from the wilderness where you feel most at home. Although ideal for honeymooners, the suite is not designed to house half a dozen dishevelled academics, and space is at a premium. Paperwork is piled on every available surface and a gust of wind from the open windows often causes a minor disaster. A large area of the floor is taken up by a young army officer named T. E. Lawrence, who is hard at work creating a map of Syria, and who tuts at his clumsy colleagues as they navigate their way around it. You are glad that you are seated at the spacious writing desk where you at least have room to stretch your arms.

You close your ears to the bustle in the bureau and concentrate on the paperwork in front of you. You hold a selection of reports on the British Empire's war against the Ottoman Empire. They make for depressing reading. The amphibious attack at Gallipoli has ended in a bloody defeat and the Indian army's advance on Baghdad has been reversed, with the attackers now besieged by the Turks at the town of Kut. Elsewhere, a stalemate reigns on the Suez Canal front, with the

Ottomans unable to force their way across and the British incapable of driving them back.

With conventional operations stalled, the British government is seeking new ways to undermine the Turks. There is a substantial Arab population within the Ottoman Empire, who have become restive under Turkish rule. Cultural, economic and religious grievances have turned the southern reaches of the Ottoman Empire into a tinderbox. A single spark could be enough to ignite a rebellion and open a new front against the tenacious Turks.

Yet you know better than any other person that Arab culture is a complex mosaic of tribes and traditions that is difficult to define, let alone unify. If an Arab rebellion is to become a reality, then a suitable leader must be identified and supported with arms, expertise and gold. Yet this challenging task is complicated by the fact that the British government and the Indian government have vastly different views on who should lead the revolt.

You turn to the documents that have been sent to you from London. The War Office has identified Hussein bin Ali as the ideal man to lead a revolt. Hussein is the Sharif of Mecca and a direct descendant of Muhammad. His stewardship of the holy city gives him powerful political and religious authority. Tribes of the region will surely respond to his call to arms, and his experience as a semi-autonomous ruler will enable him to navigate the treacherous waters of Arab politics. He has ambitions to create a unified Arab state that stretches from Mecca to Damascus. You privately doubt that the British and French governments will allow the Ottoman Empire to be replaced by an Arab Empire, but that is a problem for after the war has been won.

3. Hussein bin Ali

You can understand why the

British government favours supporting Hussein. He is an experienced leader with political legitimacy. He is also pro-British and has already begun discussions with diplomats about what aid might be made available for any uprising.

You return the paperwork to its folder and look at the documents sent to you from Delhi. The Indian government has a different candidate: the fearsome Arabian warlord Abdul Aziz ibn Saud. Ibn Saud has been waging war against Arab rivals – and occasionally the Turks – for decades and currently controls the prosperous Nejd region in central Arabia as well as much of the east coast. His conflict with the Ottomans was ended by a secret treaty in 1914, but the war has now given him an opportunity to renew hostilities and expand his territory.

Ibn Saud has far more military experience than Hussein and commands a large battle-hardened army. He is also a significant religious authority, who embraces an extremely austere form of fundamentalist Islam known as Wahhabism. His wars against rival Arab warlords have been characterised by iron discipline and evangelical zeal. The Indian government is especially interested in this last aspect. At the outset of the war the Ottoman Empire declared a *jihad* against the British Empire, designed to inflame the Muslim populations of Egypt, India and elsewhere. The call had little immediate effect, but the threat remains constant. The diplomats in Delhi hope that open support for Ibn Saud's zealous campaign will provide a lightning rod that dissipates Islamic unrest within the British Empire.

4. Abdul Aziz ibn Saud

Ibn Saud is a skilled commander who marches at the head of a formidable army. The Indian government is already in discussions with him about what aid can be provided to his cause.

Ideally it should be possible for the British Empire to provide support for both Hussein and Ibn Saud. Unfortunately, the two men despise one another. Hussein sees Ibn Saud as a religious fanatic and a long-term rival. Ibn Saud regards Hussein as 'a trivial and unstable character' and refuses to cooperate with him. You suspect that the two leaders would turn on one another without hesitation, were it not for the larger threat of the Ottoman Empire.

Behind you there is a clatter, followed by a muffled curse, as a tottering tower of books tumbles from the mantelpiece. One of your colleagues mutters profuse apologies as he tidies up the mess. You sigh and rub your eyes. As an expert in Arabian culture and politics, you must make a recommendation on behalf of the Arab Bureau.

AIDE-MEMOIRE

* The war against the Ottoman Empire is going badly. Something is needed to turn the tide or the conflict in the Middle East may be lost.
* The British government favours the Sharif of Mecca, Hussein bin Ali, as the ideal leader of an Arab revolt. Hussein is an experienced politician who commands significant religious authority. He claims that he can summon thousands of fighters to his cause.
* The Indian government argues that the warlord Abdul Aziz ibn Saud should lead the revolt. Ibn Saud is a religious zealot who commands a battle-hardened army that has conquered vast swathes of eastern Arabia.
* Hussein and Ibn Saud despise one another. Hussein regards Ibn Saud as a dangerous religious fanatic, whilst Ibn Saud

considers Hussein to be a feeble figure unfit to command.

* Hussein is the Sharif of Mecca and possesses special political authority. He will bring an air of control and political respectability to the revolt.
* Ibn Saud commands a formidable army of religious zealots. He will be able to wage a highly effective military campaign if he is made leader of the revolt.

THE DECISION

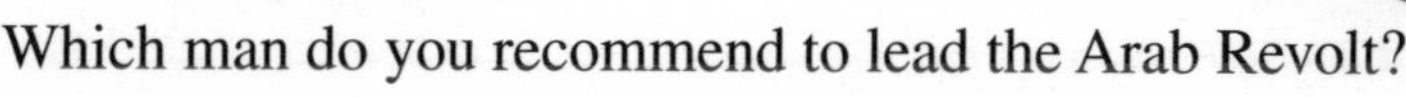

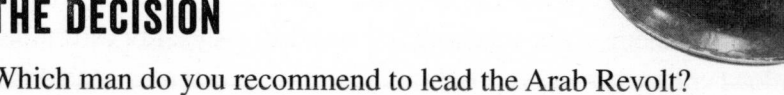

Which man do you recommend to lead the Arab Revolt?

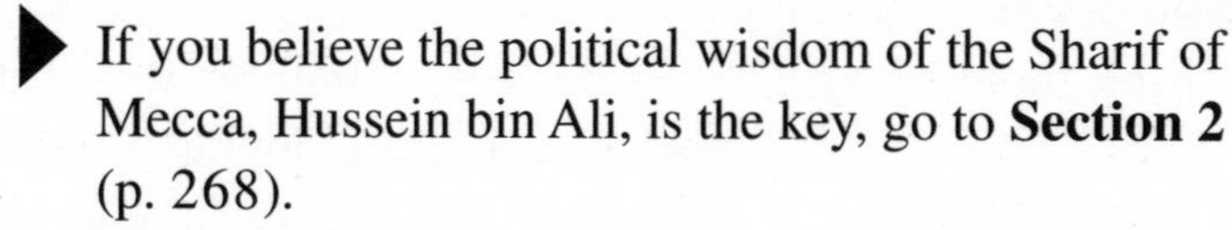

▶ If you believe the political wisdom of the Sharif of Mecca, Hussein bin Ali, is the key, go to **Section 2** (p. 268).

OR

▶ If you feel the zealous ferocity of the warlord Abdul Aziz ibn Saud is essential, go to **Section 5** (p. 286).

SECTION 2
RISK AND REWARD

14 April 1917, Wejh

It is a sweltering day in the small Red Sea port of Al Wejh. The gentle sea breeze is powerless against the dense heat. Lizards bask on rocks whilst your Arab fighters doze in the shade. A handful of your warriors amuse themselves watching red-faced British sailors struggling to unload crates from a supply ship. It seems true that only mad dogs and Englishmen go out in the midday sun.

After a tiring morning spent in delicate negotiations with tribal leaders, you are enjoying a fleeting period of tranquillity in your vast and opulent tent. The high ceiling ensures an airy atmosphere, and the walls are resplendent with red and gold tapestries. You recline against a pile of cushions laid atop a leopard-skin rug and allow yourself a few moments of contemplation. You are ***Faisal ibn Hussein***, the third son of the Sharif of Mecca, Hussein bin Ali, and the de-facto military leader of the Arab Revolt. Although you are only thirty-one years old, your inspiring presence and skilled diplomacy have welded together a disparate force

5. Faisal ibn Hussein

of tribal fighters, desert raiders and Ottoman deserters. Your army, aided by the British Royal Navy Red Sea Patrol, captured Wejh in January 1917. Since then you have mounted an effective guerrilla campaign against the 820-mile-long Hejaz Railway, which links Damascus and Mecca. Nevertheless, you are conscious that your advance has stalled and that the Ottomans are mustering their strength against you.

Your thoughts are broken as your tent flap is thrown back and a figure in white-and-gold robes enters. You face breaks into a broad smile as you recognise your friend and advisor Captain T. E. Lawrence, recently returned from a successful raid on the Hejaz Railway. You are delighted to see the blond Englishman and exchange warm greetings. Lawrence is bursting with energy, and you sense that he has some daring idea on his mind.

Before you can discuss this further, your guest-master hurries in to tell you that an important visitor has arrived at your tent. You struggle to contain your nerves as you whisper to Lawrence, 'Auda is here.' Your anxiety stems from the man's fearsome reputation. Auda is a legendary Bedouin raider who is a veteran of countless battles. After weeks of careful negotiations, he has finally agreed to join your cause. Lawrence's blue eyes light up and he immediately shouts, 'Auda abu Tayi!' to invite the newcomer in. The tent-flap is drawn back to admit a tall, sinewy man in white robes and a red Mosul headcloth. He is every inch the grizzled bandit and radiates an intimidating aura.

You exchange the proper greetings with the newcomer and invite him to join you and Lawrence to discuss the war effort. Your servants provide hot Anise tea before leaving you to draw up your plans in secret. You can see that Lawrence is itching to share his ideas. He sips the scalding tea with nervous energy, oblivious to its heat.

You outline the situation. Your force has been raiding the Hejaz Railway for several weeks with considerable success. The British authorities in Egypt are pleased with the results of this campaign and urge you to continue it, promising weapons, explosives and advisors to support your efforts. Auda murmurs his approval. Many of his followers are brigands who have joined the cause in search of plunder. Deploying his men against the railway gives them an opportunity to

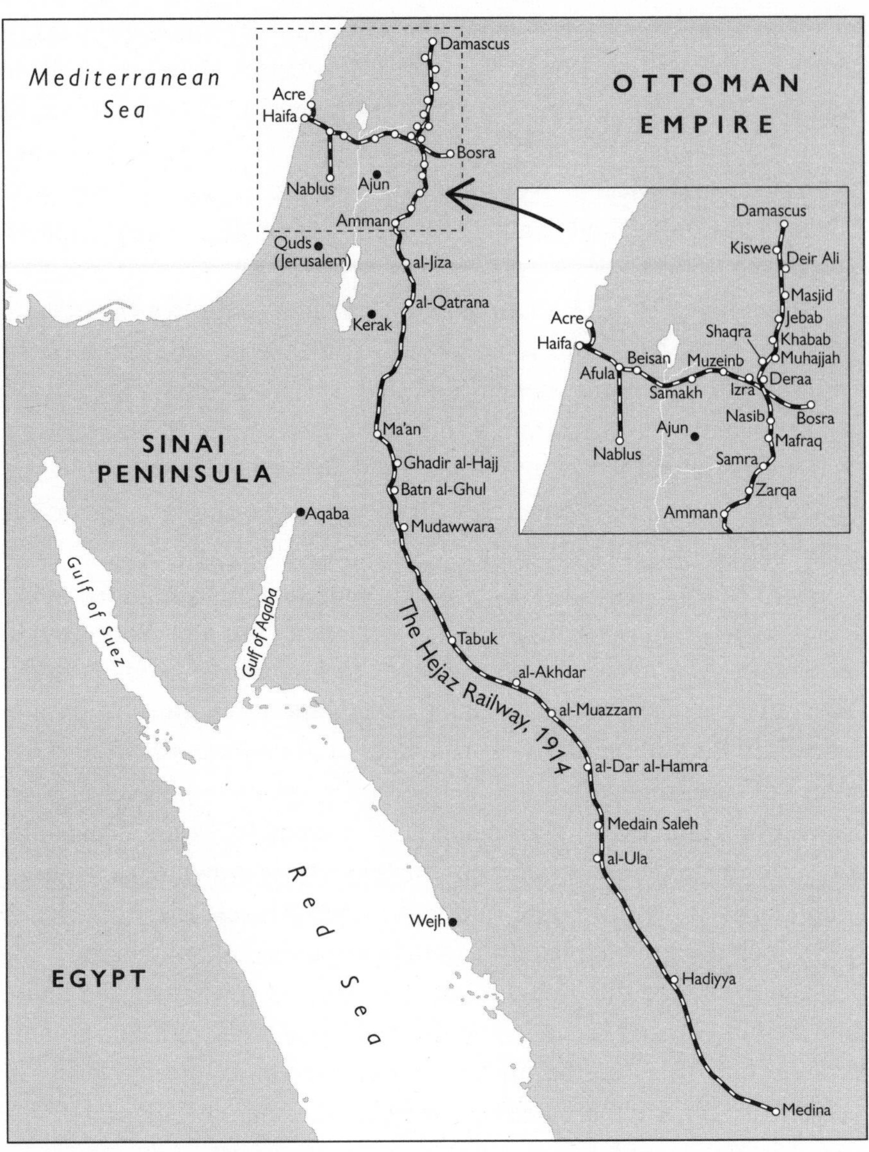

Map 1: The Hejaz Railway

loot derailed Ottoman trains. From the glint in his eyes, you can see that the prospect appeals to the veteran bandit.

You turn to Lawrence for his views. His face is flushed with excitement as he produces a ragged map and rolls it out in front of you. His finger taps at the port of Aqaba, which lies some 300 miles to the north of your position. 'Here,' says Lawrence emphatically, 'is where

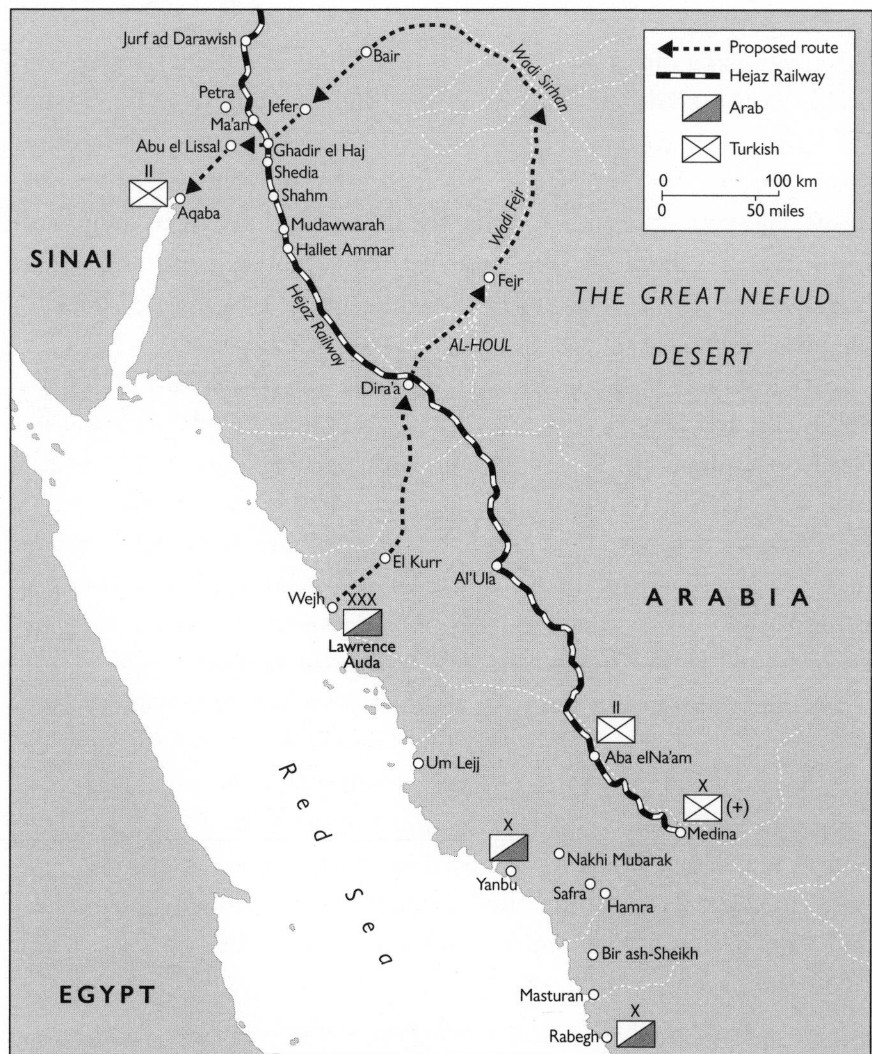

Map 2: Lawrence's proposed march on Aqaba

we must strike.' Aqaba is the last major Red Sea port under Ottoman control. If you can take it, then you will control the entire coastline. You will also place yourself on the right flank of the British-led Egyptian Expeditionary Force and will be able to draw additional supplies from their plentiful stocks. Even more tantalisingly, you will be able to advance into Syria and perhaps incite an Arab revolt that extends beyond the Arabian Peninsula.

But you have grave doubts about this plan. Aqaba is heavily defended and a direct attack upon it is suicidal. Even the British, who briefly considered launching an amphibious assault, have baulked at the difficulties involved. Furthermore, the Turks control all the valleys that surround the port. These passes are formidable defensive positions, and your spies tell you that the Ottomans have lined them with fortifications. Should Aqaba somehow be captured, your men would be powerless to advance and would find themselves trapped beneath the guns of the Turks' positions that surround the town.

You outline these objections, only to be met by one of Lawrence's enigmatic and almost arrogant smiles. You know he has been waiting for this moment. His finger traces a semicircular route on the weathered map. Instead of attacking along the coastline and into the teeth of the Turkish defences, the Englishman proposes a daring overland march that will skirt the edge of the Great Nefud desert and sweep in behind Aqaba. The attackers will pour down the valleys, taking the Ottoman defences from behind, and will seize the port.

Auda contemplates the plan as he sips his tea. His leathery hand gestures to the Great Nefud desert and he reminds Lawrence that the area has no water. Any force crossing it will have to be small and move fast, and even then a sandstorm might destroy the expedition long before it reaches Aqaba. But Lawrence is not discouraged. He proposes to lead the expedition himself and take with him only the hardiest and most daring fighters, including the men of Auda's own war band. The bandit seems a little surprised to be included in the plan, but you can see that he is impressed by Lawrence's presentation.

Lawrence turns to you for the final decision. He knows that you would dearly love to move beyond mere sabotage and lead your army into Syria, where it can ignite a widespread revolt. Yet he does not know the full weight of your responsibilities. The Arab Revolt is currently a bright flame, but one that can easily flicker and die if a mistake is made. Lawrence's plan is a daring gamble. If it succeeds, the rewards will be great, but if it miscarries it will shake the morale of your force and certainly cost your trusted friend his life. Perhaps it would be better to maintain your attacks against the railway? The British will support you, the risks are lower and your forces can easily escape if they are discovered. However, this campaign does little to further your long-term aim of advancing into Syria.

Silence falls over the tent as you contemplate your options. The weight of responsibility sits heavily on your shoulders.

AIDE-MEMOIRE

* Your campaign against the Hejaz Railway has achieved some success and comes at relatively low risk to your forces. The safest option is to continue these attacks.
* The capture of Aqaba would be a huge victory. You would advance your army almost 300 miles north and would be in a position to advance towards your eventual goal of Damascus.
* The Turkish forces facing you are growing in strength and their anti-guerrilla sweeps are becoming more dangerous. If you do not advance, you may find yourself being driven back.
* Lawrence's plan is extremely risky. The Great Nefud desert is virtually impassable, and even if his force crosses it, it will surely be exhausted and depleted. Will it then be able to fight and win a battle against the Turks at Aqaba?
* Lawrence is confident that his knowledge of the area, plus Auda's experience, will enable them to make the journey.
* If the expedition fails, then you will lose your friend and most trusted advisor, not to mention Auda and his tough veterans. Can you afford such casualties?

* If the expedition somehow succeeds, then it will represent one of the greatest victories of the Arab Revolt thus far. Is it worth the risk?

THE DECISION

Do you allow Lawrence to mount his risky expedition, or do you prefer to concentrate your forces against the Hejaz Railway?

▶ If you approve of Lawrence's daring plan to attack Aqaba from behind, go to **Section 3** (p. 276).

OR

▶ If you feel Lawrence's proposal is too dangerous and wish to focus on attacking the Hejaz Railway, go to **Section 6** (p. 290).

SECTION 3
DO OR DIE

12.30 p.m., 2 July 1917, Abu el Lissal

The rugged hills form an amphitheatre where the roar of guns is amplified tenfold. The sound of rifles and machine guns is punctuated by the sharp crack of mountain guns as the Turks burst shells over the heads of your warriors. A Bedouin fighter rises from behind cover to return fire, but is hit immediately and tumbles backwards with a gasp of pain. You glance around your position. Several of your best men have fallen, their robes stained with dark patches of blood that are already attracting clouds of flies. Other fighters are starting to edge away from the ridgeline, casting furtive glances behind them as they consider fleeing. Your warriors are close to breaking point. Your heart sinks, for defeat here means disaster for the entire Arab Revolt. Bellowing encouragement to your hesitant warriors, you stand and fire several shots at the Turkish troops in the valley below you. Enemy bullets shriek all around you, but you show no fear. Your courageous example steadies your men for now, but you know it will not last.

6. T. E. Lawrence

You are ***Captain T. E. Lawrence***, later to be known as

simply Lawrence of Arabia. Your diminutive frame – you stand five feet five inches tall and weigh no more than eight stone – conceals an inner fire that burns with frightening intensity. Prior to the war you were a promising young archaeologist at Oxford University. But now you are a key figure in the Arab Revolt and the commander of a force of fierce Bedouin warriors. You are an unlikely person to lead these desert fighters – you are blond-haired, blue-eyed and resplendent in

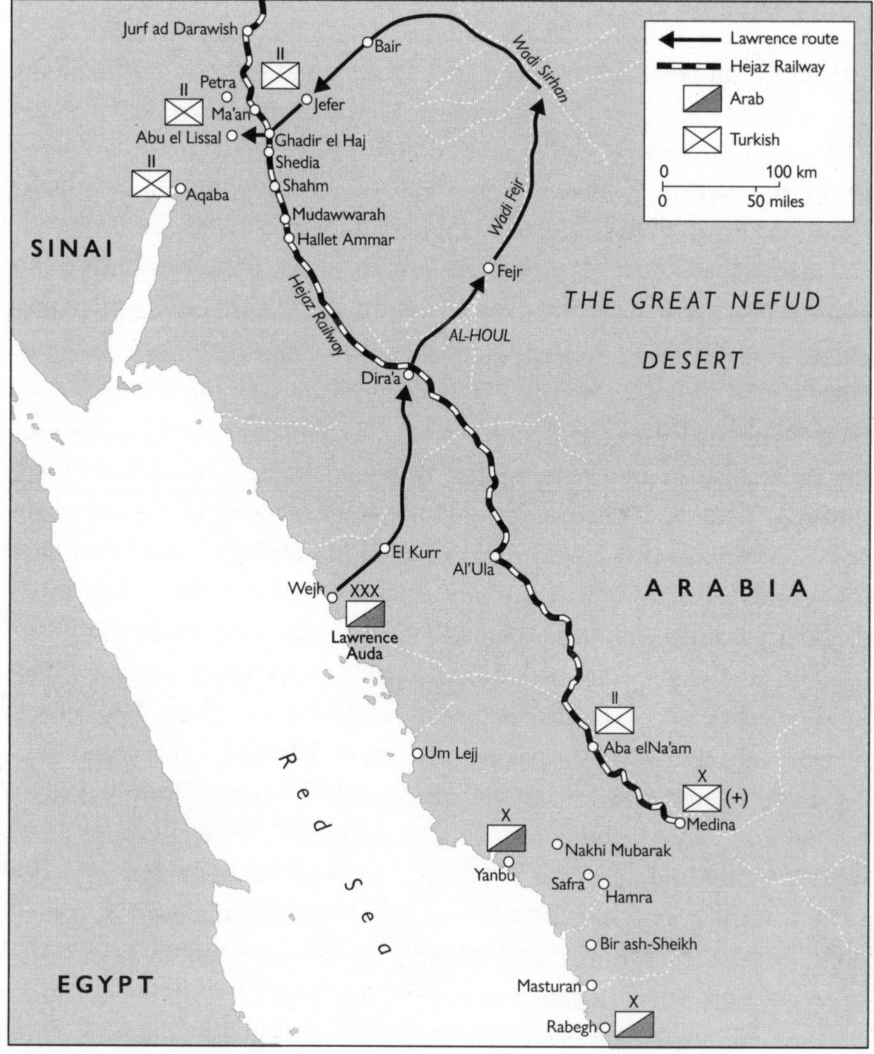

Map 3: Lawrence's advance on Aqaba

white-and-gold robes – but your expert knowledge of the Middle East, your skill with languages and your military brilliance have catapulted you into a position that you could only have dreamed of before 1914.

Yet your dream has become a nightmare. Your daring march to outflank the Ottoman defences at Aqaba has crossed 600 miles of trackless wilderness to reach this point. You have evaded Turkish patrols, completed delicate negotiations with hostile tribes and even ventured into a sandstorm to rescue a fighter who had fallen behind. Yet now fate has turned against you, for enemy reinforcements have arrived at the worst possible time. A fresh Turkish battalion strengthened their defences at Abu el Lissal mere days before your arrival, and more reinforcements arrived at Ma'an to block your retreat. Your own force was left isolated and there is no prospect of escape. With typical daring, you resolved to attack the enemy at Abu el Lissal and smash them before your own force was crushed between the Turkish pincers.

The attack went well at first. Your warriors surprised the Turks and poured fire upon them from the high ground that overlooked their camp. But the Turks rallied and took up a strong defensive position, from which they returned fire. Their machine guns and artillery gave them an edge against the Bedouin sharpshooters, and you have a growing sense of despair as you realise that your men are unable to break through. Time is of the essence. Although you have cut the telegraph line to Ma'an to prevent the Turks signalling for help, you know that the sounds of battle will eventually draw the enemy battalion at Ma'an to the field. If this happens, you will be encircled and wiped out.

The heat of the remorseless midday sun is an act of violence. The boulders that dot the landscape are so hot to the touch that they scorch the skin of anyone who rests against them. Parched, weary and despondent, you drop back from the line to seek out water. Gunfire echoes behind you as you trudge to a small muddy hollow. You crouch in it, hoping to find some relief from your raging thirst by sucking your sleeves to filter precious droplets of moisture from the mud. It brings only the smallest comfort and is marred by the constant taste of dirt.

A shadow suddenly falls over you, and you look up to see Auda silhouetted against the sun. The legendary bandit is wild-eyed with the thrill of battle as he extends a hand that helps to bring you back to your feet. He grins and asks, 'Well, how is it with the Howeitat?' He refers to his own tribe, who are the wildest of all the Bedouins of the region. He adds a barbed comment, referencing a joke you once made of his fighters: 'All talk and no work?'

You lock eyes with Auda and feel anger bubbling in your veins. He does not seem to understand the gravity of the situation. You are losing the battle and, unless you can turn the tide, then all will be lost.

You have mere seconds to decide how to respond. You could reason with Auda, explaining the situation and devising a plan to move forward and destroy the Turks before reinforcements arrive. You hope that Auda will see the logic of your argument. The chieftain is a grizzled veteran who understands what it takes to win a battle. Yet you are also aware that he is a born brigand and not a professional soldier. He and his men prize plunder and will not risk their lives without good reason. Military logic may not be enough to appeal to this mindset.

Alternatively, you could provoke Auda. The Howeitat are an intensely proud people, and a carefully calculated insult might sting the warlord into action. Yet this is a grave gamble, for Auda has a terrifying temper and kills those who insult him without hesitation. He claims to have personally slain seventy-five Arabs and perhaps even more Turks, although he does not keep count of the latter. If you push him too far, he may well add you to the list – and even if you avoid this violent end, he might punish you by withdrawing his warriors and leaving you to your fate.

The fate of the entire Arab Revolt depends on what you say next.

AIDE-MEMOIRE

* Your forces have been fighting the Turkish garrison for several hours and casualties are mounting. You must do something to turn the tide of battle.
* Turkish reinforcements are at Ma'an to the north. They will soon hear the battle and come to investigate. If this happens, you will be encircled and wiped out.

* You need a renewed effort from your warriors. If they can make one last attempt to close with the enemy, then it might be enough to break the stubborn Turkish resistance.
* Auda is a hardened warrior with a sound grasp of military tactics. You can reason with him and he will surely understand your logic for launching a fresh attack.
* He is also a born brigand. He will not risk his fighters in a doomed cause and may put self-preservation above your own objectives.
* Auda is fiercely proud of the Howeitat and will defend their honour at all costs. A carefully worded insult could provoke him to unleash the full fury of his warriors.
* Angering Auda is extremely dangerous. He will kill without hesitation, and his loyalty to you may not be strong enough to stay his hand.

THE DECISION

Do you reason with Auda or do you provoke him?

▶ If you wish to carefully explain the situation prior to planning a renewed attack, go to **Section 7** (p. 294).

OR

▶ If you would rather try and goad Auda into action, go to **Section 4** (p. 282).

SECTION 4
DEATH OR GLORY

1 p.m., 2 July 1917, Abu el Lissal

'Well, how is it with the Howeitat? All talk and no work?'

Lawrence's tanned face is lined with rage. He lifts his chin in an arrogant pose and snarls, 'By God, indeed, they shoot a lot and hit little.'

Your smile vanishes in a flash, replaced by a white-hot anger that pours into your veins like lava and makes you shake with volcanic fury. Your hand flies to the hilt of the curved dagger that you wear on your belt, and you picture yourself slicing open this impudent Englishman's throat. Lawrence shows no fear and glares at you with contempt. He is insulting not merely you, but your entire people. It is not enough to kill this man. No, you must prove him wrong!

You unclench the hilt of your dagger and instead tear off your red headdress and hurl it to the ground at Lawrence's feet – a mark of your fury, for Bedouin warriors never go uncovered – before turning on your heel and marching up the steep slope, bellowing orders to your warriors. You will show this English whelp how your tribe fights.

You are the legendary desert bandit ***Auda abu Tayi***. You are somewhere between forty and fifty years old, but your exact age is uncertain. Your life has been a saga filled with violent adventures, and your body is covered in a constellation of battle scars. You are hot-headed, ruthless and delight in seizing plunder. Yet you are also a staunch supporter of the Arab Revolt and, as a mark of loyalty to the cause, you have ripped out your false teeth because they were fitted by Ottoman dentists.

You crest the ridge and scowl at the defiant Ottoman battalion in the valley. Your appearance draws renewed fire from the Turks, but you ignore the bullets that whistle past your head and ricochet from nearby boulders as you order your warriors to prepare themselves for a cavalry charge. Lawrence struggles up the slope in your wake and you growl at him, 'Get your camel, if you wish to see the old man's work.' Lawrence nods and runs towards where his mount is tethered, calling for riders to join him.

7. Auda abu Tayi

After a final contemptuous look at the Turks in the valley, you march back down the incline and join your warriors, who are readying their horses. You swing yourself into the saddle of your magnificent Arabian charger and draw your wickedly sharp scimitar. This is no time for the words or speeches favoured by Lawrence. Instead you hold the blade aloft, admiring how the sun reflects from its surface, before lowering your sword and pointing towards the crest. You spur your horse forward, and fifty of your warriors form up alongside you. They are the bravest of your tribe and ride the fastest horses of any man in the Arab Revolt. You know that they will need all their speed and courage to survive the charge that you are about to launch – yet the honour of the Howeitat demands it. Within a few moments your cavalry has formed a fighting line around you. Your men draw their swords and wait for your signal. Their horses shift nervously and toss their heads. The tension is electric. Then, after what seems like an age, you give a blood-curdling yell, rake back your spurs and lead your wild riders over the crest and into the valley.

Your mare surges ahead as you thunder down the slope towards the stunned defenders. You ride high in the saddle, swinging your scimitar above your head and howling an ululating war cry. Bullets shriek all around you, ripping through your robes, blowing away your pistol holster, shattering the binoculars that you wear around your neck and blasting a hole in your sword scabbard. Yet somehow you ride through this maelstrom unscathed, protected by the speed of your charge and the dust kicked up by the pounding hooves of your cavalry. Your horse thunders onwards, and within seconds you are so close to the Turkish line that you can clearly see the faces of individual soldiers, their mouths open in fear as you bear down upon them with all your primal fury.

Suddenly a bullet tears through your mare's chest, killing her instantly and catapulting you from your saddle. You hit the ground hard and are nearly trampled by your riders as they charge past you and crash into the enemy. After taking a few seconds to clear your head, you scramble to your feet and rush forward to join a merciless melee between the Ottoman infantry and your cavalry. You are in your element as horses rear, rifles roar and men scream. A Turkish soldier lunges at you with a bayonet, but you turn aside his clumsy thrust and deliver a vicious riposte with your scimitar, which sends him staggering away, blood pouring from his face.

Amidst the din of battle you suddenly hear the thunder of hooves. Sweeping in from the Turkish flank comes Lawrence, riding at the head of a mass of camel-riders shrieking blood-curdling war cries and firing from the saddle. Attacked from two sides and shocked by the ferocity of the assault, the Turkish defence splinters like rotten wood. The enemy's formation collapses as their soldiers turn and flee from your onslaught. But there is no escape. The battle degenerates into a slaughter as Arab riders whoop hunting yells and pursue the terrified fugitives. Within minutes the Turkish battalion has been annihilated.

Clutching your blood-stained scimitar, you stride through the wreckage of the battlefield until you find Lawrence. Your body shakes with adrenaline and you are almost incoherent as you spit at him, 'Work, work, where are words?' Lawrence merely returns an enigmatic smile and congratulates you on your victory. The Battle of Abu el Lissal has opened the road to Aqaba.

AFTERMATH

A handful of Turkish riders managed to escape the destruction at Abu el Lissal and brought news of the disaster to Ma'an. The garrison commander was terrified that the Arabs would soon descend on the town and abandoned the position in a panic. He retreated north to await reinforcements and would pose no further threat to the campaign.

All that now stood between the Arabs and their prize was a series of garrisons that guarded the passes between Aqaba and the interior. These fortresses had been built with the expectation that any attack would come from the direction of the sea and they offered no protection against an assault that came overland. On 4 July Arab fighters swarmed up precipitous cliffs to attack the Turkish fort at Kethiria under the cover of a lunar eclipse, capturing the entire garrison without suffering a single casualty. News of this victory soon spread, and the Turks abandoned their useless defences to make a final stand at Khadram, a heavily entrenched strongpoint that overlooked Aqaba. But this position was equally vulnerable to an attack from behind. After several days of skirmishing and tense negotiations, Lawrence persuaded the garrison commander to surrender in order to spare his men the fury of an Arab assault where no mercy would be given or expected.

On 6 July Aqaba fell into Arab hands. Lawrence led a horde of gleeful warriors through the streets of the town and plunged into the surf to celebrate the victory. Rifles were fired into the air, and wild whoops echoed throughout the small port long into the night. Lawrence's daring gamble had paid off. His force had marched across 600 miles of trackless terrain, inflicted thousands of casualties upon the enemy and captured a position that was once thought impregnable. The Arab Revolt was now poised to begin an advance into Syria towards the ultimate prize of Damascus.

THE DECISION

▶ To follow the alternative route, go back to **Section 3** (p. 276).

OR

▶ To explore the decisions of the campaign, go to the **Historical Note** on p. 298.

SECTION 5
THE ARABIAN NIGHTMARE

11 May 1918, outskirts of Mecca

Dusk is descending and the battlefield has become eerily quiet. Sporadic gunfire still echoes in the distance as fugitives are pursued and the wounded are finished off by Abdul Aziz ibn Saud's merciless warriors. The Battle of Mecca has ended in a decisive victory for Ibn Saud's army. The enemy was not the Ottomans, but the forces of the Sharif of Mecca, Hussein bin Ali. The Sharif's army has been destroyed and amongst the dead lie his sons, Faisal and Abdullah.

8. Ronald Storrs

You look upon the battlefield with a grim face and a heavy heart. Figures move in the shadows as Ibn Saud's fighters search for plunder. Wounded men groan with pain and try and drag themselves to safety. A riderless camel limps past your observation post, its colourful saddle dark with blood, and disappears into the evening gloom.

You are ***Ronald Storrs***, an experienced politician from the British government of Egypt, a leading member of the Arab Bureau and one of the finest minds of your generation. T. E. Lawrence describes you as 'the most brilliant Englishman in the Near East' and your understanding of the subtleties of Arab politics has served you well throughout your career. You have a deep admiration for Egyptian and Arab culture and once had dreams of unifying Egypt and the Arab territories into a new post-war empire.

Yet now all you have worked for lies in ruins. In 1916 you had accepted the recommendations of your colleagues to support the zealous Ibn Saud instead of the politically astute Hussein. The Indian government was delighted at the decision and readily sent equipment, advisors and gold to support Ibn Saud's war effort. Yet problems soon emerged. Arab Bureau intelligence showed that Ibn Saud's forces were massing in the west and probing into the lands claimed by Hussein, rather than concentrating against the Ottoman Empire. Ibn Saud made no attempt to conceal his intentions, insisting that Hussein was a coward, a fraud and an Ottoman puppet who had to be dethroned before any war against the Turks could begin.

The Arab Bureau realised it had made a serious error in supporting Ibn Saud, but by then it was too late. The Indian government had provided his army with rifles, machine guns and explosives. The weapons, combined with his men's fanaticism and iron discipline, meant that Ibn Saud's force was more than a match for Hussein's poorly armed tribal militia.

Mounting alarm in Cairo saw you despatched as an advisor to Ibn Saud's army in early 1917 with urgent instructions to dissuade him from attacking Hussein's army. You arrived to find the warlord in high spirits and bursting with confidence. The Indian government had given him all the tools he needed to crush his rivals and create an empire that stretched from the Red Sea to the Persian Gulf. You deployed all your diplomatic wiles to try and convince him to focus on the Ottoman enemy, but he brushed aside your arguments, assuring you that they would feel his wrath after he had dealt with Hussein. Your increasingly desperate messages to Cairo and Delhi had no effect on policy. The British government had lost interest in the Arab Revolt, and the Indian government cared nothing for Hussein so long as Ibn Saud contributed to their campaign.

Abandoned by the British and facing a dangerous enemy, Hussein had no choice but to appeal to the Ottomans for aid. The Turks provided weapons and ammunition via the Hejaz Railway, with Hussein's forces providing escorts for the trains to prevent them being preyed upon by bandits. A strange proxy war raged in Arabia as the British and Ottomans supported rival Arab leaders.

By mid-1917 Ibn Saud's army was ready to begin its invasion. His heavily armed and well-organised forces crushed Hussein's courageous but disparate tribal fighters and within six months they were at the gates of Mecca, where the Sharif planned to make a final stand. Using all his religious and political authority, Hussein drew together a large but ill-disciplined army of fighters in a final attempt to turn the tide. You observed the Battle of Mecca from an observation post in Ibn Saud's army's lines. Hussein's warriors fought bravely, and you watched with awe as his men charged on camel-back into the teeth of withering rifle and machine-gun fire. Yet it was all for naught. Ibn Saud's army was too powerful and too well organised. The result was inevitable, and Hussein's army was destroyed in a hail of bullets and shells.

AFTERMATH

Ibn Saud's spectacular victory at the Battle of Mecca caused alarm amongst even the most complacent British and Indian civil servants. After eighteen months of military and financial aid, Ibn Saud had done much to secure his own position, but little to take the fight to the Ottoman Empire. Having taken Mecca, his forces gradually inched north towards Medina, but showed noticeably less enthusiasm for attacking the Turkish garrison there than they had done for fighting Arabs. There was even some skirmishing between British and Arab forces around the Red Sea coast, as the Royal Navy hastily secured ports that might threaten trade passing through the Suez Canal.

Unlike Hussein, Ibn Saud had little interest in expanding the revolt further north. He concentrated on consolidating his power in his vast new kingdom of Saudi Arabia. The lack of threat from the Arab Revolt enabled the Ottomans to concentrate their forces against the British on the heavily fortified Gaza line. The Egyptian Expeditionary Force launched three great frontal attacks on this position in 1917, but each was repulsed with heavy casualties. Further offensives were planned for 1918, but the looming threat of a massive German offensive on the Western Front meant that troops were diverted from Egypt to strengthen the defences in Europe. The Middle East became locked into a permanent stalemate.

The defeat of Germany and Austria–Hungary brought the war in the Middle East to an end. The Ottoman army still held the Gaza line and although the empire was much reduced – Ibn Saud now ruled in Arabia, and an Anglo-Indian army had secured Baghdad – it had somehow survived. British and French ambitions in the region were unfulfilled. The British secured a protectorate in Iraq and took direct control of the Red Sea ports, but the French had to settle for nothing more than preferential trading rights in Syria. Elsewhere the concept of a Jewish homeland, promised by the Balfour Declaration of 2 November 1917, was quietly dropped by the British and French governments. Against the odds, the 'sick of man of Europe' still drew breath. The Ottoman Empire would endure for decades to come.

THE DECISION

▶ To follow the alternative route, go back to **Section 1** (p. 262).

OR

▶ To explore the decisions of the campaign, go to the **Historical Note** on p. 298.

SECTION 6
A FADING FLAME

17 April 1917, Hejaz Railway, north of Medina

The Turkish scouting party inches its way forward along the railway. You can tell these men are veterans by the way they move, and you suspect they have travelled this frequently-attacked route many times before. Your entire body is electric with tension as they pass over the part of the tracks where you have laid your explosives. The man leading the party pauses and takes a close look at a small bank of sand, crouching in the dust to check whether it shows the telltale wires that lead to a detonator. After what seems like an age he stands, satisfied, and motions for his squad to move on. You allow yourself a long exhalation: they have not spotted your trap.

Several minutes later an Ottoman train comes creeping into view. Its engine is reinforced with armour plating and there are machine-gun nests atop its carriages. Yet none of this will protect it from your explosives. The engine rumbles forward and, as it passes above your bomb, you slam down the plunger on your detonator. A huge plume of flame erupts from the desert with an ear-splitting roar. The armoured engine is torn from the tracks, landing on its side amidst the sand as if it had been a toy picked up and tossed aside by a bored child. The remainder of the train buckles, the carriages crashing into one another in a maelstrom of flying wreckage and screeching metal. Several of the rooftop machine-gunners are hurled from their nests and fall, screaming, beneath the twisting carriages.

Your fighters open fire seconds later. The remaining rooftop machine-gunners are mown down before they can fire a single shot. Bullets hammer the train, blasting through gaps in the wrecked armour plate and scything through the surviving Ottoman soldiers who try to deploy from the carriages. The battle – if it can be called that – is over within minutes.

9. Abdullah bin Hussein

You are ***Abdullah bin Hussein***, the thirty-three-year-old second son of the Sharif of Mecca, Hussein bin Ali. Your younger brother Faisal is the military leader of the Arab Revolt, but you are only nominally under his control and command your own force. Although you were instrumental in persuading your father to ally with the British and begin the Arab Revolt, you dislike and distrust T. E. Lawrence, whom you feel has far too much influence over Faisal. You prefer to fight your own campaign, free from Lawrence's unsolicited advice.

The firing dies down and is soon replaced by wild whoops as your fighters burst from cover to plunder the wreckage. You make no move to restrain them. Loot is an important motivation for your men, and you will not deny them their rewards.

You slowly follow your men towards the ambush site. This is the second train you have derailed this month. The Hejaz Railway is permanently besieged and neither the Turks nor their German allies seem to have an answer to your guerrilla tactics. Standing atop a rise, you lift your binoculars and look further down the railway, where you can see the figures of the Turkish scouting party hurrying away. They have failed in their duty, but will live to fight another day. But for now, you and your men will enjoy the spoils of war.

AFTERMATH

The campaign against the Hejaz Railway raged throughout 1917. Several Ottoman trains were derailed and the line was frequently sabotaged. The Turks responded by fortifying their trains with armour and machine guns and providing cavalry escorts who could chase away Arab raiders.

The campaign tied down significant Ottoman resources, but its effectiveness was beginning to wane by the latter part of the year. Turkish tactics gradually improved, and their anti-guerrilla sweeps inflicted some stinging losses on Arab forces. There was a significant casualty in November 1917 when T. E. Lawrence vanished during a scouting mission near Deera in Syria. His exact fate remains unknown, but it is believed he was captured by Ottoman soldiers and died trying to escape.

Worse still, the fire that sustained the Arab Revolt was slowly beginning to fade. The Arab army was always a fractious coalition, held together by a combination of Hussein's authority, Faisal's diplomacy, British gold, Ottoman loot and regular doses of battlefield victory. But by the winter of 1917 the latter was in increasingly short supply. The army had not advanced an inch since the capture of Wejh in January and the campaign against the railway was losing momentum. Successful attacks on trains became rarer, whilst bitter skirmishes with Ottoman patrols were ever more common. The Ottomans exploited the darkening mood by offering generous bribes to wavering fighters and encouraging them to abandon the cause.

By early 1918 the Arab army had begun melting away as it became apparent that there would be no great advance into Syria. Some fighters drifted from the cause and returned to their homelands, others resumed long-simmering blood feuds with one another, and a handful even defected to the Ottomans. Faisal struggled to hold his forces together and was increasingly reliant on British gold to secure the loyalty of his tribal chiefs.

The war ended with a much-weakened Arab army still based around Wejh, just as it had been in early 1917. Its failure to advance meant that Faisal's dreams of a pan-Arab state lay in the dust. The British and French divided up the Middle East according to the terms of the Sykes–Picot agreement of January 1916 and left Hussein and his sons to rule over the small Kingdom of Hejaz. The new states of Transjordan, Iraq and Syria were ruled by the British and French, using malleable puppet kings. The men who had fought in the revolt were left with nothing to show for it.

THE DECISION

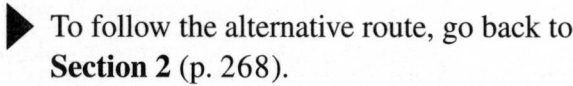

- To follow the alternative route, go back to **Section 2** (p. 268).

OR

- To explore the decisions of the campaign, go to the **Historical Note** on p. 298.

SECTION 7
LAST GASP

2 p.m, 2 July 1917, Abu el Lissal

The crackle of gunfire rumbles in the distance and the sun presses its scorching weight against your skull. Auda grins at you, clearly amused by his own wit. An uncomfortable silence fills the void between you, and the warlord's expression begins to change. But you swallow your anger with a deep breath and take a few seconds to compose yourself. There is a battle to be won and it is no use enraging your most important ally.

You are ***Captain T. E. Lawrence*** and you are unwilling to admit defeat. Despite a complete lack of formal military training, you are a keen student of military history and have an intuitive knack for leadership. Now is the time to put those skills to use and turn the battle in your favour.

10. Lawrence astride a camel

You force yourself to chuckle at Auda's quip and the tension between you immediately evaporates. Stepping away from the muddy stream, you gesture for him to join you as you crouch down and sketch out the current battlefield, making lines in the sand and placing stones. Your crude map shows the situation. The Ottoman battalion in the valley is pinned down by your sharpshooters atop the ridge. But the Turks are well armed with machine guns and artillery, and your fighters cannot advance on them without drawing withering fire. The result is a stalemate. Ammunition is running out, as is your time, for every minute wasted raises the chance that reinforcements will arrive from the garrison at Ma'an.

The key is the high ground. Your finger traces a line indicating the ridge where Auda has positioned his marksmen. You need the Howeitat to redouble their efforts to pin down the defenders in the valley. With Turks focused on the firefight, they will not see your flank attack until it is too late. Speed will be of the essence, and so you will lead a flood of camel-riders who will plunge down the steep ridge and crash into the enemy. As you reach the finale of your plan, you lock eyes with Auda and, with a sweep of your hand, you scatter the pebbles that indicate the enemy battalion. Auda grins and nods. He promises you that there will be no Turks left standing once his men open fire.

Auda strides back to the firing line, bellowing his orders, whilst you prepare for the charge. You gather your riders together and brief them on the plan, before climbing into the saddle of Namaa, your magnificent racing camel. Using the dead ground behind the ridge for cover, you move the camels into position. Once all is in place, you fire a flare gun into the air as a signal to Auda to provide covering fire. Moments later you hear the crackle of rifles as the Howeitat warriors play their part. Now is the time.

With a yell, you drive Namaa forward and burst over the ridge at the head of your riders. The slope is steep and the speed of your descent momentarily catches your breath in your lungs. As your camel hits the flat ground, you can see Turkish officers frantically gesturing for their men to turn and engage the new threat. Bullets begin to whip past your head and you return fire with your revolver. A rider to your left is hit and falls in a whirlwind of dust and flailing limbs. The thunder of hooves reverberates through your body, whilst your ears are filled with the roar of gunfire and the ululating cries of your fighters.

You can see a Turkish machine-gun crew working feverishly to swing their weapon round to bear, before it is too late. You urge Namaa onwards and the racing camel responds, her long neck almost

11. A standard bearer leads Arab fighters into battle

horizontal as she sprints over the sand. You charge directly at the machine gun, roaring your defiance, with your revolver firing again and again. You are within a few paces of the gun when it suddenly opens fire. At this range it simply cannot miss. Bullets punch through your chest and send you reeling drunkenly in your saddle. Namaa shudders as her flesh is shredded by a dozen rounds and she crashes to the ground with an agonised groan. You are sent somersaulting and land flat on your back. The stunning impact briefly numbs the agony that fills your chest. You lift your head and look down to see that your white robes are painted red with blood. Even this small effort leaves you exhausted. Your head sinks back to the ground and your breath comes in shallow, painful gasps. Despite the intense heat of the day, you suddenly feel terribly cold. You are dimly aware of the cacophony of battle around you before your world fades into silent darkness.

AFTERMATH

Lawrence's charge at Abu el Lissal turned the tide of battle. The weary Turks were surprised and were swept away by the sheer ferocity of the assault. With their formation shattered, the Ottoman battalion was run down and wiped out before it could escape from the battlefield.

But the victory came at a terrible cost. Lawrence's death left his fighters heartbroken and his army leaderless. Auda stepped into the breach as a replacement, but he lacked Lawrence's calm authority and strategic vision. The old bandit struggled to control his dispirited and increasingly fractious force. Auda's lieutenants questioned the value of Aqaba, which to them was a small and insignificant port, and urged him to turn north and loot the prosperous town of Ma'an instead.

Auda could not resist this temptation. He abandoned Lawrence's plan and marched north in search of plunder. The Arab force arrived at Ma'an to find that the Turkish garrison had retreated, leaving the town undefended. Auda and his warriors gleefully ransacked the area, carrying off supplies, gold, tapestries, carpets and furniture.

But the sacking of Ma'an was a fatal mistake. The Turks had retreated, but they had not gone far and were swiftly reinforced. The reinvigorated Ottomans launched a sudden counter-attack whilst the Arabs were busy plundering. Auda was caught unawares, struggling to rally his scattered men to mount an effective defence. A short, one-sided battle followed, before the Arabs were routed from the town with heavy casualties. Turkish cavalry pursued the fugitives and extracted vengeance for the defeat at Abu el Lissal. Auda perished in the maelstrom and his small army was broken.

The Turks understood how close the Arabs had come to capturing Aqaba and reorganised the garrisons that defended the passes, rebuilding their fortifications to provide protection from the landward side. The gateway to Aqaba was locked and the Arab Revolt would go no further than Wejh.

Faisal would continue his campaign against the Hejaz Railway, but the loss of Lawrence and his inability to advance north sapped the morale of his army. The Arab Revolt would steadily lose its momentum to the point where it had ceased to play a useful military role by 1918. Lawrence's dreams of leading the Arab army into Damascus died with him.

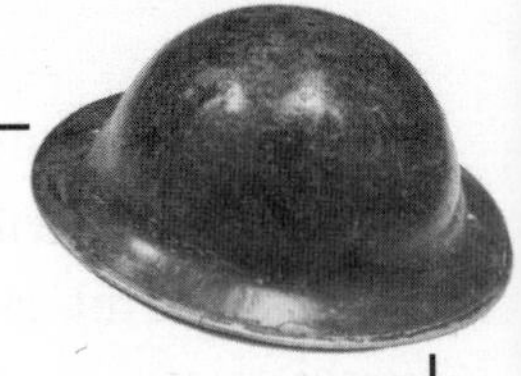

THE DECISION

▶ To follow the alternative route, go back to **Section 3** (p. 276).

OR

▶ To explore the decisions of the campaign, see the **Historical Note** below.

HISTORICAL NOTE

T. E. Lawrence remains a controversial and fascinating figure. His life has been the subject of dozens of books, articles and documentaries, but it is David Lean's epic 1962 film *Lawrence of Arabia* that immortalised him for a global audience. This chapter gives you the opportunity to explore some of the most important decisions involving Lawrence and the initial stages of the Arab Revolt.

The route begins in the Arab Bureau in Cairo. This peculiar organisation brought together a team of academics, explorers and civil servants, which operated like a modern think tank. Historically, the Arab Bureau immediately recognised the risks of backing Ibn Saud and his religious zealots and argued forcefully that the British should support Sharif Hussein (Section 1 to Section 2). The Arab Revolt began on 10 June 1916 when Hussein fired a single symbolic shot towards the Turkish garrison in Mecca. Mecca soon fell to the revolutionaries, but the Turkish garrison in Medina held out under a prolonged siege and would not surrender until after the war had ended. Worse still, Ottoman reinforcements inflicted heavy defeats upon the Arabs. The British were forced to commit increased resources to keep the revolt alive, including the despatch of T. E. Lawrence to serve as an advisor.

Lawrence's arrival changed the nature of the Arab Revolt. He forged a friendship with Faisal that served both men well. Faisal's political acumen and Lawrence's military brilliance reinvigorated the Arab war effort. Both men harboured dreams of a pan-Arab revolt that would stretch to Syria, but to achieve this the army would have to advance against the impregnable port of Aqaba. Historically, Faisal approved Lawrence's audacious plan to attack the town from its landward side (Section 2 to Section 3). This then leads to the final decision at the Battle of Abu el Lissal on 2 July 1917. This engagement was the turning point of the entire campaign. Facing defeat and desperate to crush the Turks before reinforcements arrived, Lawrence deliberately insulted Auda to provoke him into action (Section 3 to Section 4). The gamble paid off, and the Turkish battalion was crushed by Auda's cavalry and Lawrence's camel-riders.

Lawrence almost perished in the battle when he accidentally shot his camel in the head whilst firing from the saddle. He was hurled to the ground, knocked unconscious and was lucky to avoid being trampled to death as the remaining riders rushed past him. Nevertheless, the victory was decisive. Lawrence and his men had crossed 600 miles of wilderness, won a pitched battle and opened the road to Aqaba. The capture of the port enabled the Arab army to join hands with the Egyptian Expeditionary Force and advance into Syria in 1918.

But what if the Arab Bureau had decided to support Ibn Saud instead of Hussein? This would have been a disastrous choice. Ibn Saud despised his Arab rivals and was more interested in crushing them than fighting the Ottomans. Historically, Ibn Saud and Hussein's forces began skirmishing as early as July 1918 and would engage in full-scale war in 1919. British attempts to end the conflict were only temporarily successful, and a renewed war in 1924–5 ended in the conquest of Mecca and complete victory for Ibn Saud. In the alternative history, Ibn Saud, backed by the British and Indian governments, carries out this conquest much sooner (Section 1 to Section 5). The consequences for the British would have been severe. Without the Arab Revolt threatening their southern flank, the Ottomans would have been able to concentrate their forces on the Gaza line and hold it throughout 1917. Had this happened, then the Ottoman Empire might well have survived the war, albeit in a much-weakened state.

Another alternative is to concentrate on attacking the Hejaz Railway rather than approving Lawrence's expedition to Aqaba (Section 2 to Section 6). Faisal was a naturally cautious commander and the temptation to focus on the guerrilla campaign must have been great. This would have produced short-term success but guaranteed long-term failure. The Arab Revolt needed to win victories and advance to sustain its momentum. Without this, even a skilled diplomat such as Faisal would have struggled to hold the army together. By 1918 the revolt would have sunk to a low ebb.

The final alternative is to take a different approach at the Battle of Abu el Lissal. (Section 3 to Section 7). In this scenario Lawrence draws up a new plan and leads the camel charge whilst Auda provides covering fire. The attack succeeds, but costs Lawrence his life. This leads to a disastrous decision in the aftermath of the battle. Historically, Lawrence had to argue forcefully with Auda to continue the advance on Aqaba after the victory, rather than plundering the wealthy town of Ma'an. But with Lawrence dead, the Arab force would have been drawn towards Ma'an like a moth to a flame. Ransacking the town would have been a grave mistake. The Turks were nearby and would have been able to launch a fierce counter-attack that would have scattered the Arabs to the four winds and ended the campaign.

Gertrude Bell continued her work in the Middle East and was pivotal in the creation of the state of Iraq. From 1921 onwards she served as an advisor to King Faisal I and helped to create the National Library of Iraq and the Baghdad Archaeological Museum. She died of a sleeping-tablet overdose in 1926. It remains unclear whether this was an accident or suicide.

Faisal ibn Hussein served as the effective military commander of the Arab Revolt to the end of the war. He was proclaimed King of Syria in March 1920, but was swiftly deposed by the French. In August 1921 the British selected him to become Faisal I, the first King of Iraq. He reigned until his death in 1933.

T. E. Lawrence fought alongside Arab forces throughout the war. Victory brought him no comfort and he was bitterly disillusioned with the British and French betrayal of the Arab cause. He published his epic memoir *Seven Pillars of Wisdom* in 1926, but otherwise withdrew from the public eye, serving in various mundane roles in the Royal Air Force. He died in a motorcycle accident in 1935.

Auda abu Tayi led his warriors for the remainder of the struggle and rode into Damascus in October 1918. After the war he returned to Ma'an and constructed a magnificent palace nearby, paid for by wartime loot and built by Turkish prisoners of war. After a life of wild adventures, he finally died of natural causes in 1924.

Ronald Storrs became Governor of Jerusalem in December 1917 and served in this role until 1926. He struggled to manage the growing tension between Jews and Arabs and earned the hostility of both sides, despite his best efforts. He later served as Governor of Cyprus and Governor of Northern Rhodesia. He died in 1955.

Abdullah bin Hussein fought in the Arab Revolt throughout the war. He was offered the chance to become King of Iraq in March 1920, but declined the role. In 1921 he became Emir of Transjordan, and he became King Abdullah I in 1946 when Transjordan became independent. He was assassinated in 1951 by a Palestinian who was enraged by rumours that Jordan was considering making a peace deal with Israel.

7

THE ZIMMERMANN TELEGRAM:

AMERICA JOINS THE WAR, 1917

SECTION 1
CAPTAIN HALL'S DILEMMA

Wednesday 17 January 1917, Admiralty, Whitehall, London

The third winter of the Great War has been bitterly cold and much of England has recently been shrouded in snow. The inclement weather matches the mood in London as David Lloyd George's new regime comes to terms with the heavy losses suffered in the Somme Campaign, a battle that ground to a halt just a few weeks ago. The French army is exhausted and the news from Russia is less than encouraging. In contrast, the war at sea has settled somewhat and, with the German High Seas Fleet bottled up in port after the Battle of Jutland last summer, the Royal Navy has focused on holding back the menace of the enemy's U-boat fleet. For the moment the enemy's cautious tactics appear to be lending the British the upper hand.

Yet in one part of the Admiralty this morning there is a new mood of frantic activity, high anxiety and shock. Room 40, located on the first floor of the Admiralty Building in Whitehall, is the nerve centre of the navy's cryptanalysis and code-breaking operation, home to some thirty highly educated upper-middle-class academics who appear to specialise in public-school banter, peculiar affectations in garb and puerile nicknames, such as Woolly, Biffy and Barmy. Founded in the first autumn of the war, the team in Room 40 (which is actually now a collection of offices) has worked hard to make sense of the encrypted and coded German radio messages intercepted by British listening stations. There is of course no way to stop someone listening to transmitted radio messages, so encrypting and encoding them is vital to maintaining secure communications; the enemy might be able to hear the messages, but if they are securely coded and enciphered, they should not be able to make head nor tail of them. Room 40's job has nonetheless been to attempt to decipher the intercepted German messages, make sense of them and thus provide vital intelligence about enemy activity to the British military leadership and the government. Now it seems they are to play an even more crucial role in the development of the war.

You are ***Captain Reginald Hall***, the small but still imposing and charismatic Director of the Intelligence Division (DID) at the Admiralty. Though somewhat physically idiosyncratic and with an irksome tendency to blink and twitch 'like a Navy signal lamp', particularly when excited* – precipitating your sobriquet of 'Blinker' – you are highly regarded, and indeed feared, as a shrewd and ruthless operator. Your icy stare and steely, combative interrogative style are crucial assets, but your grip and leadership skills are most keenly felt; an 'admirable chief to work for', who keeps everything running efficiently and smoothly.

You have previously held command positions at sea, but poor health forced you to a desk job, perhaps fortuitously so, as your last command, the battlecruiser HMS *Queen Mary*, had exploded catastrophically with near-total loss of all hands at the Battle of Jutland. Since November 1914 you have been based at the Admiralty in London, responsible for the activities of Room 40. Over the course of the war you and your team have developed a network of intelligence sources, dramatically improved interception and deciphering capability, and have scored a range of notable successes in supporting Britain's

1. William Reginald Hall

* Probably a mild form of dyspraxia.

war effort. Now you guard your power jealously; information is true power in this context.

One of your department's greatest achievements has been the interception and deciphering of German diplomatic messages, a considerable intelligence coup. When the war broke out, the British had severed Germany's ability to send messages via the transatlantic undersea cables to its various embassies in the Americas, so the Germans had to use other methods, including long-range radio transmissions or employing a route through neutral Sweden. Washington also allowed the Germans to send a limited number of messages via their own diplomatic cable route across the Atlantic via London, even allowing them to be enciphered. Unfortunately for Berlin, all of these routes have been compromised and the British have been able to listen in. You have also developed the ability to break many of the codes and ciphers used by the Germans, and thus by early 1917 Room 40 is regularly reading messages passing across the Atlantic by whatever route.

This is not without great risk, however. In order to intercept German messages passing along the Americans' transatlantic route,

2. Room 40, Admiralty Building, Whitehall

your intelligence-gathering team has had to break into American diplomatic traffic and has been reading it also (US codes were childishly easy to break). Naturally, if Washington ever found out what the British are up to, there would be an almighty international incident. As useful as the intelligence is, the source has to be kept a closely guarded secret.

3. Nigel de Grey

On this cold Wednesday morning in January you arrived at your office in the Admiralty and, as usual, spent the first part of the day assessing the overnight dockets and messages with your assistant, Claud Serocold. In the late morning one of your key cryptanalysts, Nigel de Grey, a rather shy thirty-one-year-old publisher seconded from Heinemann, known to his colleagues as 'The Dormouse', bursts into your office in a state of high excitement. 'D.I.D,' he asks you, 'do you want to bring America into the war?' The USA has remained stubbornly neutral since the outbreak and of course it would be a great fillip to the Allies if the Americans could be persuaded to declare war on Germany, but how?

Maybe de Grey now has the answer? He tells you that he and another of your cryptanalysts, Dilly Knox, have been working on a new overnight intercept of a German diplomatic message sent via the American cable route through London by Arthur Zimmermann, the German Foreign Minister, to the German Ambassador in Washington, Johann von Bernstorff. De Grey passes you the translation. It is not yet complete, but the meaning is clear enough.

This astounding transcript that you have been handed has two crucial pieces of information that could alter the course of the war. First, it seems as though the Germans are going to launch a new escalated U-boat campaign against all shipping entering British waters – a strategy certain to bring them into further conflict with Washington, as

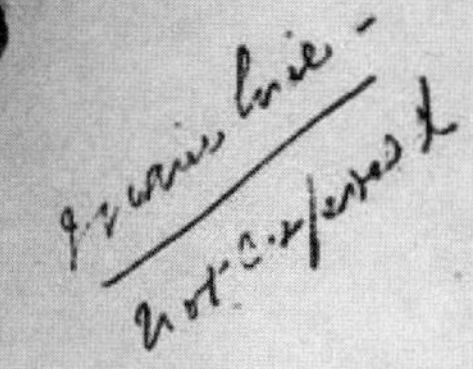

W. 158
16th Jan. 1917

Most secret for Your Excellency's personal information and to be handed on to the Imperial Minister in ? Mexico with......by a safe route.

Tel. No. 1.

We propose to begin on the 1st February unrestricted submarine warfare. In doing so however we shall endeavour to keep America neutral .....? If we should not (succeed in doing so) we propose to (Mexico) an alliance upon the following basis.

(joint) conduct of the war

(joint) conclusion of peace

Your Excellency should for the present inform the President secretly (that we expect) war with the U.S.A. (possibly)(......Japan) and at the same time to negotiate between us and Japan.....

(Incomprehensible sentence meaning please tell the President) that.....our submarines.....will compel England to peace in a few months. Acknowledge receipt.

Document 1: First decrypt of the Zimmermann Telegram

such tactics will threaten to bring about yet more American loss of life and hinder US merchant shipping. To mitigate this (and the second piece of information de Grey has brought you) is a proposal from Zimmermann that, if the Americans become belligerent, Mexico, and possibly Japan, should join Germany in any war against America. Both nations have fractious relationships with the USA, and clearly such an alliance would threaten the Americans directly and thus distract them from helping the British and French in Europe. It seems outrageous. Can it be true?

The cable decrypted by de Grey and Knox is almost certainly reliable. Room 40 has built up enough information about German and American encryption and coding methods over the last three years to provide excellent and robust intelligence. The British have been decrypting American diplomatic messages since the spring of 1915, so that much was a matter of routine. As the Germans used numerical-code groups rather than letter codes, as preferred by the USA, it had also been easy to spot the German message embedded in the cable sent from the American embassy in London. The German message consists of a thousand numerical-code groups, employing a system that has been in use since the autumn of 1916 and known in Room 40 as '7500'. Although your team has only partially broken into 7500, they know enough to provide you with the transcript in front of you, though there is much more work still to be done. Indeed, it appears as though there are two telegrams in the message and de Grey has only cracked part of one of them, but the provisional outline alone is incendiary enough.

But what to do with this information? Clearly it is likely to enrage the Americans, as the idea that the Germans are communicating with Mexico, and possibly Japan, about allying against the USA is provocative in the extreme. Even the diehard pro-German / anti-British isolationists in the Midwest and south of the US would find it difficult to pass this off as unimportant. Along with Germany's stated intention to expand the U-boat war, which would bring it into direct confrontation with Washington, America's entry into the war would now seem highly likely. It would certainly finish President Woodrow Wilson's floundering attempts to negotiate a peace settlement – something you would approve of.

Your standing orders are quite clear – such decrypted messages as the one you have just been handed should be passed on immediately to the Admiralty and the Foreign Office, for them to consider the implications for naval and foreign policy. And yet there is a grave risk attached to using the contents of the telegram: how did you come by it, would be an obvious question from Washington. Naturally, unless the source of the information is then shared, it will lack all credibility; conversely, if the source is shared, the Americans will know that you have been listening in on their diplomatic cables and this will cause no end of trouble. It would also mean that this hugely valuable source of information would be cut off; an end to finding out what both the Americans and the Germans are up to.

Yet if you did pass the message on to the Admiralty and the Foreign Office, they would be able to make appropriate preparations to combat the new U-boat offensive and work with Mexico and Japan to maintain their support. Most obviously, of course, releasing the contents of the telegram might prod Woodrow Wilson's government in Washington off its neutral perch and towards throwing their lot in against Germany. After all, Britain violating diplomatic channels is one thing, but Germany conspiring with Mexico and possibly Japan to make war on the USA is quite another. Surely the Americans would act?

What should you do? Inform the Admiralty and the Foreign Office now or withhold the information and await events?

AIDE-MEMOIRE

* Standing orders dictate that you inform your superiors in the Admiralty and the Foreign Office. It is your duty to do so.
* Can they be trusted not to expose your source? This seems unlikely as they do not truly understand the nature of intelligence-gathering.
* Releasing the telegram will surely blow your source and cause a major diplomatic

row that could undermine the impact of the telegram on American opinion.

* Yet releasing the telegram will surely provoke a major response in the USA. It could well bring them into the war and tip the balance in the Allies' favour.
* When the Germans begin their all-out U-boat offensive in a couple of weeks, it could easily cause Washington to intervene in the war anyway, without blowing your listening operations.
* If you release the telegram too quickly and without other carefully prepared political and diplomatic measures, the response in the USA could be to suspect a plot by the perfidious British to draw the Americans unwillingly into the war.
* Delaying might allow other events in the war to overtake you. Perhaps it is best to act immediately and seize the opportunity?

THE DECISION

Should you release the telegram immediately or hold fire?

▶ If you want to release the telegram, go to **Section 2** (p. 312).

OR

▶ If you do not want to release the telegram, go to **Section 3** (p. 318).

SECTION 2
A DIPLOMATIC INCIDENT

28 January 1917, Foreign Office, London

A fractious, awkward and highly unsatisfactory meeting is under way in Arthur Balfour's office at the Foreign Office in London. The weather is still cold and inclement, with grey clouds overhead and snow still on the ground, but in the meeting, tension is high and temperatures are rising. Balfour is the British Foreign Secretary, recently appointed in the wake of David Lloyd George's arrival in 10 Downing Street in December of the previous year. Balfour is meeting Edward Bell (known by his British friends as Eddie), the Second Secretary of the US embassy in London. The popular and likeable Bell is a well-connected figure in the American diplomatic service, who is good friends with Franklin Roosevelt. Bell is also the main link in the US embassy to the British intelligence services. To Balfour's left sits Captain Hall, the intense and uncompromising intelligence officer from the Admiralty who, just a few days ago, brought an important and potentially decisive piece of intelligence to the Foreign Secretary's attention. He knows Bell very well.

You are ***Charles Hardinge***, a peer of the realm with the title Lord Hardinge of Penshurst and currently Permanent Undersecretary at the Foreign Office (Balfour's most senior advisor). It is a post you had previously held between 1906 and 1910, before your appointment as Viceroy and Governor-General of India. There you had survived assassination attempts, while trying with some success to improve relations with the Indian nationalist movement, even attempting to get along with Gandhi, someone you came to admire. Despite being a natural Conservative, you have served Liberal administrations with great loyalty and returned to the Foreign Office just a few months ago, once again as its most senior civil servant. You are fully aware, however, of the personal costs of the war that your country is waging: your son, Edward, was killed in the fighting in France, aged only twenty-two. Despite this, you remain at heart cool, calm and cautious in matters of state.

The current meeting in which you are engaged had the potential to change the course of the war, but it has not gone as well as Balfour hoped. Hall had approached the Foreign Secretary with some startling intelligence a little over a week ago; it seems as though the Germans are about to launch their dreaded U-boats on international shipping once again, even though this will surely antagonise the Americans. More importantly for foreign relations and, in an effort to limit the effects of possible action from Washington, Germany's Foreign Minister, Arthur Zimmermann, has despatched a secret message to the German Ambassador in Mexico, with the intention of offering the Mexican government a military and financial alliance against the USA. It seems incredible but, if revealed to the world, Zimmermann's telegram could well provoke a belligerent reaction from President Woodrow Wilson's thus far irritatingly neutral administration in Washington.

Yet you have severe reservations about how best to handle the situation and have advised Balfour of your doubts. You have pointed out that the Americans are likely to be deeply suspicious of the telegram; it could well look like a British ruse, to Washington. The only way the telegram's veracity could be demonstrated would be by

4. Charles Hardinge

admitting where it came from, and that the British have been listening in on American diplomatic traffic. Imagine the damage that could do to Anglo-American relations, you pointed out to Balfour, and it would come out just at the moment when you would be hoping to bring the Americans into the war against Germany. You had argued forcefully that this risk was surely too great. Why not wait until you see what the impact of the new aggressive German U-boat campaign might be in Washington? Even Hall has reservations about how to leak the information to the USA.

Balfour saw merit in your arguments, but was deeply concerned that as the startling news was now loose in the Foreign Office and the Admiralty, it was only a matter of time before the Americans found out that the British had prior knowledge of the new U-boat campaign and, more importantly, of the German plan for an anti-American alliance with Mexico and possibly Japan. Balfour believed that notwithstanding the source of the information, Wilson's administration would surely see that the Germans had committed the much graver offence? Balfour, supported by the First Lord of the Admiralty, has therefore summoned Bell to inform him of the telegram.

But it has gone far more negatively than Balfour expected. You glance at the erudite and cool Foreign Secretary; even he now seems ill at ease. Bell has not reacted well to your news. Frowning, he enquires as to the source of the intelligence. At first Balfour and Hall are evasive. Bell is a good Anglophile, more than willing to do whatever he can to get the USA into the war against Germany; but without clear corroboration or provocation, Washington – and indeed the pro-neutral and anti-British press and population in America – will dismiss the whole thing as a desperate ruse by perfidious Albion to drag the USA into the war. Unless there is proof that the telegram is real, Bell enquires? Balfour and Hall exchange sideways glances, but they cannot openly admit where the telegram has come from, although Hall evasively mentions highly confidential intelligence sources. He will say no more.

Bell is deeply conflicted, it seems to you. Like most of his colleagues in the US embassy in Grosvenor Square, he is firmly pro-Allied in his outlook, as you well know. Indeed, the US Ambassador, Walter Hines

Page (Bell's boss), is so pro-British that even the State Department in Washington, generally well disposed to the Allies, thinks him too partisan and unreliable. You have heard on the grapevine that they have considered replacing him with someone a little less pro-British. But, Bell declares to you, despite the goodwill among American staff in London, the US embassy cannot be sure how this will be received in Washington.

The frowning Bell departs, offering to do whatever he can, but you are not convinced. Once he has left, Balfour remains cool and aloof, but Hall expresses his deep concerns that the Americans will surely begin exploring how the British got hold of the telegram; if they find out, it would be calamitous, he glowers. He bustles off to explore options and devise solutions. Will he have enough time? How will Wilson's government react to the telegram?

AFTERMATH

Despite the announcement by the Germans on 31 January that a new intensified U-boat campaign would begin on 1 February, all of which appeared to corroborate the legitimacy of the Zimmermann telegram to a degree, the Americans remained suspicious. Robert Lansing, the US Secretary of State, attempted to use the telegram to persuade President Wilson to commit to a more aggressive footing against Berlin, but Wilson remained steadfast: without a clear provocative act, America would remain neutral. The Americans also suspected British subterfuge – and there was no immediate evidence that Zimmermann had approached Mexico.

Four days later the contents of the Zimmermann telegram leaked to the American press (it later emerged that Hall himself had been the indirect perpetrator), but was met with scepticism and very quickly much of the narrative centred on the telegram surely being a British ruse, one that made them almost as untrustworthy as the Germans. Mexico and Japan denied all knowledge of the telegram, while the Germans remained silent. Despite efforts by much of his Cabinet, Wilson refused to intervene directly in the war, and although he broke off diplomatic relations with Germany as a result of the unrestricted U-boat campaign, he mainly intensified his efforts to bring about peace talks.

For the Allies, with the revolution in Russia, dramatically mounting shipping losses in the Atlantic, and a French army struggling with its intolerable burden, the prospects for 1917 were bleak. Although shipping losses eventually began to be brought under control, the French army 'mutinied' in the early summer and Kerensky's Russian offensive collapsed in July, precipitating chaos in the Russian army. German losses were also heavy, however, and the U-boat offensive had failed to knock Britain out of the war while simultaneously further poisoning relations with the USA. President Wilson's overtures for peace negotiations now seemed a little more palatable to all sides, who were becoming increasingly desperate.

THE DECISION

- To follow the alternative route, go to **Section 3** (p. 318).

OR

- To explore the history of the Zimmermann telegram, go to the **Historical Note** on p. 347.

SECTION 3
BALFOUR'S CHOICE

Tuesday 20 February 1917, Foreign Office, London

The international situation is in a state of flux and the Foreign Office is buzzing with activity. Just three weeks earlier the German Chancellor, Theobald von Bethmann Hollweg, announced to the Reichstag that the following day, 1 February 1917, the Imperial German Navy's U-boat fleet would begin a new intensified campaign against shipping in or entering Allied seas, a campaign that would be unrestricted in nature. Essentially, German U-boats would be free to sink – by whatever means and whenever they desired – any ship they chose; all notions of safe passage for civilians, allowing crews to leave their ships before they were sunk or limiting the risks to non-combatants would be set aside. The Kaiser's government was throwing down the gauntlet. Bethmann Hollweg stated: 'The destructive designs of our opponents cannot be expressed more strongly. We have been challenged to fight to the end. We stake everything, and we shall be victorious.'

Now, three weeks on, the Admiralty is in turmoil. What can be done to avert looming disaster? But for you, it is the diplomatic impact of the campaign that needs to be managed, for you are ***Arthur Balfour***, the British Foreign Secretary, responsible for the United Kingdom's international relations. At sixty-eight, you have had a long and highly prestigious career in politics, including a stint as Prime Minister (1902–5) and leading the Conservative Party as recently as 1911. When the coalition government was formed in 1915 you had served as First Lord of the Admiralty, and although you had been briefly mentioned as a possible successor to Asquith as Prime Minister in December of 1916, you had taken up the mantle as Foreign Secretary instead – a brief in which you had considerable experience and a major reputation, having been intimately involved in the formation of the Entente with France back in 1904. Rich and intellectual, you are also regarded as somewhat aloof and prone to displaying disinterest in many matters; a favourite saying of yours is 'Nothing matters very much and very little matters at all.' Yet in truth you are determined and resolute; it was not for nothing that your policies in Ireland earned you notoriety as 'Bloody Balfour'.

5. Arthur Balfour

Your resolve is currently being tested. The Germans' new U-boat campaign is a reaction to the very effective blockade that the Royal Navy has enforced on Germany since the outbreak of the war. The German economy is being throttled by the British blockade, and the Germans are now lashing out, despite the risks, in an attempt to hit back. The basic dilemma for Berlin, however, is that the Royal Navy's blockade may be stopping ships trying to get to Germany and confiscating their goods, but it is not causing loss of life to merchant sailors. The British might be breaking international maritime laws, but their surface ships can safely escort captured vessels and their crews to port. German U-boats, however, being small and vulnerable, do not have that luxury; in order to be really effective they have to use stealth, hide underwater and often strike without giving their position away. Unless German U-boat captains stick to careful, risk-averse tactics, there is every chance that civilians (including neutrals) will be killed. Since 1 February those cautious tactics have been abandoned and the consequences have been staggering. British shipping losses have escalated dramatically while neutral shipping, most obviously from the USA, has largely kept away. The Admiralty is still coming to terms with the problem.

But now, on this Tuesday morning of 20 February, you have been handed a critical choice to make, one that could change the nature of the U-boat campaign at sea – and, indeed, the course of the whole war. You had first been informed of the Zimmermann telegram on 5 February; Charles Hardinge, the Foreign Office's Permanent Undersecretary and most senior civil servant, had informed you of its existence. He had expressed considerable reservations about openly employing the telegram, as it would open up the British to accusations from Washington of conducting dubious intelligence-gathering operations, methods quite contrary to diplomatic niceties. Logically, in the immediate aftermath of Germany launching her new unrestricted submarine campaign, it made sense to see if this alone would trigger America's entry into the war, without having to use the Zimmermann telegram. Captain Hall was clearly frustrated by this decision and continued to lobby for use of the telegram as a means of prompting America to declare war on Germany.

While these discussions had been ongoing, you had not been idle. Setting aside the implications of the war at sea, the Germans were apparently attempting to draw Japan and Mexico into an alliance against the United States, and it was vital for you to ascertain the likelihood of this initiative succeeding, and to stymie such efforts. On 13 February you had discussed the matter with Chinda Sutemi, the Japanese Ambassador, to ascertain Tokyo's attitude to the intent of the Zimmermann telegram. The Japanese Ambassador treated the idea with a mix of bewilderment and scorn. There was 'no intention of disturbing [American-Japanese

6. Chinda Sutemi

relations] in order to please the Mexicans or to seek chimerical advantages in a country in which Japan has no vital interests', he assured you.

Mexico is a different matter, however. The British own a number of oil fields in Mexico and the possibility of war between America and Mexico threatens British interests in the region; indeed, a considerable percentage of the Royal Navy's fuel originates in Mexico. The USA has been at loggerheads with the provisional government of Venustiano Carranza in Mexico, and so there is far less clarity over how the Mexicans will react to the German initiative. The British envoy in Mexico, Edward Thurstan, as well as the Americans, have real concerns about Mexico's reliability.

Nonetheless, the most important issue remains how the contents of the Zimmermann telegram can be related to Washington without admitting British eavesdropping. Today Hardinge seems to be offering a way out of this conundrum, although the initiative originates with Captain Hall, as usual. Zimmermann's telegram to the German embassy in Washington had included a second message that was to be relayed to Berlin's representative in Mexico, Heinrich von Eckardt. He had been instructed to approach the Mexican government with the offer of an alliance, should America enter the war against Germany, and tempt them, it now seems, with the offer of recovering territories lost to the United States in the nineteenth century: Arizona, Texas and New Mexico. These implications are now far more obvious in the fully decrypted Zimmermann telegram that Hall has made available.

But Hall also now claims that he can suggest that the interception of the Zimmermann telegram took place in Mexico, and that would avoid the British exposing their interception of America's transatlantic diplomatic cables. He also suggests that the telegram could be given directly to the American government via Edward Bell, the Second Secretary of the US embassy in London, or, if necessary, leaked directly to the press in America.

Yet Hardinge still expresses his reservations. He is convinced that the Americans will be suspicious and think that the British have been up to no good; in addition, he argues, they will not be easily persuaded of the telegram's authenticity. As such, releasing the telegram could seriously compromise Anglo-American relations just at the time when

[illegible] …tor 1-8-58
…rton, State Dept.
By [illegible signature]
Date Oct. 22, 19[illegible]

TELEGRAM RECEIVED.

FROM 2nd from London # 5747.

"We intend to begin on the first of February unrestricted submarine warfare. We shall endeavor in spite of this to keep the United States of America neutral. In the event of this not succeeding, we make Mexico a proposal of alliance on the following basis: make war together, make peace together, generous financial support and an understanding on our part that Mexico is to reconquer the lost territory in Texas, New Mexico, and Arizona. The settlement in detail is left to you. You will inform the President of the above most secretly as soon as the outbreak of war with the United States of America is certain and add the suggestion that he should, on his own initiative, invite Japan to immediate adherence and at the same time mediate between Japan and ourselves. Please call the President's attention to the fact that the ruthless employment of our submarines now offers the prospect of compelling England in a few months to make peace." Signed, ZIMMERMANN.

Document 2: The fully decrypted and translated Zimmermann telegram

Washington might be cajoled into joining the war against Germany as a result of the U-boat campaign now raging in the Atlantic.

The contents of the Zimmermann telegram are incendiary and will surely provoke a major response from Washington. But releasing it is a risk, and if the Americans become suspicious, the growing pro-Allied sentiment in America caused by the U-boat campaign might well be dissipated, if opinion there considers that the British are trying to lure them into the war by treacherous means. The worst outcome of all is that the Americans believe that the British have fabricated the telegram to implicate Berlin.

What should you do? You could instruct Hall to use his contacts to alert Washington to the existence of the Zimmermann telegram or hold back and see if the U-boat campaign provokes a more robust reaction from the Americans.

AIDE-MEMOIRE

* Getting the Americans to join the war could turn the war decisively in the Allies' favour.
* Isolationist and anti-British sentiments in America are widespread. Will anyone in the USA believe the telegram to be genuine?
* The Zimmermann telegram might well be the way to tip Washington into entering the war.
* President Woodrow Wilson favours negotiations. Will the USA ever enter the war?
* If you fail to act and the Americans later find out that the British knew all long about the German plan for an alliance with Mexico and Japan, there would be major negative diplomatic repercussions for London.
* Releasing the telegram to the Americans might well expose Britain's violation of diplomatic rules and cause a breach with Washington.

THE DECISION

Should you tell the Americans about the Zimmermann telegram or keep quiet?

▶ If you want to inform the Americans, go to **Section 4** (p. 326).

OR

▶ If you do not want to inform the Americans, go to **Section 5** (p. 332).

SECTION 4
JOSEPHUS DANIELS' DAY OF DECISION

20 March 1917, Cabinet Room, White House, Washington DC

President Woodrow Wilson is convening the latest US Cabinet meeting in the White House and tension hangs in the air: the future of the Great War – and potentially the USA's role in the world – hangs in the balance. After many weeks of soul-searching, prevarication and debate, Wilson appears to be on the verge of coming to a clear decision on American participation in the war that is currently still raging in Europe. Ever since the Germans announced their new unrestricted U-boat campaign at the end of January the atmosphere in Washington, and to a degree nationally, has darkened. The publication of the Zimmermann telegram back in early March added further to the growing pressure in the capital, with increasing calls for decisive action. Has the time come for war?

As you look around the table you see many of your colleagues who have, certainly over the last two months, repeatedly called for America to declare war on Germany. But you, like the President, have been more circumspect. You are ***Josephus Daniels***, United States Secretary of the Navy, a man known for your pacifist leanings and outlook. As a pioneer of the modern American newspaper industry, you have controlled *The News and Observer*, the most influential newspaper in North Carolina, since the 1890s. You are a determined man with strong views, willing to defend adopted positions to the

7. Wilson's Cabinet: President Wilson is furthest left, Josephus Daniels is seated fourth from the left

extreme. Back in 1898 you had been the principal figure behind the only *coup d'état* in American history that had resulted in the overthrow of an elected state government by force: the Wilmington insurrection in North Carolina. Having firmly established Democrat control in the state, you have since pursued laudable causes, such as improved public education. You hold many strong convictions on religious grounds, and you are a strong teetotaller, to the extent of eradicating the use of alcohol on all US Navy ships, much to the chagrin of naval personnel. As a confirmed segregationist and white supremacist, you also firmly believe that giving the vote to black people was 'the greatest folly and crime' in American history.*

Since the outbreak of the Great War you have been working hard to maintain the anti-war voice in Wilson's administration, along with (initially anyway) William Jennings Bryan, Wilson's original Secretary of State. You have strongly railed against Britain's blockade

* Daniels' racist thinking resulted in his newspaper adopting avowedly prejudiced editorial methods and approaches, shaping Jim Crow policies and attitudes in the south of the USA.

8. Josephus Daniels

of shipping in the North Sea, which you argued flouted international law; as one wit put it, 'Britannia not only ruled the waves but waived the rules.' Yet once Germany had plunged the war into a further level of excess with its unrestricted U-boat campaigns (the first was declared in February 1915), the mood in Washington had begun to drift more and more to backing the Allies. Secretary of State Bryan, someone you admired greatly, strongly condemned both British and German maritime policies, but his equivocal position collapsed following the sinking of the liner *Lusitania* by a German U-boat in May 1915, which resulted in the deaths of more than 1,200 people, including 94 children and 128 Americans.

In the aftermath you had watched as Bryan attempted to hold off American reactions that might lead to war with Germany, but the hawks in Cabinet had insisted on a robust response, which Wilson adhered to. You had to choose between backing Bryan, with whom you agreed on the issue of neutrality and non-intervention, and backing Wilson, in whom you believed as a strong and successful political leader. You chose Wilson and kept quiet in 1915. In private, Bryan called on you to remain in the Cabinet: 'The President will need you,' he declared. Bryan was, however, ousted and replaced with Robert Lansing, a firm believer in supporting the Allies. Berlin called off the U-boats in 1915, and did so once again in 1916 when a second attempt to sharpen up U-boat operations caused a diplomatic response from Wilson, which prompted Berlin to back down.

You have viewed your approach as avowedly neutral in the war, and you have been irked over the last few months by Wilson's desire to actively negotiate peace in Europe, a policy that you believe will only result in America becoming entangled in the war. That, however, came to nothing, and it was Germany's announcement of a new U-boat campaign, followed by the publication of the Zimmermann telegram, that provoked further turmoil in Wilson's Cabinet in February and March of 1917. When the news first broke, you had persuaded Wilson to wait on Germany causing another incident similar to the *Lusitania* disaster before acting against Berlin, much to the irritation of the hawks in the Cabinet. Nonetheless, you had begun preparations to arm American merchant ships to help protect them, if war came. This measure was blocked in the Senate by anti-interventionist filibustering and Wilson had to force it through by executive order; this underscored your concerns over the divisions in American politics and society over joining the war. Consequently, and despite everything, your pacifist tendencies and concerns over the consequences of war with Germany are still prevalent.

Today, at Wilson's Cabinet meeting on 20 March, the whole issue has come to a head, in what you consider as the 'day of decision'. Wilson, still unwilling to surrender his equivocal position, announced that he deplored German militarism on land, but also British militarism at sea. Nonetheless the hawks, led by Secretary of State Lansing, make their case urging the President to declare war on Germany as soon as possible. You are considered the main opponent to war, but you are not alone, and two of your colleagues – William Wilson, Secretary of Labor, and Albert Burleson, Postmaster – have yet to speak; both are known to hold concerns over American intervention in the war and they might follow your lead in the discussion. President Wilson turns to you and pointedly asks for your opinion. What will you advise: caution or war?

AIDE-MEMOIRE

* President Wilson, a man you admire, is clearly leaning towards declaring war on Germany.
* It is still far from obvious that the American people support war, even after

the publication of the Zimmermann telegram.

* Is it worth splitting the Cabinet over this matter? If you hold out, there could be serious repercussions for the government and the Democrats.
* German U-boats are sinking ships and killing people – the Kaiser and his militarists have to be stopped.
* The British blockade is starving people in Germany, mostly civilians – children and the elderly are likely to be hardest hit. Why should America get involved when the Europeans have brought this war on themselves?

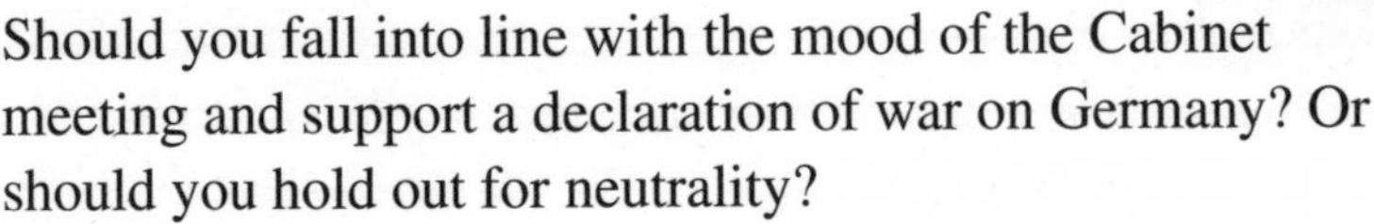

THE DECISION

Should you fall into line with the mood of the Cabinet meeting and support a declaration of war on Germany? Or should you hold out for neutrality?

▶ If you want to declare war, go to **Section 6** (p. 338).

OR

▶ If you want to hold out for continued neutrality, go to **Section 7** (p. 344).

SECTION 5
CARRANZA'S CHOICE

12 April 1917, National Palace, Mexico City

A vital meeting is taking place at the President of Mexico's official residence, a meeting that could determine the future of Mexico and, quite possibly, the outcome of the ongoing war in Europe. Leading the discussion is the President himself, Venustiano Carranza, the tall, grey-bearded and imposing political head of the Constitutionalist regime. Carranza is seeking views and opinions on how to react to the USA's declaration of war on Germany. He particularly values your views, as you are ***Cándido Aguilar***, the Foreign Minister for Mexico. A man of humble beginnings, you had become embroiled in politics and had then been drawn into supporting Francisco Madero's reforming government of 1911–13. Alas, Madero was assassinated and his government overthrown by General Huerta in a coup. Huerta's dictatorship had been short-lived, however, lasting only some seventeen months, and in the aftermath of his resignation and flight into exile you had supported Carranza's assumption

9. Venustiano Carranza

of power. Yet despite all your best collective efforts, there has been constant turmoil, with warring factions and feuds destabilising the nation.

Now you and your colleagues are confronted with an increasingly difficult diplomatic relationship with Washington and Berlin, although it is one that might yet bear fruit for Mexico.

10. Cándido Aguilar

Mexico's relationship with Berlin and Washington has been a careful balancing act since 1914. You believe the Americans to have been partly behind the military coup against Madero in 1913, in an effort to placate American investors and big business. Although Washington has subsequently accepted the reality of Carranza's government, it has yet to legally recognise its legitimacy. Your planned policies on limiting foreign ownership of land and resources in Mexico still rankle the Americans, who have invested a great deal in your country, albeit in order to make themselves rich rather than to aid Mexican development. Although your land reforms have yet to be enacted, they are a major stumbling block between your government and Washington developing better relations.

Your testy dealings with Woodrow Wilson's government are well known, however, and some dissident Mexican factions opposing Carranza's regime seem to have tried to exploit the issue. The rebel Pancho Villa – possibly in an attempt to destabilise the relationship between Mexico and the USA – crossed the border into American territory in March 1916 and attacked Columbus in New Mexico, killing eighteen US citizens and causing considerable damage.

Ruins of Columbus, N.M. after being
Raided by Pancho Villa.
W.H.Horne Co.
El Paso, Tex.

11. The ruins of Columbus after Villa's raid, March 1916

Other cross-border raids followed and the Americans eventually sent a military force of 5,000 troops after Villa. This incursion enflamed relations and brought the possibility of war between the USA and Mexico, with Wilson refusing to withdraw his troops; there were even clashes between your troops and American forces. The Americans withdrew from Mexican territory only a few weeks ago.

Relations with Washington were therefore strained throughout 1916, and you and Carranza have been exploring ways of bolstering Mexico's military power to resist further American interventions. Contacts with the Germans have developed, and it has been clear that Berlin is keen to strengthen its ties to Mexico. Negotiations about arms being supplied by the Germans have been ongoing, but it was only early in 1917 that matters began to develop.

Berlin initiated its submarine campaign against the Allies on 1 February, which saw a diplomatic rupture between Washington and Berlin a few days later. Then, on 20 February, the German envoy in Mexico, Heinrich von Eckardt, approached you with an intriguing and potentially enticing offer: an anti-American alliance between

Mexico and Germany. He mentioned money and arms, and the possibility of Mexico recovering territories lost to the Americans in the nineteenth century. Eckardt also wanted you to explore linking up with the Japanese against the Americans. All would be activated if the Americans ever declared war on Germany.

You discussed the proposals with President Carranza, but you were both sceptical about what Germany could realistically provide. What material aid could Berlin offer you? And was Mexico in any fit state to open hostilities with the USA, even if the Americans were by then focused on the war in Europe? When the Japanese proved dismissive of the whole venture, your initial interest in any deal with Berlin cooled.

Yet matters developed still further when, after much debate and discussion, and following the loss of American lives in the Atlantic, Woodrow Wilson finally decided to push for a declaration of war on Germany. Support in the USA for his policy has been less than fulsome, however, and persuading the US Congress to accept his call for war was a long and traumatic experience. But now the USA is at war with Germany, and for Mexico the moment of truth has finally arrived.

As President Carranza asks for views on whether Mexico should act in support of Germany, you are able to point out that Germany is in a position to supply only limited amounts of arms – 30,000 rifles with nine million rounds of ammunition; 100 machine guns with six million rounds of ammunition; and ten artillery pieces. Further deliveries would be possible, plus some injections of currency, and the German military leadership is obviously intent on making a gesture, but it will hardly amount to enough to start a war with the USA.

Carranza and his staff nonetheless seem interested. A military strike against the Americans might be too ambitious, as General Álvaro Obregón (the Minister of War) and the army chiefs reluctantly admit, but if German support could be drawn upon in other ways, an anti-US stance could be fruitful. The radicals in the Cabinet push the idea that you should vigorously impose the new 1917 Constitutional Laws limiting foreign ownership of property in Mexico. You are well aware that Mexico has drawn in huge amounts of foreign investment in recent years, much of it from the USA. Perhaps most importantly,

Anglo-American and other foreign companies now own some 90 per cent of the petroleum lands in Mexico.

The view in your government, particularly among the radical groupings now wielding considerable influence, is that this currently benefits Mexico very little: much of the profit simply disappears into foreign banks. If the Mexican government acts to nationalise or drastically limit the ability of foreign companies to exploit Mexico, it would add a major financial burden on the Allies; the British in particular, heavily reliant as they are on Mexican oil to fuel their Royal Navy, would be badly hit. The revenue that the Mexican government could gather in from such an initiative would be enormous.

How would Washington and Berlin react? Berlin would be minded to supply Mexico with arms and money to maintain the squeeze on the USA and Britain, while the Americans – confronted with a major war in Europe – would hardly be in a position to open hostilities against Mexico. If they did, Washington would look like the aggressors, and the German arms and supplies would aid in the defence of Mexican territory. Finally, of course, Wilson and the Americans have been interfering in Mexican affairs for too long, so such a punitive measure is all they deserve.

President Carranza is a little hesitant, but the mood of the Cabinet meeting is clear and the policy is agreed. Two days later Carranza announces the widespread seizure and tightening of controls of foreign ownership. Washington and London are furious, but with a war to be won in Europe, one in which the U-boat campaign in the Atlantic is rapidly deteriorating, there is little they can do for the moment.

AFTERMATH

The Zimmermann initiative has not quite provoked Mexico into war with the USA, but Berlin is pleased with the outcome. Mexico has turned the screws on the Allies at just the right moment and has caused a major distraction for Washington, and has imposed a further problem on Britain's Royal Navy. Nonetheless, in the summer the Allies eventually bring shipping losses under control with the introduction of convoying, and the Germans' U-boat campaign stalls. But in August a major rupture in Allied relations occurs when newspaper reports in the USA declare that the British had known about Zimmermann's telegram to the Mexicans in early February and had not informed Washington. Wilson is particularly furious because it seems the British had been intercepting American diplomatic cables, buried in which had been Zimmermann's message to the Mexicans. Anti-British and pro-isolationist sentiment grows in the USA, and President Wilson and Secretary of State Robert Lansing will have a major headache in maintaining American popular support for the war – support that has already been less than enthusiastic. With the Russians collapsing, the French army in disarray and the British only just surviving the U-boat war, the Americans start to hesitate in their commitment to the war; perhaps negotiations might be the answer after all?

THE DECISION

- To follow the alternative route, go to **Section 5** (p. 332).

OR

- To explore the Zimmermann telegram, go to the **Historical Note** on p. 347.

SECTION 6
WOODROW WILSON'S WAR

2 April 1917, US Congress Building, Washington DC

US Congress is in a state of electrified tension, awaiting a speech by the President of the United States himself, Woodrow Wilson. Many of the leading figures in American political circles have assembled to hear the words of their leader, although many suspect what is coming. In recent weeks tension has increased in Washington as a result of Germany's decision to begin a new, brutal U-boat campaign in the Atlantic, one that has threatened US trade in Europe and has already

12. Robert Lansing

caused some loss of American life. Added to this came the German Foreign Minister's outrageous attempt to draw Mexico into an anti-American alliance, although this has had less impact than some imagined it might. Now perhaps the moment of reckoning has come.

You are ***Robert Lansing***, the fifty-two-year-old US Secretary of State, and have watched the drama unfold with great anticipation. Back at the start of the war you had advocated a policy of 'benevolent neutrality', but in reality you have always held firm anti-German views, and these views hardened particularly in the aftermath of the *Lusitania* incident. You have worked tirelessly over the last few months to build momentum behind the notion that the USA should actively intervene in the war in Europe. To you, it has always seemed natural that American interests should align with those of Britain and France against the militaristic intent of Germany, and at the pivotal meeting of Wilson's Cabinet on 20 March you had lobbied hard for immediate intervention in the war; and everyone, including the dithering pacifists led by Josephus Daniels, had concurred with the feeling

13. Joint session of Congress, April 1917

of the meeting that war was inevitable. 'Well, gentlemen, I think there is no doubt as to what your advice is,' Wilson had declared, though as usual he had offered little that was specific about his own views. Some regard Wilson as a 'pussyfooter', unsuited to leading a nation in war; indeed, you suspect that Wilson himself worries about his suitability to head the USA at this time. Yet when the President announced the following day that he was convening a special joint session of Congress on 2 April, it seemed as though he had finally come to a decision.

As the political elite settle down to listen to Wilson's special address in absolute silence, you look on with some satisfaction. Wilson's speech is scintillating, and many quickly regard it as one of the best in American presidential history. 'The world must be made safe for democracy,' he declared. 'Its peace must be planted upon the tested foundations of political liberty.'

He outlines a litany of Germany's failings, including referencing (albeit briefly) the Zimmermann telegram:

> One of the things that has served to convince us that the Prussian autocracy was not and could never be our friend is that from the very outset of the present war it has filled our unsuspecting communities and even our offices of government with spies and set criminal intrigues everywhere afoot against our national unity of counsel, our peace within and without our industries and our commerce.
>
> That it means to stir up enemies against us at our very doors the intercepted [Zimmermann] note to the German Minister at Mexico City is eloquent evidence.
>
> We are accepting this challenge of hostile purpose because we know that in such a government, following such methods, we can never have a friend.
>
> We have no selfish ends to serve. We desire no conquest, no dominion.

It is the best speech you have heard from Wilson by far, and Congress is captivated and, it seems, is carried by the passion of the President.

You are firmly of the opinion that the Zimmermann telegram is, in effect, a 'smoking gun', clear evidence of Germany's aggressive intentions and belligerent foreign policy. Some in the press, particularly in Washington, have openly agreed, especially once Zimmermann himself confirmed the legitimacy of his telegram in early March – something you considered to be a dreadful 'blunder' on your opposite's part. It seems that the President now concurs, and you are greatly relieved at the tone and intent of Wilson's speech. Congress cheers wildly at the end of the speech and it is apparent that the President's call to arms will be endorsed, if not unanimously, as some hoped for.

14. *Washington Evening Star*, March 1917

AFTERMATH

Two days later, and despite some impassioned speeches against America joining the war, the Senate backed the President's stance by 82:6, quickly followed by the House at 373:50. America was now at war with Germany. Berlin's gamble on unrestricted U-boat warfare has surely failed, and Zimmermann's initiative had backfired spectacularly.

The USA's entry into the war in April 1917 was a crucial and pivotal moment in the Great War, particularly as it balanced the decline of Russia's campaigns on the Eastern Front in the aftermath of the revolutions. American entry also effectively ended any likelihood of

The Atlanta Journal. SPECIAL WAR EXTRA

ATLANTA, GA., FRIDAY EVENING, APRIL 6, 1917.

WILSON HAS SIGNED DECLARATION OF

WAR

BRAZIL MAY ENTER WAR TO AID U. S.

Situation Most Grave, Declares Foreign Secretary Muller — South American Country to Seize Ships

GERMAN PRESS IS BITTER AGAINST U. S. AND WILSON

ALLIES' GRIP NOT BROKEN BY TEUTON ASSAULTS

Picked Troops Hurled Against French Line Northeast of Rheims in Desperate Effort to Relieve Pressure

CONSECRATES SERVICE OF GEORGIA TO U. S.

Congressman W. S. Howard Tells House State Is Ready to Do Its Part in War on Kaiser

LADY OF MONTANA, IN TEARS, VOTES AGAINST THE WAR

WASHINGTON, April 6.—President Wilson has signed the war declaration and the United States is now at war against Germany.

The senate met at noon and Vice President Marshall immediately affixed his signature to the resolution declaring state of war exists between the two countries. President Wilson's signature was placed on the resolution immediately after Mr. Marshall signed it. The resolution had passed the house early this morning and the senate had adopted it late Wednesday night.

The house voted 373 to 50 for war; senate 82 to 6.

Budget of $3,401,000,000 asked for army and navy.

Bond issue of three and a half billion proposed.

German ships in American ports seized.

Thirty-two thousand industrial plants offered for government service.

Army bill calls for:

15. *The Atlanta Journal*, 6 April 1917

Berlin's U-boat campaign having any lasting impact on the war; the USA's naval and merchant shipping strength was thrown fully into the Allied effort and condemned Germany to defeat at sea. By 1918 American troops were pouring into Europe, and Germany's hopes were fading.

SECTION 7
LA FOLLETTE'S NEUTRALITY

8 April 1917, US Senate, Washington DC

It has been a week of political upheaval and turmoil in Washington, and President Wilson's authority and power base have been seriously undermined. At a Cabinet meeting just four days ago there had been ructions when the President had asked for views on adopting a more belligerent approach towards Germany over the new U-boat campaign and after the Zimmermann telegram outrage. Although the warmongers, such as Secretary of State Lansing, had lobbied hard, Josephus Daniels and others had demurred. It is even rumoured that three of the Cabinet had threatened to resign if Wilson tried to enforce his new aggressive foreign-policy stance. Wilson hesitated, but has still decided to put the idea of increased belligerency to Congress to test the waters. Much hangs in the balance, however.

You are ***Robert 'Fighting Bob' La Follette***, a progressive Republican Senator from Wisconsin and an ardent opponent of war. You have previously represented your state in the House of Representatives and acted as governor, before standing for the Republican presidential nomination in 1912, although you lost out to William Taft. Nonetheless, you have a major record of reforming policies and initiatives and are highly regarded in Washington. You have backed some of President Wilson's domestic agenda, but on foreign policy, particularly since 1914, you have had serious disagreements. Just a few weeks earlier you led the charge against the efforts of the government to arm merchant ships, because you saw it as a provocative act that might lead to further direct confrontation with Berlin.

You are convinced that the USA is being drawn into a war illegitimately and is being forced to take sides when, in truth, neither the Allies nor the Central Powers are worthy of American support. Like others in the Senate and the House, you have argued and believe that the USA should not ally with nations such as Britain and France – nations that, throughout their empires, deny basic democratic rights to millions of people and, in the case of Britain, to many of their own citizens.

16. Robert 'Fighting Bob' La Follette

Now you are leading the campaign against US entry into the war, and as a key member of the Senate Committee on Foreign Affairs you are in a strong position to speak out. At the committee meeting convened to discuss Wilson's desire to press for war, you and others argue against the call to arms. William J. Stone, the chair of the committee, helps to swing the day by arguing that he believes the USA is being pushed into war by big-money interests, hoping to profit from any conflict. The committee splits and no overarching consensus is agreed. Now the matter will be debated in the Senate.

You are far from alone in opposing war, and others speak out. Going to war with Germany would be the 'greatest national blunder in history', Senator William Stone claimed, while George Norris argued that the push for war was all about the money that could be made: 'I feel we are putting the dollar sign on the American flag,' he warned. The anti-war mood is bolstered by your own impassioned speech, one that gathers yet more support. Some simply ask why the USA is getting involved in a European war when the Germans are little worse than the British; neither side was willing to enter proper peace talks a few months earlier. The Zimmermann telegram is dismissed as a foolish gambit, if indeed it was genuine – maybe the British fed the story to Washington simply to inveigle the USA into the war, a war that really does not directly concern them?

The sense of any strong backing for the war has also clearly been sharply dented by the Josephus Daniels faction in the Cabinet refusing to support Wilson's measure. Ultimately, many in the Senate and the House of Representatives are appalled that the USA – with a fractious Cabinet and a less-than-convinced Congress – could even contemplate going to war. To make matters worse, while many newspapers on the eastern seaboard are broadly supportive of intervention in the war, elsewhere popular support is far less apparent.

Against a backdrop of such uncertainty, President Wilson falls back on his February provision of awaiting a clear provocation from the German U-boats that are now devastating Allied shipping in the Western Approaches and around the British Isles; only if American ships are sunk and there is loss of life will the President escalate. This reiteration bolsters support for a wait-and-see policy, and an immediate vote on war with Germany is pulled. You are hailed as the man who kept the peace; you have, for the moment at least, avoided war. Now what matters is seeing if German U-boat captains can avoid another international incident.

AFTERMATH

To the pro-interventionist faction in Washington, dismayed as they were by Wilson's supine climbdown, it was only a matter of time before there was serious loss of American life at the hands of the German U-boats. The carnage in the Atlantic was terrifying for the Allies, however; in April more than 800,000 tons of shipping had been sunk by the Germans, a level of loss that was quite unsustainable. With Russia convulsed by revolution, crumbling French army morale and crippling losses at sea, the prospects for the Allies looked bleak indeed.

Yet in late May the Royal Navy finally introduces a convoying system for Allied shipping, whereby groups of merchant ships begin to be escorted by Allied naval ships. With extra cover provided by Allied aircraft, this proves more than capable of driving off or deterring many German U-boat attacks. Losses start to fall back to manageable levels and the crisis is abated; Berlin's gamble has failed and Germany's long-term strategic position appears weaker than ever. Yet without full American support, the Allies' war effort begins to stall. As the summer progresses, a strategic stalemate seems to be descending – that is until August, when 160 American civilians are drowned in a ship sunk by a German U-boat. Will this be enough of a provocation to bring popular support in America sufficiently behind US intervention once and for all? Or will Wilson hesitate again? Without American intervention, the war could well descend into a protracted impasse.

THE DECISION

- To follow the alternative route, go to **Section 6** (p. 338).

OR

- To explore the Zimmermann telegram, see the **Historical Note** below.

HISTORICAL NOTE

The subterfuge and intrigue behind the whole story of the Zimmermann telegram have perhaps lent the event a greater degree of importance than it deserves. American popular opinion was at best nudged by the telegram, even though pro-interventionists in Washington seized upon its release to cajole Wilson into action. In truth, he was most infuriated by the fact that the Germans had embedded the message in an American diplomatic cable that was supposed to be used by the Germans only to facilitate peace moves, not conspire with Mexico against Washington. As a man of strong principles, it was this deception and insult that perhaps pushed Wilson into a strong reaction in April 1917.

In this scenario the historical path takes you from Section 1 to Section 3; Captain Hall did hold on to the telegram and did not inform Balfour or Edward Carlson, First Lord of the Admiralty, of its existence, as indeed technically he should have done. Undoubtedly he took a great risk, but he jealously guarded his information and power and took upon himself a major strategic decision of potentially profound proportions; it could easily have blown up in his face. Yet it would also have been a great risk if Hall had followed procedure and had passed on the contents of the telegram to Balfour immediately (Section 1 to Section 2). If the Zimmermann telegram had been leaked or released to the Americans early, to try and warn them of the impending German U-boat offensive, it would have been impossible for Hall to cover his tracks; it would have become clear to the Americans that the British had been listening in to their communications, whatever excuses the British offered. It would also have fuelled the isolationist lobby and raised serious questions about the devious British hoodwinking America into joining a war through underhand means. One outcome might well have been that Wilson resisted calls to join the war and, without American entry into the war in April 1917, the future for the Allies looked bleak.

When Hall eventually took the telegram to Arthur Balfour in early February he had established a clearer picture of the full contents and was creating a palatable cover story in order to allow the intelligence to be released to Washington. Yet there was still a risk involved for Balfour. The historical path is to go to Section 4 and inform the Americans (although in truth, Hall leaked the information to the US embassy in London before he got official agreement from Balfour – another enormous personal risk). Balfour was in reality quite hands-off with such matters and was most likely to defer to Hall's thinking, which is what occurred. But what if Balfour had listened to Hardinge's concerns and withheld the information (and we assume that Hall had not broken protocol)? This leads us to Section 5 and how Carranza's government might have reacted. Their historical rejection of the Zimmermann initiative was founded in part because it leaked out before the Americans joined the war: both London and Washington quickly pressured Mexico into openly rejecting the Zimmermann plan, once they had become aware of its existence. Yet although Carranza quickly rebuffed Berlin's offer once it was in the open, his regime had been examining it, prior to it being exposed. What if Washington had not been made aware? It is highly unlikely that Mexico would ever have declared war on the USA, but Carranza and his government had plenty of grievances against Washington and it is possible they would have exploited them, especially with Berlin's connivance. If it then came to light that London had known about the Zimmermann plan and had not informed the Americans, it would certainly have soured relations.

Once the Zimmermann telegram had become public knowledge and the Germans' unrestricted U-boat campaign had begun, how did Washington react? At the famous US Cabinet meeting in March 1917 Josephus Daniels read the room and decided to bite his tongue and accept that the advice given to Wilson was to push for war against Germany. This was the path of moving from Section 4 to Section 6 and leads to the historical outcome of an American entry into the war in early April 1917. But support for intervention across the USA was not overwhelming until Wilson went to Congress. Once war was declared, however, opinion came in behind the government, such that anti-war speakers in Congress were hounded and heavily criticised. But what if Daniels and the other 'doves' had held out – the path from Section 4 to Section 7? Although such a move was highly unlikely without the arch anti-interventionist William Jennings Bryan still being in place as Secretary of State, an obdurate Daniels might have threatened to resign and taken some others with him, which might have caused Wilson to hesitate. It might also have bolstered isolationist sentiment across the USA, headed by political figures such as 'Fighting Bob' La Follette, and precipitated a delay in US intervention, with a consequently negative impact on the Allies' war effort.

Ultimately, the Germans' unrestricted U-boat campaign pushed

America to the edge of war and the Zimmermann telegram helped to nudge Wilson into asking Congress to declare war. Hall deployed the Zimmermann leak very effectively, though it is going too far to suggest this was the decisive factor in prompting US entry into the war. It is also worth noting that Anglo-American relations in 1917 were nothing like they were in the Second World War or even today – there was certainly no 'special relationship'. There was deep-rooted suspicion towards the British (and towards Europe generally). Wilson and his Cabinet may well have favoured the Allies against Germany, but until 1917 there was no great desire in American society to enter the war.

Captain Reginald 'Blinker' Hall was knighted in 1918 and retired as Rear Admiral in 1919, before serving as a Conservative MP and lecturing on intelligence matters across the world. He remained evasive about the true sources and paths of his intelligence work, and his friend Eddie Bell from the US embassy once described him as 'a perfectly marvellous person but the coldest-hearted proposition that ever was. He'd eat a man's heart and hand it back to him.'

Charles Hardinge (Lord Hardinge of Penshurst) became Ambassador to France in 1920 after continuing to serve as Balfour's permanent secretary, before retiring in 1922. He lived to be eighty-six and acquired six knighthoods in his lifetime.

Arthur Balfour, his boss, despite having served as Prime Minister (1902–5), is probably best remembered for the Balfour Declaration, which offered British government support for the establishment of a 'national home for the Jewish people'. Balfour continued to play a role in British politics and to serve in government until 1929. His total of twenty-eight years of government service is bettered only by Winston Churchill.

Josephus Daniels was an arch segregationist and his efforts and policies helped to exclude people of colour from the political system in the USA well into the twentieth century. He retired from government in 1921 and returned to editing the *Raleigh News and Observer.* He supported Franklin Roosevelt's presidency and served as Ambassador to Mexico (1933–41), a job in which he enjoyed some success. In Raleigh in 2020 a statue of Daniels was removed from Nash Square while a school named after him in 1956 (he died in 1948) was renamed, both consequences of the political and social unrest prompted by the murder of George Floyd in Minnesota.

Cándido Aguilar married Venustiano Carranza's daughter, Virginia, in 1919 and remained loyal to the President until the latter's death in a power struggle in 1920. Aguilar initially went into exile, but intermittently returned to politics in Mexico before being expelled from the Mexican Revolutionary Party in the 1940s for exposing corruption. He was later jailed by President Alemán and was subsequently exiled to Cuba. He died in 1960.

Robert Lansing remained as Secretary of State under President Wilson, but fell from favour as he was sceptical of the Treaty of Versailles and the relevance of the League of Nations. After Wilson suffered a stroke in October 1919, Lansing eventually suggested that the then Vice President, Thomas Marshall, take over, but this was viewed as disloyalty and Lansing subsequently resigned in February 1920. He returned to the law and died in 1928.

Robert 'Fighting Bob' La Follette endured considerable criticism for his opposition to US entry into the war, but he continued to hold the government to account for its wartime policies. His radical attitudes and acceptance of socialist principles eventually caused him to run for President in 1924 on a socialist / progressive ticket, in which he won 16.6 per cent of the vote, the third-highest popular vote for a third-party candidate in US history. La Follette died shortly afterwards, but was later regarded as one of the most important and influential senators ever in American politics.

8

REVOLUTION:

RUSSIA'S AGONY, 1917–1918

SECTION 1
THE PETROGRAD UPRISING

Saturday 24 February 1917, Stavka (Russian military headquarters), Mogilev, Russian Empire

The mood around the Stavka is one of gloom and despondency. Recent months have seen a decided downturn in the conduct of the war against the Central Powers and there is a growing mountain of problems and crises to be dealt with: crumbling morale, deteriorating military capability, equipment shortages and a sense of despair. The army had not been well prepared for war against Germany in 1914 (something that seemed to have had little impact on the Tsar's decision to go to war) and only the monumental efforts of the officers and men of the Imperial Russian Army – despite the crippling losses – have kept the war going. But now, with desperate news seeping out of Petrograd (St Petersburg had been renamed as the more Russian-sounding Petrograd), matters could well be coming to a head.

1. Mikhail Alekseyev

You are ***General Mikhail Vassilievich Alekseyev***, the fifty-nine-year-old Army Chief of Staff and, in effect, the professional head of the Russian army. Despite hailing from a modest background in the Smolensk district, you have enjoyed a distinguished military career, building a serious reputation. You were appointed to the position of Chief of Staff in August 1915 and have worked remorselessly to maintain Russia's military effort, scoring some notable successes in 1916, particularly against Austria–Hungary. But, confronted with institutional torpor and corrupt patronage, your efforts have been hindered and Russia's situation has deteriorated. Unwilling (some say unable) to delegate matters to colleagues that you consider weak and ineffective, you have shouldered a heavy burden. Your health has suffered, and in the autumn of 1916 you had had to spend some weeks in the Crimea recovering from a serious kidney ailment.

Like many others in Stavka and wider government circles, you despaired at the Tsar's assumption of direct military leadership of the army in 1915, even though this had resulted in your promotion. His predecessor in the role of supreme commander, Grand Duke Nikolaevich, had been popular enough, but had been overwhelmed by the deteriorating situation. Eventually the German success at

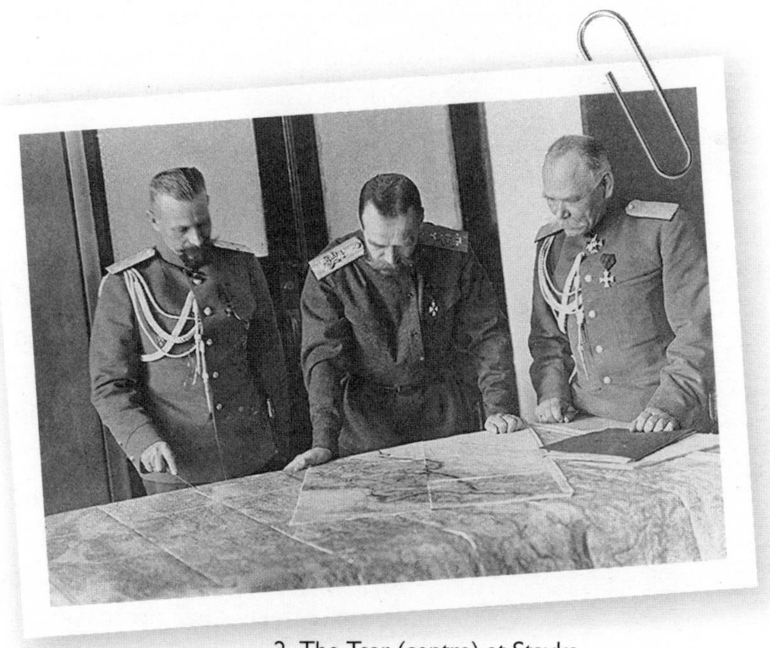

2. The Tsar (centre) at Stavka

Gorlice–Tarnów in 1915 had precipitated a calamitous Russian-army retreat and Nikolaevich had paid the price. But the Tsar is also completely out of his depth as a military commander, and it has been you who has kept the show on the road. In spite of the myriad problems, Russian military successes in 1916 – General Brusilov's offensive in particular – had bought time for the Allies and hit the Germans and Austrians hard, but the Russian losses had been crippling and the state of the army showed worrying signs of stress. Desertion and other linked indicators of the weakening resolve of the troops have grown markedly, and the Tsar is now inextricably linked to this worsening performance of the army; his reputation and standing have taken a frightful battering since his assumption of command in 1915.

3. Anti-government poster critical of the role of Rasputin

Now news from Petrograd has emerged that indicates that the situation on the home front might be even worse. Discontent in the capital has been growing for months, with the workers dismayed at the poor conditions, lack of necessities and harsh repression, whilst the political class has fumed at the decline in Russia's fortunes in the war. And of course everyone is deeply suspicious about the Tsar's German wife, Alexandra. In the opinion of many, she has exerted undue influence in government, and her German heritage – previously merely a problem – has proved corrosive to the reputation of the monarchy and has further undermined the Tsar's dwindling popularity. The recent scandal over the royal family's involvement with the appalling Rasputin has further weakened the place of the monarchy. Rumours were rife that Rasputin was woefully influential in the royal family, and even that he was intimately involved with the Tsarina. The circumstances of his death are another indication of the chaos at home.

The long-underlying notion that the Tsar is a benign national father-figure who has been let down by corrupt and malignant advisors has become a thing of the past; now the Tsar and Tsarina are viewed with suspicion and contempt. And yet they seem insulated from the reality of the nation's woes and from the discontent of the urban masses in particular. The Tsar and his family have long lived a quite separate existence from the world around them in their home at Tsarskoe Selo; now that dislocation threatens their existence.

The Duma, the Russian parliament, has attempted to take a more important role in government, but the Tsar (strongly backed by his wife) views any move to shift power from the monarchy to the Duma as an insult and a betrayal of his anointed status. Consequently there has been little progress, and the government has been increasingly paralysed in the face of the collapse in popularity. Now food supplies have been disrupted in Petrograd and discontent is threatening to explode into protest and violence. For the moment the police and the army garrison appear loyal, but the situation is getting out of control.

As you and your staff head to see the Tsar, who is based in the Governor-General's house, you wonder whether he has grasped the

4. Unrest in Petrograd

depth of the crisis confronting his regime. The government's grip on power in Petrograd is tenuous at best. How do you approach the subject? You have previously been unable to hide your disillusionment over the conduct of the war, and had even planned to urge the Tsar to develop a more inclusive regime, drawing more upon the Duma. Now might be the moment to press the Tsar to accept this as his only realistic option. You know that others around you think similarly, but are often too afraid to speak their minds. Admiral Konstantin Nilov has fatalistically mused that unless the regime acts quickly, you will all soon 'hang from lamp-posts and we shall have a revolutionary outbreak the like of which we have never had before'.

As you and the other senior Stavka officers enter the conference room to discuss matters with the Tsar and his entourage, you must quickly decide what steps to take. A new telegram from Mikhail Rodzianko of the Duma has arrived (Document 1). It is stark in its urgency:

> Serious situation in the capital, where anarchy reigns. General discontent is increasing. In the streets, uninterrupted firing, and one part of the army is firing on the other. It is necessary to nominate without delay a person possessing the confidence of the people and who would form a new government. To wait is impossible.

Standing aside could lead to the collapse of the entire regime, which would threaten the prosecution of the war – your primary concern. But what should you advise? Conciliation and compromise? Or fierce action to quell the nascent uprising?

AIDE-MEMOIRE

* The Tsar is not up to leading the war effort and the government. He must accept help now before it is too late.
* Offering concessions could make matters worse and lead to chaos.
* Being directly responsible for the war has seriously weakened faith in the monarchy. The Tsar must act now to rebuild trust.
* Cracking down on the radicals and revolutionaries - if necessary even with the Tsar's best and most loyal troops from the front - could be the only way to save the nation.
* The collapse in morale in the army and the frighteningly high desertion rates do not offer much hope of repressive policies continuing to work indefinitely.
* The government in Petrograd can seize the situation quickly and begin to defuse the crisis in a way the Tsar cannot. Is it

time to offer them some more power? (Consider Document 1, the Rodzianko telegram.)

* Adopting a more constitutional role, a little like the Tsar's cousin in Britain, King George V, might be the route to greater stability.

THE DECISION

Should you advise the Tsar to offer some real power to the Duma in the hope it can retrieve the position? Or should you back what appears to be the Tsar's instinct to put a hard man in firm control to crack down on the opposition?

▶ If you want to go to suggest that the Tsar offers more power to an elected government, go to **Section 2** (p. 362).

OR

▶ If you want to support the idea of using coercive force to crush the opposition in Petrograd, go to **Section 3** (p. 368).

SECTION 2
CIVIL WAR

Sunday 31 August 1919, HMS *Warspite*, Sevastopol, Crimea

It is a hot and close afternoon in the Black Sea and everyone is suffering in the oppressive heat, particularly those on deck of the Royal Navy battleship HMS *Warspite*. There is a tense atmosphere as the crew peers towards the city of Sevastopol, now in ruins after months of war and destruction. The city is shrouded in smoke and haze and in the distance the crew can hear the guns of the Russian republican forces as they pummel the city once more, in an effort to bring the siege to an end. The *Warspite* is about to depart, carrying a small number of the surviving leaders of the Russian royalist government. Somewhere on board is Prince Georgy Lvov, the man who two years before had attempted to rescue the Tsar's failing regime, but who in retrospect may well have been a major cause of the conflict that has consumed Russia ever since. Yet the most significant passengers the *Warspite* has been tasked with rescuing are only just arriving. A small convoy of vehicles has just pulled up at the quayside and into the sunlight the Tsar and his family emerge, protected by guards and officials – the children look confused and scared, the Tsarina carries a fixed and impassive countenance. The Tsarevich, Alexei, has to be helped, such is his failing health, whilst the Tsar himself looks haggard and exhausted, far from the upright and confident figure portrayed in the photographs and films issued by the royalist government in recent times, but then much has happened in the last few months.

You are ***Lord Jellicoe***, previously commander of the Grand Fleet

5. Sevastopol Harbour

during the Battle of Jutland back in 1916 and thereafter First Sea Lord. You had fallen from favour in 1917, brought down by a despicable and underhand plot, but David Lloyd George, Prime Minister, had subsequently appointed you as Allied Supreme Naval Commander in the Mediterranean in 1918; this at least had brought promotion to Admiral of the Fleet. Thus it had been you who was ordered to enter the Black Sea in the spring of 1919 with a combined Allied naval force to support the ailing Russian royalist army, but the situation was dire for the Tsar and his dwindling forces. By the summer your brief had turned to planning for a likely evacuation, and Winston Churchill – now back as First Lord of the Admiralty – had (you have heard, at the urging of King George himself) specifically issued you with personal instructions to ensure the safety of the Tsar and his family.

As the Russian royal family struggles onto the battleship carrying their remaining possessions, surrounded by officials hoarding boxes of documents and files, you reflect on the turn of events in Russia since the upheavals of early 1917. Then the Tsar, threatened with

6. Lord Jellicoe

catastrophe, had opened negotiations with key figures in the Duma to discuss the transition of some powers to the elected government. The Tsarina had been furious, and some hardliners implored the Tsar to impose a fierce crackdown on opposition in Petrograd, but for once the Tsar was persuaded by his officials and General Alekseyev to offer concessions. Despite the deteriorating situation in Petrograd, the Duma – headed by Mikhail Rodzianko and Prince Georgy Lvov – assumed key powers in an effort to bring much-needed reform. Some Tsarist loyalists, regarded by the Duma as incompetent and corrupt, were removed from power, but this initiated a backlash from the hardliners.

The Duma tried to keep the growing influence of the workers' Petrograd soviet under control, but efforts to work with the Social Revolutionary Party brought open resentment and criticism from the monarchists and other determined supporters of the Tsar. Lvov's reforms nevertheless headed off an immediate total collapse in support for the monarchy, although some factions still pressed for the Tsar's abdication. Rodzianko and Alekseyev meanwhile effectively took over control of government and attempted to ease the Tsar away from power and decision-making, but Nicholas was not ready to give up entirely. As in 1905, when the Tsar had previously been forced to offer reforms, he soon began to reassert his authority and began backtracking on his concessions. In the midst of this internecine squabbling a new German offensive plunged the Russian army into chaos.

Russia's allies in the West despaired of the Tsarist regime, but were fearful of a radical socialist government replacing it. Besides, even though the USA had now joined the war, Britain was suffering from the U-boat blockade and the French army had been undermined by outbreaks of mutiny. The Central and Allied Powers began grudging and tentative negotiations to bring about a ceasefire. The Tsarist regime was therefore temporarily reprieved by the end of the Great War in the summer of 1917, despite having to make some concessions to the Germans. But conflict soon broke out across Russia as different factions battled to take control. In some regions the Tsarist regime continued to hold power, while in others, particularly the major cities, the workers' soviets began to assume control. The Duma struggled desperately to retain its grip, but power drained away and the Russian government found itself issuing orders that no one was listening to. Rodzianko was assassinated, though he had long since lost control; Lvov resigned in despair; and Alekseyev, fearful of the consequences of the socialists and radicals seizing power, maintained the loyalty of some of the army to the Tsar.

By the autumn of 1917 Russia had descended into civil war, with former members of the Duma forced to take sides. The factions split into what became known as the republicans and the royalists, and fierce battles erupted across Russia. Some regions such as Poland, Finland and Georgia used the break-up to assert their independence. The Great Powers looked on, unsure who to support – the royalist forces appeared incompetent and weak, whilst the republicans were riven by dissent and factions. To the outside world, Alexander Kerensky appeared to speak for the republicans, but French and British agents were convinced that more radical socialist revolutionaries really held power. In an odd turnabout, Germany, greatly concerned about the possibility of outright revolution in Russia, supplied the Tsar with equipment in 1918, but it was to no avail.

By the spring of 1919 the royalists were in full retreat and were forced into a few enclaves in the south, including the Crimea. A final summer offensive saw the Tsar holed up and under siege in Sevastopol while General Alekseyev was forced to surrender in Odessa.

Fearful over what might happen to the Tsar and his family, the British government began planning to rescue Nicholas, but it took some weeks for the Tsar to fully recognise his plight. Now, with thousands lying dead and wounded in the beleaguered city of Sevastopol, he has accepted his fate and agreed to escape. As you look on, you wonder if Russia's turmoil is over. Will the flight of the Tsar bring peace or will it herald a further battle for power?

AFTERMATH

The ending of the first phase of the civil war brought some respite for Russia, but very quickly infighting within the new regime generated yet more instability. The republican forces had always been a loose coalition – liberal survivors of the Duma, radical socialists such as the Mensheviks and outright revolutionary hardliners such as the Bolsheviks, headed by Vladimir Lenin. Repeated attempts by Lenin and his

7. The Tsar and his family

supporters to rule through the soviets during the war had strengthened their power base, but over the next few months they were attacked by those seeking an elective parliamentary democracy as the source of government in Russia. The tussle, laced with violence and assassinations, continued for months, but without the extreme urgency and pressures of war the Bolsheviks were unable to assert full control. Threatened with arrest, Lenin and Trotsky fled into exile.

The Tsar and his family meanwhile retreated into retirement and obscurity in the English countryside, something that the family-loving Nicholas appeared to prefer. Few in Russia lobbied for his return in any form. He and his cousin, King George V, and their respective families remained close, but they were unable (and indeed unwilling) to rebuild links with the Kaiser who, after the peace treaty of 1917, remained as head of state in Germany, albeit in a much less powerful and more constitutional position.

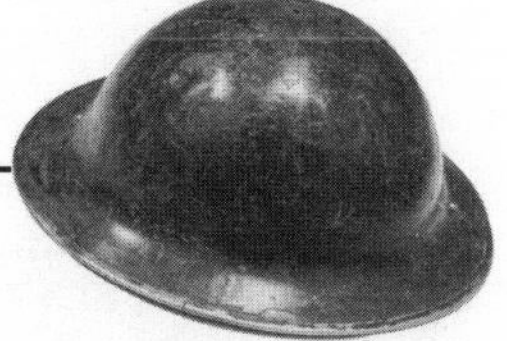

THE DECISION

- To follow the alternative route, go to **Section 3** (p. 368).

OR

- To explore the revolutions in Russia, go to the **Historical Note** on p. 403.

SECTION 3
THE SEARCH FOR PEACE

Saturday 20 October 1917, Foreign Affairs Committee, Council of the Republic

A difficult and tempestuous meeting of Russia's Provisional Government is in full flow, with contrasting views on how Russia can survive its ongoing crises and agony. The Foreign Minister, Mikhail Tereschenko, has over recent days once again reiterated his view and underlined his policy that Russia must continue to participate in the war against the Central Powers. He acknowledges that peace is preferable, but maintains it can only be realised through conventional diplomatic means and only then from a position of strength. It is essential, he argues, that Russia continues its role with the Allies, standing alongside France, Britain and the USA – anything else, such as a separate peace with Germany, would be catastrophic for the home front and disastrous for army morale,

8. Aleksandr Verkhovsky

and in any case could only be achieved by surrendering too much to Berlin.

You, however, have begun to consider the previously unthinkable – the possibility of Russia dropping out of the war – and you hold some sway in these discussions, for you are ***General Aleksandr Ivanovich Verkhovsky***, the recently appointed Minister for War. At thirty years old, you are young and dynamic and have enjoyed a substantial military career, one that has also led to you adopting reformist and radical politics – indeed, you are a member of the Socialist Revolutionary Party. You actively supported the February Revolution and subsequently became an elected deputy in the Sevastopol Council of Workers. You have been willing to use force and coercion to maintain control and discipline in the armed forces in defence of the revolution, but since taking over as Minister of War in late August you have become increasingly disillusioned about the ability of Russia to continue as a belligerent in the war against Germany. There are far too many problems to resolve.

Indeed, ever since the new government emerged in the aftermath of the Tsar's removal in February, Russia has staggered from one crisis to another, and there remains a distinct lack of grip in government. A crucial element in this has been the uncertainty over who actually holds power in the new Russia – the Provisional Government or the workers' councils known as soviets. The Tsar had attempted to enforce his will back in February, but this had sparked mass riots and protests, and the army proved unwilling to carry out his orders. A few days later the Tsar was compelled to abdicate and a new Provisional Government announced. But it had been the Petrograd soviet and the workers who had sparked the collapse, and the politicians and generals had merely delivered the *coup de grâce* to the monarchy. From then on there has been a dual power structure in Russia, and the soviets have grown stronger everywhere, while the Provisional Government has wrestled unconvincingly with the crushing problems confronting Russia.

War against Germany and Austria–Hungary has remained the open wound in Russia. Yet there was little dissent when the Provisional

Government's first Foreign Minister, Pavel Miliukov, announced that Russia would fight 'shoulder to shoulder' alongside their Allies and 'fight their common foe to the end'. The Provisional Government's policy was that Russia's war had been badly bungled so far, but now that the Tsar's inept government had been swept away, much better progress would be made. Initially there was even talk of continuing to fight for serious territorial gains from the Central Powers, including Constantinople and the Dardanelle Straits. The Petrograd soviet took a different view from the start – they advocated a general call for all people to resist the war and to take 'decisive action in favour of peace'. 'We will stop the horrible butchery which is disgracing humanity,' they proclaimed. Yet even they were unsure how to achieve this. Measures to convene a socialist peace convention in Sweden of the different parties from across the major powers foundered, but the Petrograd soviet leadership at least pushed the Provisional Government into accepting that a peace without territorial demands was a surer path to success. Even this confrontation in April had precipitated a major crisis that threatened the government.

9. Alexander Kerensky

But many in the soviet were also deeply concerned that if Russia sought a separate peace with Germany, the socialist revolution in Russia would be threatened and potentially undermined if the terms were too harsh and damaging. Only the more extreme elements in the soviet, including the Bolsheviks, repeatedly pressed for immediate peace. Against their better judgement, members of the Petrograd soviet leadership were drawn into the Provisional

Government and thus shackled to the foreign policy that Russia had to work towards a collective peace settlement with the Central Powers.

In an effort to cajole Germany into a more amenable position, Alexander Kerensky, the new head of the Provisional Government who was appointed in July, pushed for a fresh military offensive by the army, partly to shore up support for the Russian cause. Seeing no other alternative, the soviet leaders in the Provisional Government acquiesced; they hoped it would lead to a peace settlement, whereas inactivity would only lead to slow disintegration. Unfortunately the offensive failed disastrously and the Russian army soon began to haemorrhage, precipitating a new crisis in which protestors and demonstrators at home called for 'all power to the soviets'. Lenin himself fled to Finland to avoid arrest and await events. Fear of a right-wing coup, headed by General Lavr Kornilov, resulted in a series of sackings and recriminations that further weakened support for the Provisional Government.

10. Protests in Petrograd after the failed military offensive

After becoming the Minister for War in this increasingly dire situation, your assessment of Russia's ability fight is bleak in the extreme. For the first time the notion of Russia abandoning the war, come what may, emerges. Even if Germany extracts its pound of flesh from Russia in any negotiation, the alternatives are simply worse – the total collapse of Russian government, civil war and an extreme left-wing-inspired revolutionary coup are all possibilities. It is in this high-pressure environment that you begin to brief the Foreign Affairs Committee, and you start to outline the perilous position Russia finds itself in. You highlight five key points (Document 2):

1. The reduction of the army to a sustainable size cannot be carried out for strategic reasons. It would leave Russia hopelessly exposed if the army was reduced in size.
2. The current size of the army is too big to enable the soldiers to be fed.
3. The army is similarly too big to be adequately clothed.
4. Command systems are breaking down – no one is in effective control.
5. Bolshevism is continuing to corrupt our combatant forces.

Mikhail Tereschenko, the Foreign Minister, rounds on you. What would you have us do, he demands? We cannot simply surrender or give in, especially not after the heavy human cost of the war so far. It is the moment of truth. Do you press openly for a separate peace, whatever the cost, or do you maintain the aim of keeping the war effort going, as the price of failure would be even worse?

AIDE-MEMOIRE

* The Russian army is at breaking point. The war cannot be maintained (see Document 2). Estimates indicate that some two million Russian soldiers have already abandoned their posts.

* The army has to hold on, for a retreat or collapse will result in the end of Russia.
* Whatever deal the Germans impose, it will still be better than total chaos and collapse.
* Russia is dependent on Allied support and loans - a separate peace will fracture these links and bring about economic ruin.
* The extremists and the Bolsheviks are openly calling for the overthrow of the government. Without immediate peace, it is a distinct possibility that a revolutionary coup will succeed.
* A ruinous peace settlement will precipitate further, and potentially calamitous, unrest at home, as well as destroying what remains of the army's morale.

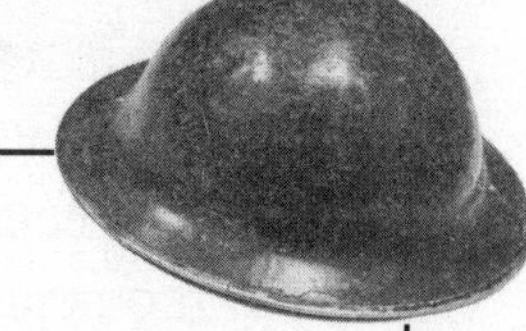

THE DECISION

Should you back government policy of working for a collective peace settlement alongside your Allies or should you press for peace now, before disaster ensues?

▶ If you want to keep fighting, go to **Section 4** (p. 374).

OR

▶ If you want to sue for peace, go to **Section 5** (p. 382).

SECTION 4
PEACE OR WAR?

Monday 18 February 1918, Central Committee meeting, Winter Palace, Petrograd

It is a cold, grey and overcast day in Petrograd, in stark contrast to the intensity and furore erupting across the capital of the new Soviet government of Russia. The city is in uproar and the regime in turmoil, for the ceasefire with the Germans has recently ended and the enemy is advancing everywhere; Petrograd itself is in danger, and frantic preparations are beginning to evacuate the seat of power to Moscow. Much of the city is in despair at the parlous nature of Russian defences, though those opposed to the Bolsheviks are relishing their potential 'liberation' from the communists. It seems that bourgeois Russians might prefer German rule to Bolshevik domination.

11. Leon Trotsky

In the midst of this crisis you are working feverishly to salvage something, for you are ***Leon Trotsky***, Russia's thirty-eight-year-old Foreign Minister and one of the key architects of the new regime. Born into a wealthy Ukrainian Jewish family, you had become involved in radical politics in the 1890s, embracing Marxism. You had later been a major figure in the failed 1905 revolution, resulting in your imprisonment in Siberia, from which you escaped. Much of your life has been spent in exile or in prison, but you remained committed to the concept of revolution and radical change in Russia and the wider world. When the February Revolution swept through Russia in 1917 you had been in New York, and it took you until May to reach home. Once in Russia, you backed the Bolshevik position, even though often you had not seen eye-to-eye with Lenin in the past (he had previously described you as 'Little Judas'). Soon, however, you were in a senior position in the Petrograd soviet and played a leading role in the Bolshevik overthrow of the decrepit and incompetent Provisional Government. This had proved remarkably straightforward; its greatest error had been in continuing the war against the Central Powers and, even as Russia had bled to death, its members had clung to their bourgeois ways of thinking. It was a mistake that you and Lenin were determined not to repeat: Russia had to get out of the war.

12. Vladimir Lenin

Yet while seizing power had been relatively easy, dealing with the reality of exiting the war without bringing down the revolutionary regime at the same time has not. Lenin had, however, promised 'Bread, peace and land!' to the workers and peasants, so you had to deliver on ending the war. You had taken on this Herculean task when you became Foreign Minister in November 1917 and initially your policies worked well enough. The Germans were amenable to a ceasefire, probably in expectation that they would then be able to impose their will from a position of relative strength. By the time of the ceasefire, German forces had occupied Poland and Lithuania, with troops also advancing into Ukraine. But of course the Germans also wanted to close down the Eastern Front as quickly as possible to enable a redeployment of their armies to meet the threat from the West, now boosted by the involvement of the USA in the war.

You had despatched Russian delegates to the Russo-German border town of Brest-Litovsk in December 1917 to negotiate a peace

13. Russia and Germany sign the armistice in December 1917

settlement with the Germans, and at first some progress appeared to be made. The German demands were damaging (their calls for independence for Poland and Lithuania being the most obvious bones of contention), but they could have been worse. It was clear that the elite German negotiators and commanders regarded the Bolsheviks with contempt (in their eyes, because your party included women, convicted criminals and Jews, you were to be frowned upon), but a convivial atmosphere was created by the Germans – you suspect in an effort to schmooze and manipulate the inexperienced Bolshevik team.

When you arrived a few days into the talks you were determined to put an end to this cosy atmosphere, and you proceeded to create a distinctive 'them and us' environment. Your approach was based on arguing for a 'peace without concessions' concept, even though you knew the Germans would never accept such an idea. You debated, quibbled and distracted constantly. In truth, you were playing for time, stalling in the hope that the wider situation in the war would shift against Germany, or that the expected and hoped-for rising of the working classes in Germany and elsewhere would soon bring an end to the war. You sensed that your provocative tactics were frustrating and infuriating the Germans; your methods were certainly buying time for your new Bolshevik government to begin to seize power fully across the country. But German patience began to fray, and hardliners in Berlin started to apply pressure to squeeze more out of Russia. In January they increased their demands, possibly because their situation in the war generally was worsening or because they needed a resolution before any major offensives in the west began. You left the talks to return to Petrograd to 'confer' with your government – it was not the first time you had used this ruse. You did, however, have to balance your insight into the negotiations with the realities confronting Russia, both of these being shaped by the contrasting views of the different factions in the revolutionary government.

The Bolsheviks still had no agreed policy on how to bring about the end of the war, and you were rather caught in the middle of this battle. On one side stood Lenin himself, who had been lobbying for the Central Committee to accept Germany's terms for some weeks; opposing him was Nikolai Bukharin, who rejected any peace treaty

14. Nikolai Bukharin

with Germany or even support from the corrupt Western imperialists. Bukharin, one of the more radical thinkers in the new regime, was vehemently supportive of a worldwide revolution as the only sure path to a long-lasting settlement. He was in favour of raising a revolutionary army of workers to stymie and hinder the Germans whilst awaiting an uprising against the German leadership from their soldiers and workers. Lenin rejected such thinking as unrealistic; peace now was the only way to save the revolution.

At the beginning of February the Germans upped the ante and offered you a nine-day break to consider whether to agree to the terms now on offer. Lenin wanted to accept the deal in case matters got worse, but you stalled and argued that you should announce that the war would be terminated without a formal agreement – a 'no war, no peace' notion. A dubious Lenin agreed to try. The measure failed.

The situation was then blown apart on 18 February when the Germans, frustrated and perplexed by your stalling and evasion, began a new offensive against what remained of the Russian armed forces. It soon became clear that they were now aiming for much more than they had been pressing for just a few weeks earlier; there was a clear hardening of their stance. Your Russian forces soon began to collapse; the old army had long since begun to disintegrate, whilst the new Red Army has yet to coalesce into a real fighting force. In reality, the German advance is probably being limited not by the resistance offered by the Russians, but by the logistical constraints imposed by the resources and supplies available to the German commander, General Max Hoffman. The Bolshevik propaganda machine is desperately churning out leaflets and material to weaken the commitment of

German soldiers to the war; it does not seem to be having much immediate effect. The situation looks bleak indeed.

Lenin has been trying to force through his demands for immediate peace and for Russia to sign the agreement with Germany, almost at any cost. Yesterday he almost succeeded, losing the Central Committee vote by just one – six to five. Today, as you assemble, the news is graver than ever. German troops are pushing deeper into Ukraine to support the newly announced anti-Bolshevik secessionist regime there, and Dvinsk and Lutsk have fallen to the advancing German army in Russia itself.

Consequently, in such a pressured situation, the meeting of the Central Committee is electric. Lenin again argues forcefully for

Map 1: The dire situation facing Russia in early 1918

Russia to sign the agreement with immediate effect: 'You must sign this shameful peace in order to save the world revolution!' he implores. He even indicates that he may resign if the measure does not pass. You suggest asking the Germans to restate their demands, and Josef Stalin momentarily sides with you. Bukharin and his faction oppose any agreement and argue for revolutionary war, guerrilla-style if necessary. But Lenin counters, 'History will condemn us for betraying the revolution' and even if Estonia and Finland have to be surrendered, such 'sacrifices will not ruin the revolution'. The room is split, possibly down the middle – yours appears to be the deciding vote. What should you favour? Immediate if humiliating peace or a protracted revolutionary war?

AIDE-MEMOIRE

* Lenin is usually very sure-footed on such matters. Maybe it is time to cut your losses before it all gets much worse?
* Conceding on the terms outlined by the Germans would be calamitous for Russia (see the map).
* The Germans are closing in on Petrograd. You must act now to head this off.
* You can withdraw to Moscow if necessary and continue the resistance from there.
* Russia could descend into chaos and civil war if the German terms are accepted as they stand.
* The revolution can only survive if you secure what you have right now.

THE DECISION

Should you sign the terms offered by the Germans immediately and hope this will buy you breathing space to save the revolution? Or should you fight on and resist through a guerrilla-style campaign – an approach that might ultimately spread revolution into Germany?

▶ If you want to fight on, go to **Section 6** (p. 390).

OR

▶ If you want to sue for peace immediately, go to **Section 7** (p. 398).

SECTION 5
THE TREATY OF WARSAW

Tuesday 15 January 1918, Belweder Palace, Warsaw

It is a bitterly cold day in Warsaw, a city soon to be the capital of a newly independent Poland. At the Belweder Palace, the plush, ornate home of great ceremonial occasions in Poland, a great array of delegates is congregating to witness the signing of a new peace treaty between Russia and the Central Powers, an agreement that will bring to an end the Great War on the Eastern Front. The German delegation is headed by Richard von Kühlmann, the Foreign Minister, with a glowering General Erich Ludendorff at his side. The Austrians and the Ottomans group closely together, muttering about the situation. Are they satisfied? In the west the conflict rages on, though as everyone assembling here now suspects, it will be greatly intensified once peace establishes itself in Eastern Europe and German troops begin transferring to the Western Front to confront the British and French armies, now being bolstered by the increasing flood of American troops into Europe. A global settlement to the war still seems some way off.

However disappointing and frustrating this may be, it is much less of a problem for you, ***Alexander Kerensky***, President of the Russian Republic. You have massive internal challenges to overcome, food shortages, workers' and peasants' protests and revolutionary factions to deal with – all with greatly reduced resources and an army in a poor state of health and security forces barely able to maintain order. But you are resolved to improve the situation and guide Russia towards a socially restructured, fairer and democratic future. With a background

15. Belweder Palace, Warsaw

in law, you have been deeply involved in pushing for democratisation and reform, dating back to the time of the 1905 revolution; you even defended some of those later implicated in that revolt. You had been imprisoned for a time for political activities; you were no extreme revolutionary, but you do adhere to the loose principles of socialism, and for many people in upper- and middle-class Russia that made you dangerous. In 1912 you were elected to the Duma as a member of the Trudoviks, a small grouping within the wider Socialist Revolutionary Party. When war broke out in 1914 you lobbied hard to try and push the Tsar into reforms and concessions to unite the country, but to little avail. When the February Revolution swept away the Tsar, as an ardent and well-known anti-monarchist you were propelled into high office as a representative of the Petrograd soviet and a participant in the Provisional Government.

You had wrestled with the vast problems facing Russia, eventually becoming the leader of the government in July 1917. The situation

16. Kerensky meeting the troops in 1917

was still dire, and you had to deal with threats from the radical left who wanted immediate transformation, and from the right who feared outright social revolution. For much of this time you and your colleagues – and indeed most of those in the Provisional Government – stuck to the policy that Russia had to continue to prosecute the war against the Central Powers, despite the manifold problems this was creating for the people and the institutions of the nation. You wanted peace, but only as part of a collective settlement, one that would see Germany defeated. It was also argued that if Russia withdrew from the war unilaterally, French and British financial support would end, and that might well spell economic disaster.

Yet in October, with the Russian army disintegrating, with growing criticism from the right and with the militant left calling for revolution, you were confronted with a moment of truth. The new War Minister, General Aleksandr Verkhovsky, urged an immediate ceasefire with Germany to avoid the total collapse of Russia's defences. Many objected, but it was also becoming clear that unless you acted quickly, power could be seized from you, either by revolutionaries or by the pro-monarchist forces.

Despite it provoking a number of resignations, you accepted the enormity of the situation and finally agreed to contact the Germans to establish a ceasefire ahead of opening negotiations for a wider peace settlement. Although there was outrage in some quarters in Petrograd, the army was relieved enough to offer firm support. General Aleksei Brusilov, largely regarded as the best battlefield commander at Russia's disposal, had been packed off to Moscow after the failed summer offensive in 1917, but he remained popular and rallied to your cause – he had always sympathised with the new Russia you were trying to build. You despatched him to Petrograd to bolster your control of the capital. It proved to be not a moment too soon, as the Bolsheviks attempted to seize power themselves in a *coup d'état* just a few days later. The announcement of a ceasefire, the prospect of a peace settlement and Brusilov's appointment stirred the army in Petrograd to stand firm and, despite some bloody fighting, the Bolsheviks were defeated – Lenin was captured, Stalin was killed and Trotsky and Bukharin fled. The loyalty of the Petrograd soviet was seriously questioned in the aftermath, but as a key link with the remaining leaders you were able to temporarily calm the situation.

17. Aleksei Brusilov

It had been a close-run thing and there were still serious pockets of resistance across the country, with some even declaring for the return of the Tsar. You announced a renewed timetable for the creation of a fully elected legislature, with elections arranged for the spring of 1918; this, you hoped, would stymie some of those who still echoed Lenin's call for 'all power to the soviets!' But although a democratic future was tantalisingly on offer now, it had become

18. Georgy Lvov headed the Russian delegation

essential that you delivered on peace, to provide a more stable environment for all of this to be achieved.

Some in the Provisional Government remained opposed to unilateral peace with Germany, however, and forming a reliable delegation to attend the peace talks in December at the town of Brest-Litovsk in Poland proved troublesome. Tereschenko had resigned as Foreign Minister in October, so you despatched Georgy Lvov backed by General Verkhovsky to lead the negotiations; much as you wanted to lead the talks yourself, you remained fearful that if you left Russia your position might be threatened, probably by a right-wing-inspired coup. Surprisingly, the talks went well enough. The Germans' demands were stiff, but not crippling, and it was apparent that they were deeply concerned about their own situation too, certainly with the USA now sending troops to the Western Front. General Max Hoffman, who headed the German team was keen to establish an understanding, but his job was complicated by more hardline forces working in the background, pressing for harsher terms to be imposed.

When the terms were discussed in Russia there was consternation and dismay in some quarters, particularly among the upper- and middle-class nationalists. Under the terms of the proposed deal, Poland and Lithuania would be established as independent states and Serbia would be confirmed as part of the Austro-Hungarian Empire, alongside some other minor measures. Talk of outright independence for Ukraine or Finland was blocked, however, and although Russia was saddled with a bill for reparations, you and others in the Provisional Government argued for acceptance. A political battle ensued, but Brusilov and the army were horrified by the idea of reopening the conflict in the near future, whilst the soviets were willing to accept the terms as a means of securing the rights and powers earned by the revolution. Many believed that revolution might well spread across Europe anyway in the future, and this would open up options to a different long-term solution.

Unsurprisingly, your Western Allies were appalled at your decision to negotiate peace with the Germans, but although financial claims and penalties were thrust in your direction by Paris and London, there was little they could do. Obviously, however, Russia's standing

Map 2: Treaty of Warsaw: Poland and Lithuania were established as independent states (initially under German influence)

and place in the international order had taken a severe battering, but there was little alternative, you mused.

With a degree of surprisingly understated ceremony in the circumstances, the Treaty of Warsaw – as the peace deal is now being described – is signed by the various interested parties, leading to a round of cheering and applause. You and your team smile thinly, for you realise that getting Russia out of the war may prove to be an easier task than drawing the disparate and fractious elements of Russian society into accepting and supporting the future that you have opened up to them.

AFTERMATH

The Treaty of Warsaw was hugely divisive in Russia and further exposed the already deep schisms opening up in all areas of the state. Traditionalists and radicals, socialists and liberals, monarchists and republicans, workers and peasants – all jostled for power and a voice, while the security of settled law and order proved elusive. Kerensky's government was buffeted throughout 1918 and 1919, with disputed elections, uprisings and declarations of cessation from Russia abounding. Financial and economic stability was initially compromised by French and British demands for Russia to honour its debts, but the USA, seeking a longer-term solution to Europe's woes, was more amenable. In early 1920 a settlement was agreed, something the Allies were grudgingly willing to work with, as their victory over Germany and Austria–Hungary in the spring of 1919 had brought a modicum of hope to global affairs. Some in Russia hoped that Allied victory would allow them to recover their lost territories, but a loose concept of national self-determination was imposed by the Allies, particularly by the American President, Woodrow Wilson, on these territories.

The Russian Republic wrestled with its problems throughout the 1920s, but a sense of order and acquiescence slowly emerged. Through dominance at the ballot box, the socialists drove through a programme of reforms and change, but there always remained unease about the lingering threat of a conservative-monarchist resurgence. Calls for the Tsar to return from exile in France never quite went away.

THE DECISION

▶ To follow the alternative route, go to **Section 4** (p. 374).

OR

▶ To explore the revolutions in Russia, go to the **Historical Note** on p. 403.

SECTION 6
THE FALL OF MOSCOW

Wednesday 16 April 1919,
The Kremlin, Moscow

It is a warm, sunny day in central Moscow, but the city has long since been shrouded in smoke and dust, consequences of the bitter fighting that has engulfed the new capital of Russia in recent weeks. The streets are littered with the dead from the fighting, buildings lie in ruins and everywhere the scars of a long and vicious war abound for all to see. In and around the Kremlin – until a few hours ago, the seat of what remained of Bolshevik power – victorious troops of the Imperial White Russian Army celebrate joyously at what they believe is the end of the civil war. Whilst the remaining bedraggled members of the Red Army, captured as they grimly tried to defend the Kremlin, are jostled and jeered by White Army soldiers, a cavalcade of armoured cars and vehicles pushes its way through the crowds. It halts, and victorious generals and leaders emerge to wave at their soldiers and soak up the atmosphere.

Among this group of senior officials and dignitaries is you, ***General Lavr Kornilov***, the military Commander-in-Chief of the Imperial White Russian forces. You are of Siberian-Cossack heritage and joined the army in 1885, eventually becoming an intelligence officer, an attaché and then, when the Great War broke out, you rose to become corps commander.

After the February Revolution in 1917 you tried to restore order in the Petrograd garrison, and then in the summer of that year you were implicated in a plot to seize power from the ailing Provisional

19. The Kremlin, site of Bukharin's last stand in 1919

20. Lavr Kornilov in Moscow

Government. In your view, you were trying to save a floundering regime that appeared ready to collapse at any moment. Banished for your plotting, you were in prison when Kerensky's government was eventually swept away by the Bolshevik coup in October 1917, but you were rescued by your supporters and were established in Novorcherkassk in the deep south as a rallying point for anti-Bolshevik forces – a movement that became known as the White Russian forces. When Lenin's regime crumbled under the German offensives in the spring of 1918, especially after they refused to accept Berlin's peace terms, there was chaos in Russia. Lenin quit, Bukharin took over and the Bolsheviks fell back on Moscow, while the Germans pressed on to occupy Petrograd. Russia lay in ruins, with local soviets attempting to rule urban centres while the countryside descended into anarchy. Yet the Germans and their allies were still fighting the Allies in the west and did not have the resources to occupy all of Russia. In the vacuum, you and other nationalist leaders coalesced from a loose coalition into a new Provisional Government, initially based in Rostov in the south.

In an attempt to prevent a return to monarchism, revolutionaries gruesomely murdered the Tsar and his family, a move that merely inflamed feeling against the Bolsheviks still further. Bukharin's forces attempted to rally troops in and around Moscow and other major cities, whilst initiating preparations for revolutionary and guerrilla-style warfare. But the Bolsheviks' credibility was limited, hope was draining away and in truth they could exert little control.

You and your White Russian Provisional Government colleagues also lacked credibility however, and there were many bickering factions and vested interests within your ranks. Unsurprisingly, London, Paris and Washington preferred you to the Bolsheviks and Western forces soon arrived in Russia, occupying Murmansk and Archangel, thus providing some limited support to your regime. Your government's status was later boosted by Grand Duke Michael, the Tsar's brother, finally accepting the position of head of state as Tsar Michael II.

He accepted the role as a much more constitutional position, and on the proviso that there would eventually be elections to a Constituent Assembly that would wield real political power in Russia. Although some were suspicious about a return to monarchy (including you),

Michael's determination to head a more legitimate state drew in support even from factions that were more inclined to autocratic rule. Consequently, and alongside some military successes and continuing splits and recriminations in the ranks of the Bolsheviks and other revolutionary groups, the momentum in the civil war swung back to you.

21. Tsar Michael II

In the autumn of 1918 you were appointed as Commander-in-Chief of the new Tsar's Imperial White Russian armies, with General Brusilov as your deputy. Your fierce and determined leadership was well regarded and feared; you claimed that, if necessary, you would 'set fire to half the country and shed the blood of three quarters of all Russians' to eradicate the blight of the Bolsheviks. A number of cities and provinces fell into your hands and the collapse of the Central Powers in November enabled you to recover territory in Ukraine. This drew in more support from the outside world, but there were question marks over the brutality of your army, especially when dealing with captured revolutionaries. Mass executions were not unknown, but the imposition of the rule of the new Imperial Government was paramount for many, and thus they were willing to turn a blind eye to such atrocities.

In the spring of 1919, and with you as their commander, your forces began a concerted drive on Moscow, one of the few remaining bastions of Bukharin's Bolshevik regime. Although your troops still had to deal with widespread bands of revolutionary groups who attempted to impede your progress, by early April your army was on the outskirts of Moscow. Bitter fighting ensued and there were heavy casualties, and indeed the advance stalled for a time. After two weeks of intensive fighting, however, the Red Forces gave way, Bukharin fled and Trotsky was killed. Of Lenin, there has been no news for some time.

As you and your staff inspect the Kremlin and congratulate your soldiers, a dishevelled figure is dragged in front of you – it is Josef Stalin, one of Bukharin's loyal lieutenants and a major figure in the

22. Imperial forces liberate Kharkov in 1918

civil war since 1917. A cursory order results in him being hauled away for immediate execution.

There is of course still much to be done. The Bolsheviks might have been scattered for the moment, but opposition to the new Tsar's regime remains across the country, and disparate parts of the White Russian movement are still to be brought fully behind the new government. There also remains a lingering desire among some in your forces for the imposition of deeply autocratic rule, to eliminate the chance of a return to unstable democratic government. Russia faces a long road to recovery.

AFTERMATH

Conflict in Russia did not immediately abate with the defeat of Bukharin's Bolsheviks. Many regions still had to be brought to heel, and war also broke out with Poland, which raged for two years. In some ways this

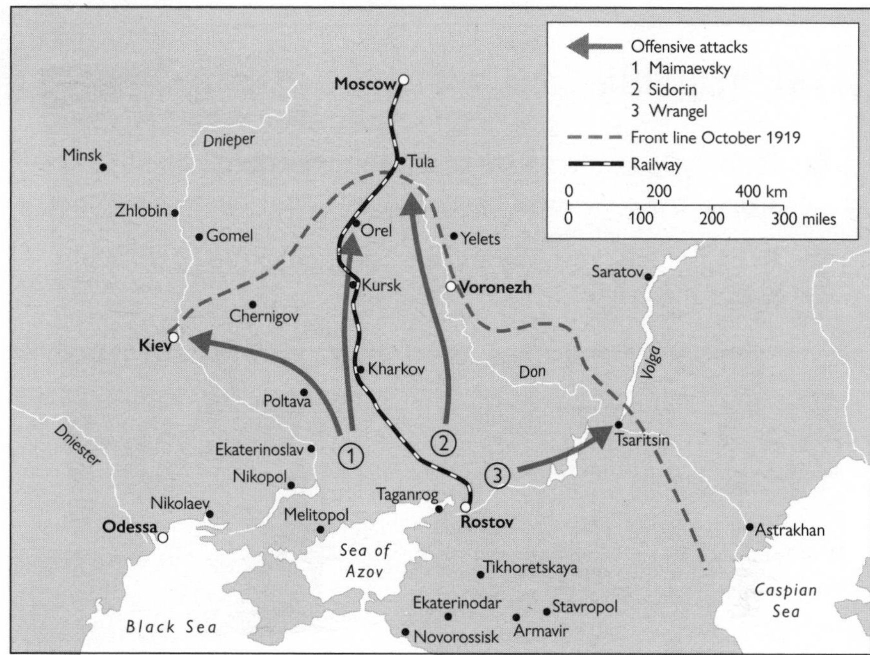

Map 3: The Kornilov Offensive

united different factions behind the government against a common enemy. Socialist revolutionaries continued to cause trouble, with violence, plots and assassinations aplenty, whilst right-wing ultra-nationalists inflicted harsh and unauthorised repressive countermeasures against the population, often enflaming the situation and turning the people against the government.

The Tsar stood well clear of politics, but his desire for the establishment of a democratic assembly remained unfulfilled for many years as different autocrats delayed elections, fearful of the outcome stripping them of power. The Imperial Government attempted to impose the rule of law and order, but an age of warlords emerged, which created uneven and illegitimate rule. Throughout, the people were forced to endure repression and miserable living conditions. A decade later the population was still crying out for stability, and Russia remained caught between fierce autocratic rule, revolutionary pressure and floundering democracy.

THE DECISION

▶ To follow the alternative route, go to **Section 7** (p. 398).

OR

▶ To explore the revolutions in Russia, go to the **Historical Note** on p. 403.

SECTION 7
THE REVOLUTION SAVED?

Sunday 3 March 1918, Brest-Litovsk, Poland

The deed is about to be done. Urged on by Lenin himself, the new Russian government has finally agreed to the terms offered by the Germans to end the war on the Eastern Front, cripplingly harsh as they are. Indeed, the deal imposed by Berlin now is significantly worse than the one that had been offered back in December; but then a good deal has happened since then to weaken Russia's negotiating position. Even as Trotsky stalled in an effort to buy time in his talks with the Germans, Russia's military strength had drained away, and when the Germans had tired of his tactics and reopened military operations, Russia's defences all but collapsed. Lenin was right: almost any terms were preferable to total disaster, and the leadership had fallen into line to back him.

23. Grigory Sokolnikov

You had been one of those who grudgingly accepted the reality, for you are twenty-nine-year-old ***Grigory Sokolnikov***, a key member of the new Soviet regime and a member of the first Politburo. Of Jewish heritage, you had long been an associate of Nikolai Bukharin and a Bolshevik revolutionary. After escaping from exile in Siberia in 1909 you had gained a solid background in economics in Paris and had been a member of the exiled revolutionary group in Switzerland during the war. Along with many colleagues, you had accompanied Lenin in his special train when in April 1917 the Germans transported you all to Russia, in an attempt to foment unrest and opposition to the Provisional Government.

Once the Bolsheviks had seized power, you worked for Trotsky at the Foreign Ministry and had been part of the first team sent to negotiate with the Germans. Initially you had backed the stalling methods employed by the Russian delegation, but in February 1918 the position had collapsed. The Germans were back on the attack and the Russian armed forces were crumbling. Despite hesitation and opposition, and urged on by Lenin, the Central Committee voted to accept the German terms before the situation deteriorated still further. Lenin then had to endure the wrath of some members of the All-Russian Central Executive Committee declaring him a traitor. Trotsky stepped aside and was replaced as Foreign Minister by Georgy Chicherin, but Chicherin certainly did not want to be responsible for signing any hugely damaging deal with the Germans, and nor did any of your colleagues. Despite your best efforts to shift the responsibility, you were delegated by the Central Committee to go to Brest-Litovsk and sign the treaty.

The Germans were now demanding independence for Finland, Belarus and Ukraine, and for the Baltic nations to be established as entities with German princes as their heads of state. German concepts of independence in truth equated to German domination. Russia would also lose one-third of its population and more than half of its industrial capacity, as well as having to pay huge reparations to the Central Powers.

You loathe having to go through with this appalling task, and during the meeting with the Germans you make it perfectly clear that you resent the treaty and everything connected with it. 'We are going to sign immediately,' you declare, 'but at the same time refuse to enter into any discussion of its terms.' It is clear to you that everything that is corrupt about avaricious and exploitative capitalist regimes is amply

Map 4: Territorial implications of the Treaty of Brest-Litovsk, 1918

24. Signing the treaty

demonstrated by the demands and attitudes of the Germans. You conclude by informing the German delegation that their success will be short-lived. This seems to sour the mood of the signing ceremony somewhat, but you have made your point.

You depart from Brest in despair, for you know that the terms imposed are crippling for the new Russia, but you cling to your hope that the contradictions in German society will eventually cause its unravelling. For the moment, however, you and your comrades must devote your efforts to saving the revolution in what remains of Russia, for there are emerging threats everywhere. Newly arising hostile states on your borders, counter-revolutionary forces at home, divisions within your own ranks, and now your former Western Allies seem intent on intervening in Russia: can the revolution survive?

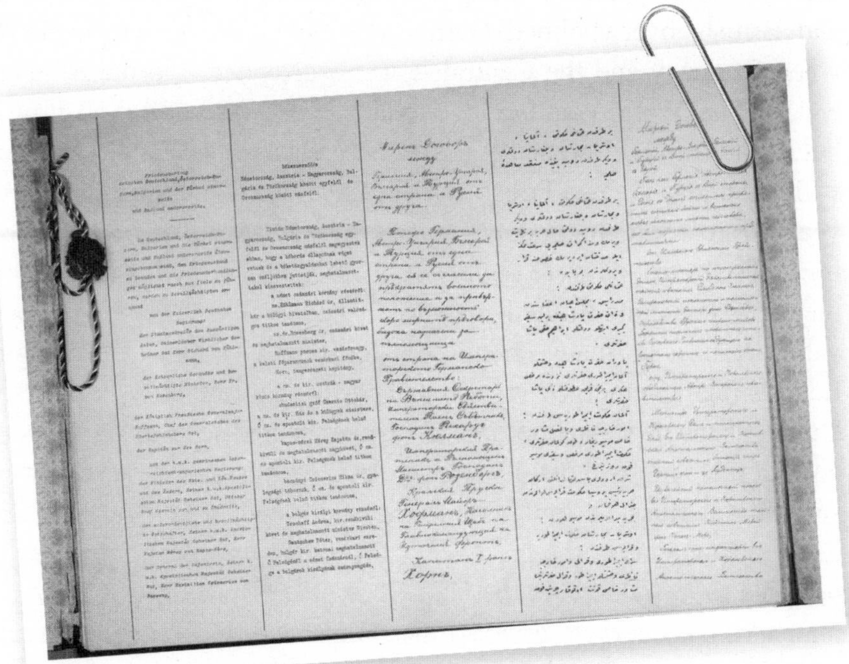

25. The Treaty of Brest-Litovsk

AFTERMATH

The Russian civil war continued, in spite of the Treaty of Brest-Litovsk, which – though it served to keep the Germans at bay – fuelled opposition at home and from the West. Conflict erupted ever more violently across Russia, and the Bolsheviks struggled to keep control. The counter-revolutionary White Russian forces continued their fight, supported by foreign powers, and in the midst of the chaos the Tsar and his family were brutally executed by revolutionary guards, to head off any chance of the monarchy ever returning to power.

In some ways the Treaty of Brest-Litovsk did not aid Germany that much. Although some troops were freed to switch to the Western Front in 1918, many were still deployed in the east, maintaining Germany's grip and supporting the newly created independent states. Ultimately the German offensives in the west – intended to end the war before the growing strength of the USA, alongside the French and British, overwhelmed Germany – failed. In November 1918, when Germany and the Central Powers surrendered to the Allies to end the First World War, Lenin renounced the Treaty of Brest-Litovsk, but it made little difference as the fighting continued. War also erupted with the newly created Polish state in 1919 and raged for more than a year before a settlement could be found, after severe and bitter fighting. Western troops were deployed in the Russian civil war although their role was quite limited, and slowly but surely the Red Army prevailed against its many enemies. It took until 1923, but eventually Lenin's regime emerged victorious and for the time being the Soviet Union, as the new state became known, appeared secure. It still faced considerable global hostility nonetheless, with many Western powers smarting at Russia's unilateral withdrawal from the Great War and deeply suspicious at the presence of a communist state diametrically opposed to its values. As the post-Great War era developed, it was a matter of considerable urgency that Lenin and his comrades should embed and strengthen the position of the Soviet Union's base, before a likely confrontation with the forces of the imperialists and capitalists.

HISTORICAL NOTE

The revolutions in Russia in 1917 were defining moments in the history of the Great War and for the whole of the twentieth century. From the moment of the Bolshevik Revolution in October 1917 until the end of the Soviet Union in 1991, the wider world's relationship with Russia dramatically shaped interwar diplomacy, the Second World War and the Cold War. In Section 1 we explored the inevitability (or otherwise) of the February 1917 Revolution, which was a consequence of long-term social and political unrest alongside wartime mismanagement and pressure. The Tsar and his staff decided upon repression and force to contain the outbreak of opposition in Petrograd, which is the historical path and takes you to Section 3. The other option was a negotiation and handing-over of powers to the Duma in an open and visible manner, which takes you to Section 2. Historically, this was unlikely as the Tsar, backed by his wife, was a true believer in his divine right to rule as he saw fit. His insulated life, away from the privations of his people and social reality, hindered his decision-making regarding the need for change, but by February 1917 it was probably too late. Even if he had agreed to a 1905-style solution, it is unlikely to have made that much difference; rebellion and civil war were probable outcomes, as discussed here, though they may have taken a different path, perhaps between republican and royalist factions. If the Tsar had repeated his grievous errors of the post-1905 era and had attempted to retake control and power, his demise was likely indeed.

If the February Revolution had swept the Tsar away and the Provisional Government and the soviets had shared power, the most crucial choice to make was whether and how to get Russia out of the Great War, because for most people this was the most pressing problem. Yet for many in the Provisional Government it was unthinkable to withdraw unilaterally from the war, even after the abortive summer 1917 offensive under General Brusilov had collapsed. In contrast, for Lenin it was blindingly obvious that – whatever the cost – Russia had to end the war. For Kerensky's regime, there was perhaps a fleeting moment when the new War Minister, Aleksandr Verkhovsky, raised the notion of imminent collapse if the Russian army carried on fighting, a point explored in Section 3. Historically, Verkhovsky backed away from suggesting unilateral withdrawal, even though he had outlined that continuation would bring down disaster upon them all. However unlikely, if he had pressed the point and then persuaded Kerensky to act immediately to call for a ceasefire with the Central Powers, the Bolshevik Revolution, then already in preparation, might have been stymied. The army in Petrograd was key, and the announcement of a ceasefire might have swayed enough of the units there to stay with the government, a prospect explored by taking the path from Section 3 to Section 5. Here we explore the possibilities of the Provisional Government surviving and accepting the terms offered by the Germans in the autumn of 1917, terms that were far less severe than those Lenin historically accepted three months later. Would the Russian republic survive in these circumstances? It is fanciful, but this route possibly offered Russia the best prospect of surviving the war without further upheaval and full-scale civil war.

The historical path takes you from Section 3 to Section 4, in which the October Revolution destroys the Provisional Government, leaving the Bolsheviks to contemplate a peace with the Germans. Their willingness (probably against Lenin's better judgement) to stall and wait for a widening revolution to engulf Germany was not so outlandish, because upheaval did eventually sweep across Germany, albeit after the collapse of their war effort. Ultimately, Lenin and his committee were confronted by a worsening and collapsing situation in February 1918 and they bit the bullet and accepted Germany's harsh terms for peace, the path that takes you from Section 4 to Section 7. However painful it might have been, and however damaging, the choice probably saved the revolution and bought enough time for the Bolsheviks to cling to power and, slowly but surely, emerge from the chaos of civil war, foreign intervention and war with Poland, to arrive as the Soviet Union by the mid-1920s.

The alternative (Section 4 to Section 6) would probably have brought down Lenin's regime. Refusal to end the war on the terms offered by Germany would have damaged the Bolsheviks enormously and would possibly have given sufficient ammunition and purpose to the White Russian forces that emerged in 1918 to seize Moscow and drive what remained of the Bolsheviks from power. The Germans may have occupied Petrograd, but with the growing threat from the Allies in the west, they would not have had the resources to completely occupy Russia. The White Russians were a disparate and poorly coordinated group historically, but the scenario here sees them getting their act together; against a weakened Bolshevik regime, it might have been enough to seize power. The aftermath of this looks very uncertain, however, and a warlord era with despots and harsh autocratic rule might well have followed.

Mikhail Alekseyev was a key figure in the Provisional Government in 1917 and headed off the Kornilov coup. After the Bolshevik takeover, he commanded White Russian forces in 1918, but struggled to work with Kornilov. He died of heart failure in the autumn of 1918.

Lord Jellicoe was damaged by the failure of the Grand Fleet to win a great victory at Jutland in 1916, and although he later served as First Sea Lord, he was regarded as only a qualified success. Later he was Governor-General of New Zealand, and he died at home in Kensington in 1935.

Aleksandr Verkhovsky survived the Bolshevik Revolution and served in a variety of roles in the Red Army, including as a military theorist and professor. He was arrested and imprisoned in 1931, released in 1934, and then later caught up in the purges of the late 1930s. He was executed on the basis of trumped-up anti-Soviet activities in 1938.

Leon Trotsky, despite his crucial role in the establishment of the Soviet Union, fell foul of Stalin's brutal seizure of power in the 1920s and was driven into exile in 1929. He spent the remainder of his life criticising Stalin. Condemned to death *in absentia* in a show trial in 1937, he survived various attempts on his life, but was clumsily assassinated in Mexico City in 1940 at the age of sixty.

Alexander Kerensky was driven from power by the October Revolution and fled into exile. He supported neither the Reds nor the Whites in the civil war and eventually settled in the USA, where he lectured and broadcast on Russian history. He lived until 1970, dying at the age of eighty-nine – one of the last major players in the tumultuous events of the Russian revolutions.

Lavr Kornilov was implicated in a plot against the Provisional Government in 1917, but later returned to influence as a senior commander of White forces in the civil war. He was a determined and fierce fighter against the Bolsheviks, although his own sympathies were largely as a straightforward Russian nationalist. He was killed by artillery in April 1918.

Grigory Sokolnikov fought to save the revolution in the civil war and later played a role as Finance Minister in the 1920s. However, he became disillusioned by Stalin's policies and rule and, despite having little English, was posted to Britain as ambassador. In 1936 he was implicated in plots against the Soviet Union and Stalin, tried and convicted on spurious evidence. Although only sentenced to ten years of hard labour, he was murdered in prison in 1939 on the orders of Stalin.

ACKNOWLEDGEMENTS

We are grateful to friends and colleagues for providing advice and inspiration during the creation of this book, especially Stephen Badsey, John Hussey, Jacob Prytherch, Gary Sheffield, and Phil Weir.

Thanks are also due to our Sunday evening games colleagues, Howard Fuller, Martyn Shipley and Andrew Southall, for their insights and ruminations over many years.

REFERENCES

On counterfactual history

Richard Evans, *Altered Pasts: Counterfactuals in History* (2014).

Niall Ferguson, *Virtual History* (1997).

The July Crisis

Christopher Clark, *The Sleepwalkers: How Europe Went to War in 1914* (2013).

Fritz Fischer, *Germany's Aims in the First World War* (1967).

Margaret MacMillan, *The War that Ended Peace: How Europe Abandoned Peace for the First World War* (2013).

The Guns of August

Richard Holmes, *Riding the Retreat: Mons to the Marne 1914 Revisited* (2007).

Spencer Jones, *The Great Retreat of 1914: Mons to the Marne* (2014).

Spencer Jones (ed.), *Stemming the Tide: Officers and Leadership in the British Expeditionary Force 1914* (2013).

Gallipoli

Christopher Bell, *Churchill and the Dardanelles: Myth, Memory and Reputation* (2017).

Rhys Crawley, *Climax at Gallipoli: The Failure of the August Offensive* (2014).

Robin Prior, *Gallipoli: The End of the Myth* (2009).

Jutland

Andrew Gordon, *The Rules of the Game: Jutland and British Naval Command* (1997).

Robert Massie, *Castles of Steel: Britain, Germany and the Winning of the Great War at Sea* (2007).

V. E. Tarrant, *Jutland: The German Perspective* (1999).

Battle of the Somme

Spencer Jones (ed.) *At All Costs: The British Army on the Western Front 1916* (2018).

William Philpott, *Bloody Victory: The Sacrifice on the Somme* (2010).

Gary Sheffield, *The Somme: A New History* (2015).

Lawrence of Arabia

Robert Johnson, *Lawrence of Arabia on War: The Campaign in the Desert 1916–18* (2020).

Michael Korda, *Hero: The Life and Legend of Lawrence of Arabia* (2011).

T. E. Lawrence, *Seven Pillars of Wisdom* (1926).

The Zimmermann Telegram

Patrick Beesly, *Room 40: British Naval Intelligence 1914–1918* (1984).

Thomas Boghardt, *The Zimmermann Telegram: Intelligence, Diplomacy, and America's Entry into World War I* (2012).

Robert Tucker, *Woodrow Wilson: Reconsidering America's Neutrality 1914–1917* (2015).

Revolution

Peter Kenez, *Red Attack, White Resistance: Civil War in South Russia 1918* (2007).

Evan Mawdsley, *The Russian Civil War* (1987).

Richard Pipes, *The Russian Revolution* (1990).

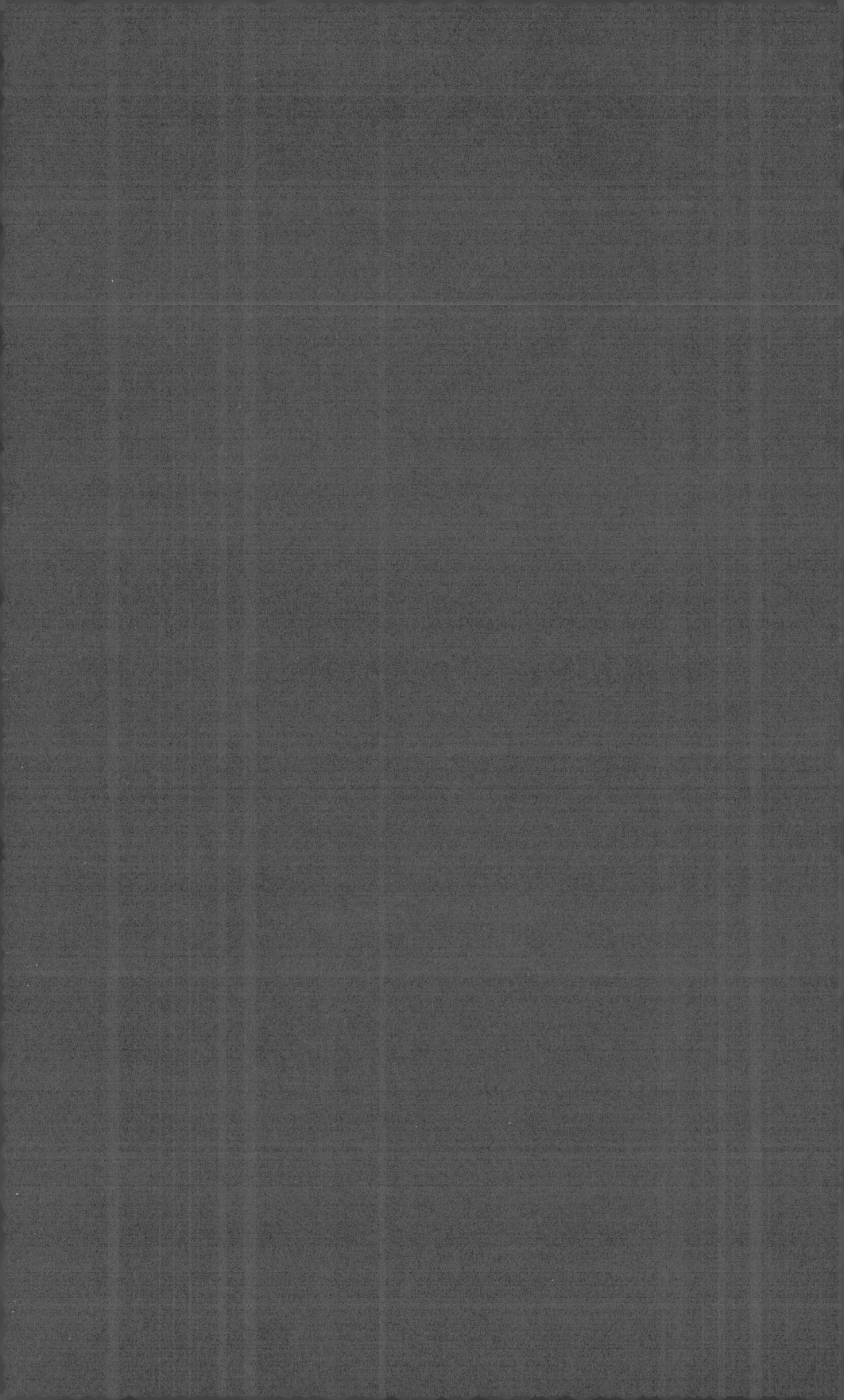